PARADOXES OF INDIVIDUALITY

Dedicated to Jaap de Koster, born February 25, 2011

Paradoxes of Individualization
Social Control and Social Conflict in Contemporary Modernity

DICK HOUTMAN, STEF AUPERS and WILLEM DE KOSTER
Erasmus University Rotterdam, The Netherlands

ASHGATE

Published by
Ashgate Publishing Limited
Wey Court East
Union Road
Farnham
Surrey, GU9 7PT
England

Ashgate Publishing Company
Suite 420
101 Cherry Street
Burlington
VT 05401-4405
USA

www.ashgate.com

British Library Cataloguing in Publication Data
Houtman, Dick.
  Paradoxes of individualization : social control and social
  conflict in contemporary modernity.
  1. Individualism. 2. Conformity. 3. Social control.
  4. Social conflict.
  I. Title II. Aupers, Stef, 1969- III. Koster, Willem de.
  302.5'4-dc22

Library of Congress Cataloging-in-Publication Data
Houtman, Dick.
  Paradoxes of individualization : social control and social conflict in contemporary
  modernity / by Dick Houtman, Stef Aupers and Willem de Koster.
      p. cm.
  Includes bibliographical references and index.
  ISBN 978-0-7546-7902-8 (hbk) -- ISBN 978-0-7546-7901-1 (pbk)
  1. Individualism. 2. Individuality. 3. Social conflict. 4.
  Social control. I. Aupers, Stef, 1969- II. Koster, Willem de. III. Title.
  HM1276.H68 2011
  302.5'4--dc23

2011017631

ISBN 9780754679028 (hbk)
ISBN 9780754679011 (pbk)
ISBN 9780754697749 (ebk)

Printed and bound in Great Britain by the
MPG Books Group, UK

Contents

List of Figures and Tables

Figures

Tables

List of Contributors

Peter Achterberg (1977) is Associate Professor at the Centre for Rotterdam Cultural Sociology (CROCUS) at Erasmus University Rotterdam, The Netherlands. He is a cultural sociologist mainly interested in the culturalization of politics in contemporary modernity.

Stef Aupers (1969) is Associate Professor at the Centre for Rotterdam Cultural Sociology (CROCUS) at Erasmus University Rotterdam, The Netherlands. His principal research interests are religious change and spirituality, play- and game culture, Internet culture and conspiracy culture.

Samira van Bohemen (1987) is a PhD candidate at the Centre for Rotterdam Cultural Sociology (CROCUS) at Erasmus University Rotterdam, The Netherlands. Her principal research interests concern the performative aspects of gender and waxing intolerance in contemporary secularized societies.

Sebastiaan van Doorn (1980) is a PhD candidate at the Rotterdam School of Management at Erasmus University Rotterdam, The Netherlands. His principal research interests are corporate entrepreneurship, upper echelons, network theory and decision making.

Dick Houtman (1963) is Professor of Cultural Sociology at the Centre for Rotterdam Cultural Sociology (CROCUS) at Erasmus University Rotterdam, The Netherlands. His principal research interests are the spiritualization and revitalization of religion and the culturalization of politics in contemporary modernity.

Roy Kemmers (1980) is a PhD candidate at the Centre for Rotterdam Cultural Sociology (CROCUS) at Erasmus University Rotterdam, The Netherlands. His research focuses on contemporary populism and, more generally, cultural conflicts in the West.

Willem de Koster (1984) is Assistant Professor at the Centre for Rotterdam Cultural Sociology (CROCUS) at Erasmus University Rotterdam, The Netherlands. He studies virtual communities as well as the genesis and manifestations of contemporary cultural conflict in Western countries.

Ineke Noomen (1979) is PhD candidate at the Centre for Rotterdam Cultural Sociology (CROCUS) at Erasmus University Rotterdam, The Netherlands. She is finishing her dissertation on religion and spirituality on the Internet, which addresses issues of marketization and mediatization.

Jochem Verheul (1981) obtained his MSc in Sociology at Erasmus University Rotterdam, the Netherlands, specializing in economic sociology. In 2009, he founded the internet consultancy agency *It's a virus*.

Jeroen van der Waal (1974) is Assistant Professor at Erasmus University Rotterdam, the Netherlands. His principal research interests entail the impact of economic globalization on social inequality, and the consequences of cultural change for value orientations and voting behavior in the West.

Acknowledgments

This book has its origins in a symposium titled *Paradoxes of Individualization*, organized on April 13, 2006, at the initiative of Marjolein Kooistra, public relations officer at Erasmus University's Faculty of Social Sciences. Its formal aim was the presentation of a handful of research projects conducted at what would later become the Centre for Rotterdam Cultural Sociology (CROCUS) to an interested academic and non-academic audience. Intellectually speaking, however, the organization of the seminar challenged us to explore the common ground underneath apparently distinct and isolated research projects, addressing issues ranging from computer gaming to political conflict and from holistic spirituality to consumption. It quickly became clear that what constituted their common denominator was the theoretical problem of individualization, or more precisely: the increased social significance of moral individualism, this modern cultural ideal *par excellence*, which has not only massively proliferated in Western countries in the last half century, but has in the process grown into a major source of moral, religious and political conflict, too.

All three of us believe firmly that it is up to the social and cultural sciences to make the social world that we live in more comprehensible rather than obscuring it only further by taking refuge in idle postmodern or statistical messing around. This is why our plan to elaborate the seminar presentations into a full-blown book in Dutch elicited the ironic suggestion from one of us (Willem) that 'We must definitely make sure that the book becomes at least as complex as social reality itself.' A conversation with Ashgate's Neil Jordan in the Summer of 2008 convinced us to change course, however, and made us decide to write the book in English instead. From that moment on the project unfortunately started suffering from delay, particularly due to massive teaching assignments and a broad range of competing publication projects that demanded our precious time and attention. Because of that, the project could only start in earnest after two of us had been exempted from parts of their heavy teaching assignments from September 2009 onwards, although even then it had to compete with other publication projects that had suffered from delay.

The progress of this book has been impeded by two iron laws of contemporary academic life, in short: teaching always receives priority over research, and short-term journal articles always receive priority over long-term book projects, principally due to the ceaseless stream of revisions and resubmissions invoked by the former. We are grateful to Neil Jordan for his patience and his understanding that academia is no longer the quiet and easygoing environment for peaceful reflection, deliberation and discussion that it used to be in the past. The final obstacle to the completion of this book came as recent as February of this year, even though it had been forecasted with scientific precision no less than nine months in advance: the birth of Jaap de Koster, son of Willem and Masja van Meeteren. If only for this brave and stubborn, yet in the end fortunately unsuccessful, attempt to incur further delay on this book, it would be unfair to dedicate it to anyone else but him.

Even though it is very much the outcome of ongoing discussions at the Centre for Rotterdam Cultural Sociology (CROCUS) at Erasmus University, Rotterdam, the Netherlands, this book's argument has first been systematically developed in the inaugural address by one of us (Dick, see Houtman 2008), which as such informs much of the introductory chapter. Finally, we are grateful for permission to reprint (more or less revised versions of) three journal articles:

- Chapter 3, Beyond the Spiritual Supermarket: Why New Age Spirituality is Less Privatized Than They Say It Is, is based on: Aupers, S. and Houtman, D. 2006. Beyond the spiritual supermarket: The social and public significance of new age spirituality. *Journal of Contemporary Religion*, 21(2), 201-22.
- Chapter 5, 'Stormfront is like a Second Home to me': Social Exclusion of Right-Wing Extremists, is based on: De Koster, W. and Houtman, D. 2008. 'Stormfront is like a second home to me': On virtual community formation by right-wing extremists. *Information, Communication & Society*, 11(8), 1153-75.
- Chapter 7, Two Lefts and Two Rights: Class Voting and Cultural Voting in the Netherlands, 2002, is based on: Houtman, D. and Achterberg, P. 2010. Two lefts and two rights: Class voting and cultural voting in the Netherlands, 2002. *Sociologie*, 1(1): 61-76.

Rotterdam, 2011
Dick Houtman, Stef Aupers and Willem de Koster

Chapter 1

Introduction: The Myth of Individualization and the Dream of Individualism

Introduction

'However plausible, and at first sight convincing it is to see an autonomous, self-directing, self-realizing individual emerging from the ashes of scarcity, religious belief, tradition, and authority, the diagnosis of individualization is empirically untenable', Mark Elchardus (2009: 152) concludes about the theory of individualization brought forward by sociologists like Zygmunt Bauman (1995, 1997, 2001a), Anthony Giddens (1991) and Ulrich Beck (1992, Beck and Beck-Gernsheim 2002). If individualization would really have occurred, he maintains, strong relationships between 'standard sociological characteristics' (idem: 150) or 'standard sociological variables (such as class, level of education, gender)' (idem: 148) and how people think, feel and act would clearly be the last thing one would expect to find. With this argument Elchardus echoes Paul de Beer, who brings in similar evidence to demonstrate that what people think, feel and do is still strongly related to 'their objective characteristics' (2007: 394).

But how could it be otherwise? Sociologically speaking, such a notion of individualization is not at all 'plausible, and at first sight convincing', but is in fact absurd since it suggests that the discipline's distinctive approach to social life—based on the notion that people are inevitably socially shaped—can and needs to be treated as a testable hypothesis. Because of this, the question of whether or not 'individuals' are still socially shaped, produced and controlled is too general and non-sociological and hence needs to be replaced by the more feasible question of whether, why and how modes of social control are undergoing a process of transformation. We have, however, major doubts about whether a theory based on the notion that individualization is an inherently non-cultural process, as Elchardus and De Beer proclaim, can provide much of an answer to this question.

Even though it remains perfectly obscure why De Beer chooses to include religiosity as one of his 'objective' independent variables, while treating people's moral and political values as 'subjective' dependent ones (idem: 394), the theory of individualization critiqued by him and Elchardus is informed by a distinction between 'objective' independent and 'subjective' dependent variables. This assumes that culture is basically irrelevant and non-consequential—that it is merely a 'reflection', 'consequence' or 'outcome' of a 'more fundamental' and 'more real' 'underlying' social reality. Such a positivist account of culture as causally insignificant, Jeffrey Alexander (2003: 13) explains, assumes that:

explanatory power lies in the study of the "hard" variables of social structure, such that structured sets of meanings become superstructures and ideologies driven by these more "real" and tangible social forces', whereby culture 'becomes defined as a "soft", not really independent variable: it is more or less confined to participating in the reproduction of social relations.

To demonstrate how difficult it nonetheless is to dispel the specter of culture from a sociological theory of individualization, we start with an interrogation of the ambiguities of De Beer's (2007) and Elchardus's (2009) treatments of individualization and individualism. We then outline our own cultural-sociological theory that gives individualism, this modern cultural ideal *par excellence*, its full due as central to the process of individualization. Analogous to the late Bryan Wilson's (1982: 149) conceptualization of secularization as 'that process by which religious institutions, actions, and consciousness, lose their social significance', we hence define individualization as 'that process by which a moral notion of individualism increases in social significance.' In doing so, we conceive of individualism as central to a (post)modern worldview that operates not unlike its religious counterparts in providing the world with meaning and informing the social actions of those who accept it (for example, Campbell 2007, Chaves 1994, Weber 1963 [1922]).

The Myth of Individualization and the Dream of Individualism

Individualization without Individualism?

De Beer's (2007) and Elchardus's (2009) notion that individualization can be understood as an inherently non-cultural process is not only remarkable for its sociologically naïve assumption that it is actually conceivable that selves are *not* socially shaped, so that this needs to be empirically studied, but even more so because the ambiguities in their own critiques confirm how difficult it actually is to dispel the cultural specter of individualism from a theory of individualization. Indeed, at a closer and more critical look, their accounts contain the seeds of a sociologically richer treatment of individualization that opens it up as a cultural-sociological problem.

For a start, De Beer (2007: 390) explains that the Netherlands constitutes an ideal case for the study of individualization because of 'social and cultural trends over the last 25 years that (...) are most aptly characterized by the term "individualization"' and also, referring to Ronald Inglehart's work about 'postmaterialist values' and 'postmodernization', which both 'clearly centre on the individual', because this country 'moreover [*sic*] stands out as one of the most progressive and liberal countries.' Whereas the word 'moreover' suggests that these 'cultural trends' are somehow unrelated to and different from the non-cultural conception of individualization De Beer sets out to critique, he simultaneously asserts the exact opposite when he claims that the Netherlands is an ideal case study because of its marked progressive and liberal emphasis on liberty, cultural tolerance, postmaterialism, etcetera, which makes it one of the most individualized countries of the world.

Having thus effectively defined individualization in two competing ways, De Beer subsequently leaves his readers puzzled when he proclaims that 'one must, of course, first define individualization' (idem: 390), stating as a matter of fact that '*individualization should clearly be distinguished from individualism*' (idem: 391, our emphasis). Given the immediately preceding argument about the Netherlands as an ideal case, it remains unclear why this is 'clear' and his explanation that 'individualism is *commonly* understood as a personal attitude or preference' (idem: 391, our emphasis) fails to convince for its absence of literature references and its failure to critique such a naïve and non-sociological conception of individualism. Indeed, towards the end of his article De Beer no longer asserts confidently that moral individualism has 'clearly' nothing to do with individualization, but more modestly acknowledges that his own analysis 'does not shed any light on *this interpretation of individualization which I prefer to call individualism*' (idem: 406, our emphasis). Needless to say, this leaves him caught between two competing notions of individualization, which urges him to defend the thesis that the Netherlands is highly individualized (the cultural basis for its selection), yet is not really individualized (going by the relationships between variables he has found). The principal conclusion to draw from De Beer's article, then, is that despite his desire to dispel individualism, conceived as a cultural emphasis on individual liberty and cultural tolerance, from the theory of individualization, the awareness that it has in fact everything to do with it looms so large that it even informs his case selection.

A similar ambiguity can be found in Elchardus's article (2009), which in its opening pages also insists on a distinction between 'individualization' and 'individualism'—'a property of the choices people make' and 'a discourse or a vocabulary of motives', respectively (idem: 147)—, to enable him to effortlessly bash the resulting ('plausible, and at first sight convincing') sociologically naïve straw man to death. Having rejected the non-sociological notion that individual selves may be decreasingly shaped by social forces, Elchardus then proceeds to outline a more sociologically informed theory of individualization, central to which is the notion that the latter does not entail a disappearance of social control, but rather a transition to a new mode of social control: 'This new mode of control is centered around the self. It is, literally, self-control, not in the 19th century meaning of self-restraint, but in the sense of control of the self through the self …, using among other things individualism as a vocabulary of motives, socially constructed as an individual that views itself as a choosing agent' (idem: 153). So there we are again: at second thought, Elchardus, much like De Beer, abandons his positivist notion that what people do is not culturally informed, so that cultural discourse is made causally irrelevant and comes in only as a legitimation of what they have already done. At the same time Elchardus recognizes that a good sociological theory of individualization must be a theory of social control, according to which people are increasingly socialized and stimulated to think of themselves as individuals, so that a cultural notion of individualism needs to be central to it after all.

Similarly, Atkinson (2007: 536) critiques the notion that the class constraints of the past have somehow made way for free, reflexive and unconstrained lifestyle choices within the context of an ongoing process of self-construction, pointing out that such a theory misses an awareness of 'the role of resources and processes of inscription by privileged others in producing self-identity.' The major problem with this type of individualization theory, Atkinson (idem: 542) echoes arguments made by Bellah et al. (1985), is that it cannot explain 'why, exactly, … different individuals and groups choose different lifestyles', commenting on Giddens that 'it is hard to see how lifestyle choices, including the decision to change lifestyle altogether, could be made *without being guided by the orientations furnished by the lifestyle already adopted.* Either the self must somehow, in a way left unexplained by Giddens, be able to transcend the orientations of its lifestyle in order to choose or else lifestyle choices are not as "free" as he would like to make out' (his emphasis).

Individualism as a Middle-Class Moral Ideal

The strain of individualization theory brought forward by Bauman, Giddens and Beck, Atkinson furthermore points out, moreover 'resonates only with the experiences of the middle classes' (idem: 536), informed as it is by middle-class longings for personal agency that are inappropriately generalized to Western populations as a whole. And indeed, as any number of studies conducted since the 1950s has demonstrated, he could hardly be more correct. It is, after all, the middle class that embraces 'tolerance towards non-conformity' (for example, Nunn et al. 1978, Stouffer 1955) and 'self-direction' rather than 'conformity' as a parental value (Kohn 1977 [1969], Kohn and Schooler 1983, Kohn and Slomczynski 1990). This goes particularly for the 'new' middle class with its 'postmaterialist' value orientation that puts individual freedom and democracy above 'materialist' needs of security and social order (Inglehart 1977, 1990, 1997). To be more precise, the moral type of individualism that these notions capture is not so much embraced by 'the middle class' or 'the affluent' in an economic sense, as these and other 'Marxist-lite' theories have suggested since Lipset (1959) launched his theory of 'working-class authoritarianism' half a century ago. It is instead typical of those with a high level of education, particularly with degrees in non-economic, non-technical, and non-administrative fields—by the well educated conceived as a socio-cultural rather than a socio-economic category, in short (Houtman 2003).

Indeed, the fact that this moral type of individualism is intimately tied up with education does as much to demonstrate that the social shaping of selves is not over and done with, as it does to point out that a sociological theory of individualization worth its salt needs to place the social processes at its center through which this individualism is constructed, transmitted, appropriated and acted upon. This, however, is not what De Beer, Elchardus and Atkinson do. Whereas they correctly identify the notion of a disappearance of the social shaping of the self as a modern myth, they hesitate to take individualism's role in shaping contemporary social life very seriously, suggesting instead—however ambiguously and inconsistently, as we have seen—that 'individualization has nothing to do with individualism.' In this book, we aim to overcome this ambiguity by adopting an explicitly Weberian cultural-sociological understanding of individualization, central to which is the increased social significance of individualism.

The dual aim of this opening chapter is to develop this theoretical argument and to put some first empirical flesh on its bones so as to set the stage for the remainder of the book. We demonstrate that Max Weber's classical cultural sociology already hinted in the direction of such a theory of individualization, although he was unfortunately hesitant to draw out the full implications of his theory of the disenchantment of the world. Critically confronting the latter with Durkheim's struggle with the problem of individualism over the course of his career, however, reveals that he should have done so. The thesis that we propose in this chapter, in short, is that carefully fleshing out and comparing Weber's and Durkheim's analyses of modern cultural discontents and their corollaries, yields a powerful cultural-sociological theory of individualization that is empirically supported by changes that have particularly unfolded since the counter culture of the 1960s.

Modernity and Cultural Disenchantment

Max Weber and the Disenchantment of the World

Weber's narrative of the gradual disappearance of the metaphysical 'Hinterwelt' that once provided the Western world with solid meaning continues to evoke debate and arouse the intellectual imagination. This process of disenchantment took off, Weber argued, with the emergence of Judaic anti-magical monotheism in ancient times and was pushed a decisive step further forward when the Protestant Reformation unleashed its attack on Catholic magic and superstition in the sixteenth century. The latter's further expulsion from the modern world has since been firmly supported by modern intellectualism's imperative of pursuing truth and nothing but truth, significantly contributing to a world increasingly devoid of meaning—a world in which 'processes … simply "are" and "happen" but no longer signify anything' (Weber 1978 [1921]: 506).

Modern science, because of its anti-metaphysical and empirical orientation, cannot help but further the disenchantment of the world. Potent though it is, it cannot provide answers to what are ultimately the most significant questions faced by mankind—the meaning of life, the purpose of the world, and the life plans to pursue or refrain from: 'Only a prophet or a savior can give the answers' (Weber 1948 [1919]: 153). As an essentially 'irreligious power' (idem: 142), all science can do is rob the world of its remaining mysteries by laying bare causal chains: '[T]he disenchantment of the world ... means that principally there are no mysterious incalculable forces that come into play, but rather that one can, in principle, master all things by calculation', as Weber summarized his position in the probably most cited passage of his essay 'Science as a Vocation' (idem: 139). Once technologically instrumentalized, such causal chains yield a superior and quintessentially modern mode of controlling nature that further marginalizes magical practices: '[O]ne need no longer have recourse to magical means to master or implore the spirits, as did the savage, for whom such mysterious powers existed. Technical means and calculations perform the service' (idem: 139). Technology liberates human beings from circumstances their ancestors simply had to bear and is meanwhile even deployed to improve and optimize their own bodies and minds (for example, Fukuyama 2002).

Although the variety of uses to which technology can be put is virtually infinite—ranging from curing diseases, increasing profits or countering global warming to exterminating ethnic or religious others—, science can only remain silent about the ends worth pursuing. It can only provide means to *given* ends, because it is unauthorized in the domain of moral values: '... it [cannot] be proved that the existence of the world which these sciences describe is worth while, that it has any "meaning", or that it makes sense to live in such a world' (Weber 1948 [1919]: 144). Although Weber acknowledged that, much to his horror, there are 'big children in the natural sciences' (idem: 142) who believe they can bestow 'objective' meaning upon the world, he firmly rejected such a position himself. Science, he insisted, simply cannot decide between competing value claims.

More than that: science can only further disenchantment by progressively destroying the metaphysical foundations on which mutually conflicting religious doctrines and political ideologies rely. Science hence inevitably creates and aggravates modern problems of meaning. The fate of modern man, Weber held, is to face this stern reality as it is, without illusions—to heroically bear the modern fate of meaninglessness without taking refuge in utopian dreams or promises of religious salvation, because there simply is no way back. Although he took great efforts to take this imperative seriously in his own life as a man of science, the struggle with his 'inner demons' that resulted in a mental breakdown in the period 1897-1902 demonstrates how difficult a task this actually was (Radkau 2009).

Does Disenchantment Spark Reenchantment?

There is much to commend Weber's analysis of the progressive dissolution of solidly grounded meaning in the modern world. Perhaps more than anything else, the emergence of postmodernism since the 1960s confirms Weber's position. Contemporary culture, as postmodern thinkers have argued, has after all lost much of its metaphysical foundation now that most people no longer believe that they live in 'natural' or 'solidly grounded' social worlds, but instead inhabit a world ruled by insidiously rhizoming simulations that entail a virtual disappearance of 'real' or 'authentic' reality (Baudrillard 1993 [1976], Houtman 2008), a world in which depth has been superseded by surface (Jameson 1991) and in which even science's authority to legislate truth has progressively dissolved (Bauman 1987, Rorty 1980). Hardly surprising, the Christian churches, these guardians of religious metaphysics in the West, have also lost much of their former appeal in this cultural climate (for example, Brown 2001, Houtman and Mascini 2002, Norris and Inglehart 2004). The progressive disenchantment of the world, predicted by Weber a century ago, seems a mere truism.

Or is it? Interestingly enough, the cultural climate in Weber's own intellectual circles in the German city of Heidelberg at the turn of the nineteenth and twentieth century already suggested otherwise. There and then, many a philosopher, psychologist, and artist took refuge in utopian experiments, alternative religions, and esoteric movements, such as Rudolf Steiner's anthroposophy and the philosophy of life of Henri Bergson and the like. Even Weber's own brother Alfred, the cultural sociologist, attempted to convert him to the latter. And during the Spring of 1913 and 1914, Weber paid visits to Monte Verita in Ascona in the Alps, where his contemporaries indulged in free sexuality and alternative forms of religion. There is hence no doubt that Weber was acutely aware of these attempts by many of his fellow-intellectuals to re-enchant a progressively disenchanted world by infusing it with new meaning (Radkau 2009).

Weber himself nonetheless adopted a rationalist stance and firmly dismissed spiritual tendencies such as these as 'weakness not to be able to countenance the stern seriousness of our fateful times' (1948 [1919]: 149)—and more bluntly: 'this is plain humbug or self-deception' and one should 'bear the fate of the times like a man' (idem: 154-5). Remarkably and unfortunately, this aversion seems to have withheld him from a detailed and systematic analysis of these tendencies, particularly so because the latter are in the end fully consistent with his own cultural sociology. The latter after all postulates that there is a universal human need to give meaning to an essentially meaningless world and hence conceives of culture as 'the endowment of a finite segment of the meaningless infinity of events in the world with meaning and significance from the standpoint of human beings' (Schroeder, quoted by Campbell 2007: 11).

This point of departure of Weber's cultural sociology implies that loss of plausibility of cultural and religious worldviews—due to disenchantment or otherwise—inevitably sparks processes of 'cultural rationalization', aimed at cultural reconstruction to safeguard the reassuring notion that the world is a meaningful place rather than a chaotic, meaningless and nihilistic void without any inherent purpose or direction (Weber 1963 [1922], see also Campbell 2007). Following a Weberian cultural-sociological logic, then, the destruction of a metaphysical 'Hinterwelt' does not simply aggravate problems of meaning, but does also spark attempts at reenchantment to replace the worn, implausible and obsolete myths of the past by ones that are better adapted to the modern world and less susceptible to disenchantment and loss of plausibility.

A New Era of Individualism?

Constructing such a new cultural myth to sustain morality in modern societies was the principal ambition of Weber's French contemporary Emile Durkheim, who hence embarked on an intellectual project that contradicted Weber's. Whereas for Weber, science can only destroy the notion that the world has a solid meaning, it is for Durkheim the only means left to firmly ground morality. For him, it provides a tool to distinguish between what is 'normal' and what is 'abnormal' ('pathological') and hence points out directions for social reform, amelioration and progress. Watts Miller (1996: 1) hence correctly characterizes Durkheim's work as a 'search for a passage from "is" to "ought"', or a 'route from science to ethics.' He recalls in this context Georges Gurvitch's notion that Durkheim is the sociological equivalent of Columbus: whereas Columbus sought a new route to the east and discovered America, Durkheim sought a secular and scientific route to ethics and discovered sociology.

Individualism in Durkheim's Early Sociology

'In a word', Durkheim expressed this ambition in the final sentences of his first book, *The Division of Labor in Society* (1964 [1893]: 340), 'our very first duty at present is to create for ourselves a morality.' Likewise, in his methodological treatise *The Rules of Sociological Method* (1964 [1895]: 60-61) he underscores that the scientific method is actually capable of informing rationally-based judgments about what is 'good' and what is 'bad', what is 'normal' and 'abnormal': 'A phenomenon can ... persist throughout the entire range of a species although no longer adapted to the requirements of the situation. It is then normal only in appearance. Its universality is now an illusion, since its persistence, due only to the blind force of habit, can no longer be accepted as an index of a close connection with the general conditions of its collective existence.'

According to Durkheim's first book, moral norms rooted in shared cultural myths of a religious nature, could only constitute the basis for social cohesion in premodern societies, while this 'mechanical' type of solidarity erodes as modernity unfolds due to the expansion of the division of labor. This argument constitutes a direct attack on Auguste Comte's claim that modern societies, just like traditional ones, need collective religious myths to underpin morality and safeguard social cohesion: 'In his *Division of Labor* ... Durkheim was not gropingly moving toward an appreciation of shared moral norms; he was, in fact, moving away from Comte's emphasis on their significance in modern society' (Gouldner 1958: xiii). Rather than being based on cultural similarities between people, Durkheim proposed that in modern industrial societies solidarity comes instead from economic and functional differences between people: differences in capacities and occupational activities, as crystallized in the industrial division of labor. It is indeed awareness of the mutual dependence entailed by the latter that lies at the basis of the social cohesion of modern industrial societies: 'mechanical' solidarity gives way to 'organic' solidarity (Durkheim 1964 [1893]).

In his disagreement with Comte, Saint-Simon's sociology constitutes Durkheim's most important source of intellectual inspiration. Since in the end both industrial classes have an interest in the preservation and expansion of industrialism, Durkheim echoes Saint-Simon, this is exactly what serves as the basis for the social cohesion of modern society (Fenton 1984: 16). Durkheim's appropriation of Saint-Simon's sociology is hence drastically different from Marx's, who was deeply influenced by it too, most notably during his stay in Paris in the 1840s (Coser 1977: 56-62). The principal difference is how the two imagine the relationship between labor and capital, understood as inherently interdependent and cooperative by Durkheim and as essentially antagonistic by Marx. Whereas Durkheim consequently views exploitation, labor conflicts and class struggle as 'abnormal' excrescence, that can and should be avoided by a more 'rational' type of industrial organization, Marx sees them as 'normal' and 'inevitable' side effects of capitalism. This is Durkheim's line of thought when under the title 'Some Notes on Occupational Groups' he advocates cooperation between labor and capital in the famous foreword to the second edition of *The Division of Labor in Society* (1964 [1893]: 1-38), with the aim of nourishing awareness of mutual dependence so as to further industrial peace and reinforce organic solidarity.

This foreword hence reveals that for Durkheim organic solidarity is in fact so 'normal' that it does not even need to exist in the real world to qualify for this status, exposing one of Durkheim's typical movements from 'is' to 'ought.' In terms of Max Weber's theory of knowledge (1949 [1922]), this is a metaphysically informed value judgment, more or less skillfully disguised as an 'empirical fact'. Marx's strikingly different account is also informed by a pretension of having knowledge of a 'real' reality beyond culture that can authoritatively inform moral evaluations of what is 'normal' and 'abnormal', 'good' and 'bad'. For Marx, after all, workers who feel they have the same interests as capitalist entrepreneurs have a 'false' class consciousness: they do not simply hold 'different' moral and political values, but they are wrong, mistaken and do not understand what the world is 'really' like. Only those who have a 'true' class consciousness, and hence like Marx himself 'know' that modern industrialism is 'really' or 'essentially' about labor's exploitation by capital, and who translate this 'knowledge' into political action against capitalism, display a 'rational' understanding of what the world is 'really' like.

The fact that Durkheim and Marx follow the same positivist logic, yet nonetheless arrive at incompatible moral evaluations of what is 'normal' and 'abnormal', 'good' and 'bad', does much to demonstrate how deeply problematical this logic actually is. It is informed by nineteenth-century Enlightenment rationalism and its quest to not simply dethrone a 'false', 'superstitious' and 'traditional' religiously-informed morality, but to simultaneously replace it by a superior and scientifically-informed one (Seidman 1994: 19-53)—precisely the ambition unmasked by Weber as futile and intellectually dishonest. The only way to evade this positivist logic is by giving culture its full due, that is, refusing to reduce it to a 'less-than-real' reality, that as such only obscures a 'more real' and 'more fundamental' non-cultural social reality, assumed to reside 'behind' or 'underneath' it.

Individualism in Late-Durkheimian Sociology

This reductionist treatment of culture disappears in Durkheim's more mature work, however, which marks a change in precisely the direction he initially did not want to go. He came to recognize the role of religious myths in grounding morality and securing social cohesion and came to understand religion as an inevitable feature of all human societies, be they 'primitive' or modern (Seigel 1987). Because religion constitutes the sacralization of a society's most cherished values, he came to argue, modernity cannot mean the end of religion, but can only entail its transformation. This analysis, brought forward in his last book, *The Elementary Forms of Religious Life* (1965 [1912]) could hence not differ more from the one presented in his first book, which offered nothing less than an attack on this very notion.

The difference between the early and the late Durkheim is particularly visible in his treatment of individualism. Although there are multiple references to 'individualism' and 'the cult of individualism' in *The Division of Labor in Society*, all of these are dismissive and 'decidedly negative' (Chandler 1984: 571). This is because although Durkheim was keenly aware of individualism's presence and influence, acknowledging that in modern society 'the individual becomes the object of a sort of religion', he then still understood it as the antithesis of morality, underscoring that 'it is not to society that [the cult of individualism] attaches us; it is to ourselves', so that 'it does not constitute a true social link' (Durkheim 1964 [1893]: 172).

He abandoned this antithetical understanding of the relationship between individualism and morality during the Dreyfus affair that shook France in 1898. In his essay 'Individualism and the Intellectuals' (Durkheim 1973 [1898]), he responded to the anti-Dreyfusards' charge that the liberal individualism of the intellectuals paved the way for anarchy, disorder, and anti-social egoism. Quite to the contrary, Durkheim argued, because one needs to make a sharp distinction between two different types of individualism. On the one hand, there is the 'utilitarian' type of individualism that he, just like in *The Division of Labor*, associates with 'the strict utilitarianism and the utilitarian egoism of Spencer and the economists' (idem: 44) and characterizes as an 'egoistic cult of the self' (idem: 45) and as 'morally impoverished' (idem: 44). On the other hand, however, there is a 'moral' type of individualism, 'the individualism of Kant and Rousseau, of the idealists—the one [of] the Declaration of the Rights of Man' (idem: 45), in which '[the] human person … is considered sacred in the ritual sense of the word' (idem: 46).

In his article, Durkheim now defended this moral type of individualism as 'the only system of beliefs which can ensure … moral unity …', thus spectacularly reversing his initial position to now even claim that it is 'a simple truism' (*sic*) that 'religion alone can produce ... moral unity' (idem: 50)—exactly the position that *The Division of Labor* set out to attack. This is because this moral type of individualism does not value that which separates people from one another, but rather sacralizes their shared humanity. It 'springs not from egoism but from sympathy for all that is human' (idem: 48) and holds that '[t]he rights of the individual are above those of the state' (idem: 46) and that '[t]he dignity of the individual [comes] ... from the higher source ... [of partaking] in humanity' (idem: 48). '[T]his religion of humanity ... is the only one possible', Durkheim now argued, because under conditions of modernity people have 'nothing in common except humanity' (idem: 51), which serves to give this 'religion of humanity' the status of a 'religion in which man is at once the worshipper and the God' (idem: 46). In stark contrast to *The Division of Labor in Society*, in short, in his later work Durkheim came to construe individualism as the religion of modernity *par excellence*, that is, as providing moral cohesion to modern societies.

Indeed, in his last book *The Elementary Forms of Religious Life*, Durkheim conceives of religion as a major source of solidarity and cohesion in any type of society, 'primitive' and 'modern' alike, defining religion as 'a unified system of beliefs and practices relative to sacred things, that is to say, things set apart and forbidden—beliefs and practices which unite into one single community ... all those who adhere to them' (1965 [1912]: 44). Whereas he prefers to call this community a 'church' to convey 'the notion that religion must be an eminently collective thing' (idem: 44), it seems preferable to retain the latter notion without evoking the 'church' concept with its narrow Christian connotations. Of particular interest is his brief discussion of speculations among his contemporaries about 'whether a day will not come when the only cult will be the one that each person freely practices in his innermost self' (idem: 43), a cult that as such 'would consist entirely of interior and subjective states and be freely constructed by each of us' (idem: 44). Equally aware of these aspirations as his German counterpart Weber, Durkheim likewise dismisses them as sociologically naïve and socially infirm, sticking to his strictly sociological conception of religion and commenting that 'if that radical individualism has remained in the state of unrealized theoretical aspiration up to now, that is because it is unrealizable in fact' (idem: 427).

And indeed, these desires should not be confused with Durkheim's 'religion of humanity', because the former sacralize the particularities of people's personal emotional inner worlds, while the latter sacralizes what people have in common, that is, their shared humanity. This reveals how much the humanistic universalism of 'Individualism and the Intellectuals' is informed by an Enlightenment rationalism that forges a close link between intellectual rationalism and moral individualism, with the two presupposing and reinforcing one another. Without a hint of irony, Durkheim writes about the 'dogma of autonomy of reason' and the 'doctrine of free inquiry' (1973 [1898]: 49) as undergirding the religion of humanity and he calls upon his readers to 'make use of our liberties to seek out [from 'is'] what we must do ... [to 'ought']' (idem: 56).

Individualism and Subjectivism since World War II

When half a century and two world wars later counter-cultural protests started voicefully expressing modernity's cultural discontents, it became abundantly clear that Durkheim had been only half right when he proclaimed moral individualism as modernity's new religion. He was right in acknowledging its role as a major moral resource, but clearly wrong in believing that this basically negatively defined type of liberty (in the sense of Berlin's (1969) 'freedom from') sufficed to endow modern life with new meaning and purpose. The counter culture proved that it did not and further stimulated the subjective turn Durkheim and Weber already witnessed in their own days and dismissed as 'weak' and 'socially infirm'. The subjectivism of the counter culture added a less negatively defined notion of individual liberty to solve the problem of 'freedom for what?', neglected by Durkheim's individualism-cum-rationalism. It does so by encouraging people to seek self-development and personal growth, and to be true to themselves by taking their intuitions, experiences and emotions seriously.

The Counter Culture and the Dream of Individualism

Enter the Counter Culture

The counter culture of the 1960s was informed by modernity's cultural discontents that took shape as 'a deepening condition of "homelessness"' or a 'metaphysical loss of "home"' (Berger et al. 1973: 82) and that sparked attempts at cultural reconstruction to overcome this alienation. The counter culture was hence not so much an attempt at political revolution by middle-class youth that eventually failed, that disappeared as sudden as it appeared, and that is now over and done with, but it was rather an acceleration in an ongoing process of cultural transformation that has meanwhile changed Western societies virtually beyond recognition (Campbell 2007: 234-9, Marwick 1998: 13-15). This is why British historian Arthur Marwick prefers to refer to the counter culture as a 'cultural' rather than a 'counter-cultural' revolution, emphasizing that it 'did not *confront* [mainstream] society but *permeated* and *transformed* it' (idem: 13, his emphasis).

Critiquing 'the System'

Central to the counter culture was a deep disgust of rationalized modern institutions with their elaborate division of labor and hierarchical power structures that demand people to conform to narrowly and technically defined roles. Playing such roles was understood as alienating and being reduced to a mere functionally defined cog in a rationalized machine. Max Weber had already suggested that these discontents were responsible for the spiritual and experiential longings among his academic peers and students in Germany in the first decades of the twentieth century, noting that 'What is hard for modern man … is to measure up to *workaday* existence', and adding that '[the] ubiquitous chase for experience stems from this weakness' (1948 [1919]: 149, his emphasis). In the 1960s, for reasons we cannot go into here, these cultural discontents became central to a full-fledged cultural critique of modernity's increasingly rationalized institutional orders (see Campbell 2007: 184-249). This shows that, much like Weber already suggested in his own days, these institutions' relentless quest for rationalization, efficiency and effectiveness undermined their cultural meaningfulness and moral legitimacy. A positive identification with these 'abstract', alienating and unduly restrictive institutions and with the technically defined roles they consisted of had become increasingly difficult (Zijderveld 1970).

State bureaucracies, capitalist corporations, universities and research institutes alike came to be understood as standing in the way of what people could actually be: free, creative and autonomous individuals, aiming to live their lives to the fullest. In this cultural climate, informed by a marked individualism that insisted on the primacy of individual liberty and personal authenticity, 'the system' and those in charge of it were demonized as obstructing the latter. The source that reflects this best is Theodore Roszak's (1969) book *The Making of a Counter Culture: Reflections on the Technocratic Society and Its Youthful Opposition*, itself a counter-cultural pamphlet as much as a social-scientific study. It serves to underscore that counter-cultural protest was not simply directed against vestiges of moral traditionalism, conformity and obedience like the Christian churches (Brown 2001), but just as much against bulwarks of Enlightenment rationalism like the bureaucratic orders of the state, the corporate world, and the knowledge industry. Daniel Bell (1976: 143) has even gone so far as to maintain that 'though [the counter culture] appeared in the guise of an attack on the "technocratic society" [its ideology] was an attack on reason itself.'

Roszak's portrayal of 'the system'—itself, tellingly, one of the most widely used concepts within the counter culture—as a brute, dehumanizing agent did of course not stand alone. Jean-Paul Sartre and others reshaped Marxism into existentialism, critiquing the 'thingification' (*chosification*) of human beings by science and technology as a major threat to human freedom. The Frankfurt School, and particularly Erich Fromm, Max Horkheimer, Herbert Marcuse and Theodor Adorno, added a sizable dose of Freud to Marxism, thus replacing the 'old Marx' (the one of the 'economic laws of capitalist development' and the 'inevitable' socialist revolution) by the 'young Marx' (the one who critiqued capitalism for its alienating tendencies, that is, its dehumanizing reduction of workers to mere cogs in the machine).

In the hands of the Frankfurters, faith in an inevitable socialist revolution gave way to the ambition to liberate the self from psychologically harmful, externally imposed limits, indoctrinations and illusions. It goes without saying, the Frankfurters basically maintained, that capitalist corporations and the state have a vested interest in making people believe that they are actually free and happy inhabitants of a tolerant and democratic society, but whoever is willing to take the effort of looking more carefully and more critically, will quickly discover that what is masked as 'real' tolerance is in fact mere 'repressive' tolerance and that even people's deepest and most cherished personal dreams, needs and desires have been molded and manipulated (Marcuse 1964). Horkheimer and Adorno's (2002 [1944]) influential critique of the culture industries, charged with keeping people in a shiftless, complacent and uncritical state of half sleep so as to veil the harsh realities of the real world and seduce them to believe that their profound alienation is in fact a state of satisfaction and happiness, constitutes a major case in point. The climate of system paranoia back then made theories such as these immensely enticing, credible and popular, which shows how much a marked individualism, insisting on the primacy of individual liberty and personal authenticity, was indeed central to the counter culture.

Escaping 'the System'

The religious domain witnessed much the same cultural discontents and turbulence. Churches and church authorities were critiqued for straitjacketing believers in religious orthodoxy; for refusing to provide room for doubt and critical discussion about Christian doctrines and traditional teachings about sexuality, women's roles, homosexuality, marriage and the family; and for refusing to take personal spiritual experience very seriously (Brown 2001). These discontents sparked a veritable exodus from the churches that has in less than five decades transformed Christianity into a minority position in the formerly Protestant countries of northwestern Europe (Houtman and Mascini 2002). With their 'New Theology', Protestant theologians like Rudolf Bultmann and Paul Tillich attempted to make Christianity less vulnerable to the newly emerged cultural climate, but could only do so by reinterpreting the Bible as containing neither 'literal truths' nor 'God's word' and by instead emphasizing the vital importance of the self and its experiences. Tillich, for instance, 'urged people to look for God in the "depths" of their life, in the very "source" of their being, and to recognize God in their most ultimate concerns' (Campbell 2007: 273).

   Outside the Christian churches, counter-cultural critiques of 'the system' sparked a spiritual turn to the deeper layers of one's own consciousness, allegedly not infested by the outer world and as such providing 'real' freedom, 'real' liberty and 'real' meaning (Zijderveld 1970). This 'turn within' sparked interest in non-Western religions like Hinduism and Buddhism, and of course much more so in their meditation practices than in their doctrines, theologies and sacred texts (Campbell 2007). The New Age movement, which advocated such a 'turn within' and promised an imminent Age of Aquarius that would bring an end to alienation, became an attractive option in this climate. It is informed by the notion that people have basically not one, but two selves: a 'mundane', 'conventional' or 'socialized' self that is demonized as the 'false' or 'unreal' product of society and its institutions, and a contrasting 'higher', 'deeper', 'true' or 'authentic' self that is sacralized as basically unpolluted by society and its institutions and hence conceived as 'who one is by nature.' The principal goal in life according to the deeply romantic strain of religion that New Age is, is to disconnect from the former self and connect to the latter by means of a range of available psychological and spiritual therapies and meditational practices. It understands this as embarking on an essentially infinite journey of personal spiritual growth that coincides with a gradual overcoming of the state of alienation one is kept in by society and its institutions (Heelas 1996a). Wouter Hanegraaff (2002: 259), an international academic expert in this field (Hanegraaff 1996), is hence correct to underscore that 'New Age spirituality is strictly focused on the individual and his/her personal development', adding that 'this individualism functions as an in-built defense mechanism against social organization and institutionalization', thus explaining New Age's appeal within the boundaries of the anti-institutional counter culture.

Psychological and spiritual therapies and meditation were, however, not the only ways of escaping modernity and its alienations. Firstly, the experiential 'road within' was also followed with the help of hallucinogenic drugs like LSD, mescaline and magic mushrooms. Indeed, his advocacy of LSD owed Timothy Leary, whose 'turn on, tune in, drop out' would become the creed of the counter culture, his reputation as a psychedelic guru. Secondly, and much like nineteenth-century romanticism (think of Rousseau's 'noble savage'), the counter culture sparked a fascination for cultures seen as untouched by modern civilization. This led to the establishment of small tribe-like communities in pastoral or natural environments, away from modernity's urban centers, where those concerned hoped to be able to live a life in harmony with nature and like-minded others. Examples are Arcosanti in the United States (founded in 1970) and Findhorn in Scotland (founded in 1972), but one can of course also think of temporary events and festivals like Woodstock (1969). A third case in point, finally, was the hippies' enthusiastic embracement of romantic fiction, fairy tales and fantasy novels about pristine civilizations in imaginary pasts. The best illustration is Tolkien's *Lord of the Rings* with its mythical world Middle Earth, inhabited by hobbits, elves and wizards. When it was released as a paperback in 1965 it was embraced as 'immediately familiar, upon first reading, with an apparently imaginary place and/or time' (Curry 2004: 118) and it was 'absolutely the favorite book of every hippie' (Hinckle, quoted in Ellwood 1994: 201).

Just as much as counter-cultural critiques of 'the system', in short, its romantic desires of finding refuge in less alienating inner, exotic, natural and fantasy worlds were informed by markedly individualist longings for personal authenticity and 'real' liberty. Meanwhile, almost half a century later, these ideals have far from withered away. They have rather transformed mainstream Western society virtually beyond recognition and can now no longer be dismissed as 'deviant' critiques from society's 'margins' (for example, Furedi 2003). They have become the dominant culture.

Individualism from Counter Culture to Mainstream

The individualism that was so voicefully expressed by the counter culture has meanwhile developed into the cultural logic that governs the very domains and institutions that were still critiqued as alienating only half a century ago (Houtman 2008). Authoritarian and bureaucratic management regimes, stifling churches and religious orthodoxy, the mass consumerism of the culture industries, and last but not least politics that refused to take cultural demands for individual liberty seriously, have all transformed in ways informed by the thrust of the counter-cultural critique.

Breaking Free from Systems and Roles

When the counter culture raged against bureaucratic conformism, against authoritarian management regimes and against the creative dullness of the corporate world, it basically echoed and amplified critical voices already heard in the 1950s. Back then, critical books about industrial organization, work and management, informed by concerns that were very similar to the ones the hippies would come to embrace later on, were already remarkably well received. The best known examples, which have meanwhile all attained a classical status in management studies and the sociology of organizations, are Elton Mayo's *Hawthorne and the Western Electric Company: The Social Problems of an Industrial Civilisation* (1949), C. Wright Mills' *White Collar* (1951), William H. Whyte's *The Organization Man* (1956) and Douglas McGregor's *The Human Side of Enterprise* (1960).

The counter culture's rootedness in the preceding decade shows that a replacement of Henry Ford's Fordism and Frederick Taylor's 'scientific management' (Braverman 1974) was already incipient by the time the hippies started repeating and amplifying these critiques in the 1960s. Since then, a 'new spirit of capitalism' (Boltanski and Chiapello 2005) has emerged—a spirit that boasts job autonomy, self-management, and personal creativity and as such poses a major break with the massively bureaucratic organizational forms of the past. Management bestsellers like *The Seven Habits of Highly Effective People* (Covey 1989) and *In Search of Excellence* (Peters and Waterman 1982) are saturated with notions of 'flexibility', 'autonomy', 'creativity', 'innovation', 'excellence', 'activity', and 'readiness for change', alongside 'client-orientation', 'people first', and 'human resources', all tapping into notions of freedom, self-transcendence and overcoming alienation. 'Instead of predicating work upon the premise of sacrificing the integrity of the whole person', Costea et al. (2007: 250) rightly point out, concepts such as these 'draw around work the discursive contours of liberating the entire "self", releasing it from the erstwhile shackles of "Taylorism"/"Fordism" or the "Protestant ethic".' Due to this transformation, '[work] becomes a stage for self-expression' and 'the site of control is ... displaced to a significant extent from external authority to inner attributes of the subject who is urged to self-manage' (idem: 253). This basically comes down to 'substituting *self-control* for *control*' (Boltanski and Chiapello 2005: 191, their emphasis).

Desires to break away from structures and formalized roles remain neither limited to the corporate world of capitalism, nor to management more generally. Politicians are also increasingly expected to adopt more personalized styles, further adding to an already marked 'personalization' of politics (for example, Mughan 2000, Wattenberg 1991). They increasingly try to maintain a critical distance from their formal political roles by showing the public who they 'really' are—that is, who they are as 'private', 'non-role-playing' persons. Supported by skilful campaign teams, public relations officers and spin doctors, they stage their authenticity in carefully directed media appearances, not hesitating to throw in their spouses, babies or personal hobbies if that appears helpful.

A few examples from our own country suffice. Christian-Democratic party leader Wim van de Camp built his campaign for the European elections of June 2009 around his personal hobby of motorcycle racing, and even went so far as to launch it clad in a motor suit. In the period preceding the national elections of June 2010, Job Cohen (back then mayor of Amsterdam, now leader of the Labor Party), acted as a guest editor for Dutch women's magazine *Margriet* and was as such featured on its cover. He avidly used the opportunity to treat the magazine's readers (mostly middle-aged women) on, among other things, a look inside his official residence, an interview with his wife and his favorite bicycle tour through Amsterdam. At roughly the same time, minister of agriculture Gerda Verburg (Christian Democrats) managed to get her own personal glossy *Gerda* published, in which she eagerly displayed her life in the countryside and shared some of her favorite recipes.

From Churched Religion to Personal Spirituality

Rather than a transition from Christian religion to a moral individualism-cum-rationalism as advocated by Durkheim at the beginning of the twentieth century, a massive subjective shift towards spirituality has taken place since the 1960s (Houtman and Aupers 2007, Houtman and Mascini 2002). In the opening pages of their book *The Spiritual Revolution*, Paul Heelas, Linda Woodhead and their colleagues summarize this transition as follows:

> in the West those forms of religion that tell their followers to live their lives in conformity with external principles to the neglect of the cultivation of their unique subjective-lives will be in decline. Many churches and chapels are likely to fall into this category. By contrast, those forms of spirituality in the West that help people to live in accordance with the deepest, sacred dimensions of their own unique lives can be expected to be growing. (2005: 7)

Although this increasingly popular type of spirituality is historically rooted in New Age and its utopian promises of an imminent Age of Aquarius, the latter notion with its socially critical implications, and indeed the label 'New Age' itself, has lost most its former appeal. Nothing would be more mistaken than to conclude from this that the associated type of spirituality has meanwhile disappeared, too, however. Rather to the contrary: it is more accurate to conclude from this that New Age, with its characteristic rejection of restrictive religious traditions, institutions and doctrines, and its emphasis on the primacy of subjective-life and personal experience, has become full part of the Western cultural mainstream. This has particularly occurred from the 1980s onwards, when it was lovingly and massively embraced in the media and popular culture (think of Shirley MacLaine in the 1980s, James Redfield and his *The Celestine Prophecy* in the 1990s, Oprah Winfrey, Dr. Phil, etcetera).

This growing popularity of New Age from the 1980s onwards sparked an awareness among its advocates, or at least a fear, that it was on the way of becoming an established religious tradition just like any other and this motivated a tension with its ethic of self-spirituality. According to the latter, being a member of an established religious tradition with its own heritage, canonical texts, routines and doctrines, and (perhaps worst of all) herd of dedicated followers, after all, comes alarmingly close to the New Age rendition of the Christian notion of 'sinfulness.' This dynamics explains why the term 'New Age' lost currency and why New Agers have turned towards more indeterminate labels like 'spirituality' ('Are you a New Ager?'; 'No, I am not; I am very interested in spirituality, though!'):

> [B]y the beginning of the 1990s, more and more people attracted to alternative spirituality began to distance themselves from the label New Age .... During the 1980s it was still possible to investigate the New Age movement ... simply by questioning people who identified themselves as involved in New Age; during the 1990s, participants have increasingly refused to identify themselves as such, preferring vague and non-committal terms such as 'spirituality'. (Hanegraaff 2002: 253, see also Heelas 1996a: 17)

The demise of the label 'New Age' does hence not indicate that longings for a personal spirituality have disappeared, but rather proves the opposite. Heelas et al. (2005) have even suggested that a 'spiritual revolution' may be underway, consisting of a major transition from 'religion' to 'spirituality', and Campbell (2007: 41) even goes so far as to observe 'a fundamental revolution in Western civilization, one that can be compared in significance to the Renaissance, the Reformation, or the Enlightenment.'

'Think Different!': Rebellious Consumers

Counter-cultural discontents about mass consumerism, understood as driven by narrow-minded conformism and jealousy of the size of the tail fins of the neighbor's car ('keeping up with the Joneses'), and the banal emptiness of the products of the culture industries were already expressed in the 1950s, too (Slater 1997: 11-

12). This critique has most influentially left its traces in David Riesman's book *The Lonely Crowd* (1950), allegedly the most sold sociology book ever. When the counter culture critiqued and ridiculed the conformity of mass consumerism, marketing concepts were already changing in ways consistent with it.

Marketing gradually gave way to branding, associating products with young, hip, cool, adventurous and non-conformist images and lifestyles. Corporations started challenging consumers to assert their self-dependence and personal authenticity by setting themselves apart from the dull gray masses. A 'hip consumerism driven by disgust with mass society itself' emerged, which 'promises to deliver the consumer from the dreary nightmare of square consumerism', resulting in a 'perpetual motion machine in which disgust with the falseness, shoddiness, and everyday oppressions of consumer society [is] enlisted to drive the ever-accelerating wheels of consumption' (Frank 1998: 31-2). Contemporary consumer culture has come to breathe the rebelliousness and non-conformism of the 1960s' counter culture, in short, even to the extent that 'the critique of mass society has been one of the most powerful forces driving consumerism for the past forty years' (Heath and Potter 2004: 98).

The iconic status attained by Che Guevara's portrait with military beret and wild mane is a major case in point. It is today no longer merely featured on posters and T-shirts, but on an immense collection of knickknacks, ranging from calendars, wallets and cigarette lighters to wristwatches, suspenders, and coffee mugs. A symbol of counter-cultural protest against capitalism and imperialism half a century ago, Che has now become the icon of a consumer culture driven by individualism, non-conformity and rebelliousness. And it is not difficult to find other examples of advertisements and commercials appealing to such dreams. Apple Macintosh, and particularly its award-winning *1984* commercial directed by Ridley Scott—known from movies like *Alien* (1979), *Blade Runner* (1982), *Thelma & Louise* (1991), *Gladiator* (2000) and *Robin Hood* (2010)—is of course an outstanding example.[1] The commercial presents Apple as a brand for rebellious individualists who have the moral stamina to withstand the dull grayness and slavish conformity of those who willingly and knowingly defer to the whims, caprices and impulses of those who happen to be in power. Apple's well-known *Think Different* campaign boasts a similar message and leaves just as little to the imagination.

One could of course counter that Apple, particularly through its charismatic front man Steve Jobs, is atypical in that it is more directly rooted in the counter culture than most other companies, but this would neglect the many other examples that are available. There is, for instance, Ikea's 'Design your own life' and even sound and reliable German BMW is nowadays flirting explicitly with a rebellious

---

1   The commercial can be found on Youtube: http://nl.youtube.com/watch?v=OYecfV3ubP8 [accessed February 24, 2011].

and non-conformist image in its campaign *Company of Ideas*.[2] Jack Pitney, Vice President Marketing BMW, USA, explains: 'We are eager to unveil this smart and original campaign that communicates BMW's culture of creativity so thoroughly. BMW has carved out a unique niche in the industry by placing a premium on constant innovation and inspiration and this campaign will reveal the company behind The Ultimate Driving Machine.' 'Was anything truly extraordinary ever achieved by compromise?', the campaign's printed ads ask rhetorically, to immediately give the obvious answer in an even larger font: 'In a word, no.' Roy Spence, president of advertising agency GSD&M (Austin, Texas), recounts that 'BMW's performance is legendary, but how they get there is an important part of the story as well. They get there through passion and inspiration—they aren't hindered by idea-killing bureaucracy.'

Also in our own country, the Netherlands, advertising slogans boasting ideals of personal authenticity galore: 'Always yourself' (HEMA department store); 'Being purely yourself for a moment with the refined blends of Pickwick' (Pickwick tea); 'The best you can become is yourself' (Content temporary employment agency); 'Ample room to be yourself' (Landal GreenParks holiday resorts); 'Be yourself—There are already so many others' (7Up); and 'Stay yourself until the end' (Monuta funeral insurances). Contemporary marketing and consumer culture, we conclude, is permeated by articulations of an individualist and non-conformist ethic that is drawn upon to endow commodities with auras of personal rebelliousness and to associate them with cultural ideals of personal authenticity. The counter-cultural spirit of individualism has not disappeared, but now fuels the engines of consumerism.

The Rise of Cultural Politics: Political Conflicts about Individual Liberty

The counter-cultural quest for individual liberty also sparked a new type of cultural politics in which old-style distributive class issues have become overshadowed by cultural desires for expanding individual liberty, overcoming alienation and furthering democratic participation. New-leftist parties emerged besides the established parties on the left and the notion that particularly well-educated voters feel attracted to the former, because they embrace individual liberty more enthusiastically than the less educated do, became a theoretical mainstay in the study of politics (Houtman 2003).

This increased political salience of cultural issues pertaining to individualism has sparked a gradual decline, and in some instances even a reversal, of the familiar pattern of a leftist-voting working class and a rightist-voting middle class that old-school class theories of politics have since the nineteenth century accepted as virtually 'natural'. Indeed, book titles such as *The Death of Class* (Pakulski and

---

2   See, for example, http://goliath.ecnext.com/coms2/gi_0199-5507576/BMW-Unveils-New-Advertising-Campaign.html and http://danwarne.com/why-sony-cant-compete-against-apple-or-why-you-should-always-say-no-to-compromise/ [accessed February 24, 2011].

Waters 1996), *The Breakdown of Class Politics* (Clark and Lipset 2001) and *The End of Class Politics?* (Evans 1999) underscore the continuing prominence of these theories until the present day and this theoretical blindfold has caused many a student of politics to misunderstand the cultural dynamics that underlies the fading of the once allegedly 'natural' pattern (see in particular Nieuwbeerta's research: 1995, 1996, 2001, Nieuwbeerta and De Graaf 1999). For it has meanwhile become clear that the past half century has not so much been witnessing a decline in class politics, but rather a massive proliferation of cultural politics, central to which are cultural conflicts between educational categories, revolving around cultural issues pertaining to individual liberty (Achterberg 2006a, 2006b, Achterberg and Houtman 2006, Houtman 2001, 2003, Houtman et al. 2008a). To theoretically grasp the dynamics of conflict in contemporary cultural politics one hence needs to give the moral individualism that was so powerfully articulated in the 1960s counter culture its due, and particularly needs to recognize its increased politicization from the 1980s onwards.

Until the 1980s the new moral individualism remained by and large uncontested and hence constituted the dominant political discourse. The political culture of this period was hence consistent with the work of Inglehart (1977, 1997), who has characterized it in terms of a marked shift away from the old 'materialist' value priorities of the old economically-oriented socialist left to the new 'postmaterialist' priorities of a new and markedly culturally-oriented left that instead emphasizes personal liberty, individual freedom and self-expression. This is of course not to deny that even in the heydays of the 1960s there were pockets of rightist-authoritarian resistance and critique, driven by desires of curbing the new moral individualism and re-establishing social order (Ransford 1972). Conflict and polarization even occurred among university students, who more than any other group carried the spirit of cultural and political protest, pointing out that the new emancipatory cultural politics of the left has never been unanimously embraced in even these circles (Klatch 1999, Lyons 1996).

Nonetheless, dissident voices remained discursively marginal until the 1980s. From that decade onwards, however, a new-rightist backlash gained political strength all over Western Europe and new-rightist and populist political parties won considerable shares of the vote (Ignazi 1992, 2003, Veugelers 2000). In this decade, new-leftist politics in effect got its new-rightist counterpart, with the new-rightist parties, much like their new-leftist predecessors, emphasizing cultural issues (in their case curbing immigration and fighting crime in particular) rather than the economic and distributive issues of the good-old politics of class. From the 1980s onwards, Western European politics hence no longer merely boasts two lefts, but two rights, too.

Despite minor new-rightist electoral successes in the 1980s, the breakthrough of new-rightist politics occurred much later in the Netherlands than elsewhere in Western Europe. It only took off in 2001, when the late Pim Fortuyn started successfully attacking new-leftist moral-political taboos about immigration and multiculturalism. His landslide victory in the national elections of 2002 marked the breakthrough of new-rightist populism in the Netherlands and his ghost haunts Dutch politics until the present day. Geert Wilders's Freedom Party is nowadays most successful electorally in articulating new-rightist populism, making it Fortuyn's LPF's principal heir.

The interesting thing about this new Dutch populism is that it is rooted in the individualist longings of the counter-cultural 1960s in various ways. Much like in most other Western European countries, it is of course first of all a political reaction to and hence rejection of the latter, conceiving of problems relating to mass immigration, crime and unsafety as direct outgrowths of the overly tolerant new-leftist politics of the baby-boom generation (Mascini and Houtman 2011). Whoever listens carefully to what new-rightist politicians like Fortuyn and Wilders actually have to say, can not fail to miss that their discourse is also informed by the counter culture in a much more direct way, however, even to the extent of constituting a veritable 'counter culture 2.0'. For one thing, there is the populist aversion to a state seen as illegitimately catering to unproductive bureaucratic and political elites, who are more interested in their own salaries, their own careers and their own (to put it in Geert Wilders's terms) 'leftist hobbies' (like cultural, artistic and multicultural projects) than in making serious efforts to solve the problems hard-working and law abiding citizens face on an everyday basis. Despite the new populism's new-rightist political leanings, these complaints are not unlike the counter-cultural discontents about a bureaucratic state that is unresponsive to what the people really want.

The freedom-loving spirit of the counter culture can be heard even more loudly and clearly in populism's ruthless critiques of Muslims and Islam. These critiques are directly informed by an embracement of freedom of speech and women's and gay rights: 'In fact, if they are unwilling to become just as progressive and tolerant as we Dutch are, these Muslim immigrants ought to leave our country: they should give their own and our women more freedom and respect, they should stay away from our gays, and they should leave our freedom of speech alone.' Now that in heavily secularized Dutch society the moral principle of individual liberty has become virtually universally accepted, this type of exclusionary populist rhetoric has proven difficult to counter for progressive political parties.

Paradoxes of Individualization: Outline of the Book

Since the counter culture of the 1960s, in short, ideals of individual liberty, personal authenticity and tolerance have come to permeate the core institutions of modern, Western countries. This informs two paradoxes that will be addressed in this book. The first paradox is that this process of individualization entails a new, yet often unacknowledged, form of social control. Even though individuals now relentlessly aim to act out their originality, uniqueness, and personal authenticity, and almost obsessively insist on remaining true to themselves, they paradoxically do so in social environments that expect and demand them to do precisely that. Ideals of individual liberty, personal authenticity and tolerance have in short become social facts in the classical sense of Emile Durkheim (1964 [1895]).

Chapter 2 demonstrates that the 'agony of choice' that contemporary theorists of individualization attribute to consumers' need to continuously make selections from wide ranges of available options does in fact hardly exist. As we will see, consumers make their decisions virtually without effort and even understand them as enjoyable and meaningful opportunities to display their personal authenticity and uniqueness. Ironically, however, this effortlessness stems from the fact that their ideals of personal authenticity are firmly rooted in a pre-given cultural habitus that enables them to evade agony of choice by dismissing most of the options available to them as 'unacceptable for people like me' in the first place.

Chapter 3 further probes the social shaping of individualism by means of a study of New Age spirituality, typically portrayed in the scholarly literature as radically privatized with individuals freely and actively constructing and reconstructing strictly personal packages of meaning. This image is not so much false, but one-sided and incomplete, because it neglects that these practices of individual *bricolage* stem from a doctrine of self-spirituality that is itself collectively embraced and basically uncontested in the spiritual milieu. According to this doctrine, people *must* in fact be true to themselves and follow their personal spiritual paths. Participants are socialized in this doctrine through spiritual books and therapies and it has even come to play a significant role in the world of work, demonstrating that New Age spirituality is decidedly less privatized than it is typically taken to be.

Chapter 4 pushes the social construction of individual liberty a step further by demonstrating how the computer game industry actively engineers, produces, markets and sells it. The freedom celebrated by gamers in their enchanting yet commodified virtual worlds is pre-scripted, encoded and engineered by game designers and the industry actively markets it as enabling self-expression. As such, the freedom enjoyed in computer games constitutes a carefully crafted ideology that veils the economic interests of the game industry and helps retaining players in the game of modern capitalism.

Chapter 5 then analyzes how ideals of individualism and cultural tolerance paradoxically spark social exclusion of those who refuse to accept these ideals as morally binding. It does so by means of a case study of *Stormfront*, an online discussion forum for right-wing extremists, who prove to experience stigmatization and social exclusion by the liberal-individualist Dutch mainstream. Simultaneously, however, this right-wing extremism constitutes the most extreme and radical tip of a much larger iceberg of moral and political discontents about allegedly 'excessive' individualism and cultural tolerance. As such, this case study also serves to introduce the second paradox of individualization addressed in this book: precisely due to their increased social significance in the last half century, cultural ideals of individual liberty and cultural tolerance have become increasingly morally and politically contested.

Chapter 6 addresses religious contestations about individualism. It does so by means of a study of the struggles and dilemmas encountered in religious and spiritual appropriations of the Internet through web design. Web designers who identify with New Age spirituality embrace the decentralized, open and individualized new medium as an almost natural habitat for sharing spiritual wisdom and connecting with like-minded others. Particularly Catholic web designers, however, encounter major difficulties that stem from conflicts and disagreements about the legitimacy of Church authorities imposing limits on web content, linking policies, etcetera.

Chapter 7 then demonstrates the role of cultural conflict in contemporary Dutch politics. It does so by means of an analysis of survey data collected briefly after the historical national elections of May 2002 that brought Pim Fortuyn his landslide victory. Choosing between the old-leftist Labor Party and the old-rightist Conservative Party proves to constitute 'class voting', with a vulnerable economic position leading to leftist voting informed by desires for economic redistribution. Choosing between Fortuyn's new-rightist Populist Party and the new-leftist Greens, however, entails 'cultural voting', with a lack of cultural capital leading to rightist voting due to an authoritarian emphasis on maintenance of social order instead of a libertarian one on individual liberty.

Chapter 8 addresses cultural conflict in contemporary Dutch society by studying how secularization affects cultural tolerance. Whereas according to one theory the process increases general levels of ethnic tolerance, another maintains that it rather decreases the latter. We demonstrate that both theories are too crude and too general, because the former applies to the higher educated and the latter to the lower educated. Secularization does hence not unequivocally lead to either a more or a less tolerant general cultural climate, but affects different educational groups differently and hence increases cultural polarization and conflict about ethnic (in) tolerance between them.

Chapter 9, finally, addresses intolerance of Islam, one of the most hotly debated issues in Dutch politics in recent years. We demonstrate that this phenomenon is more complex than the good-old explanations in terms of ethnocentric prejudice among the lower educated suggest. We do in fact find evidence of a newly emerged cultural conflict between the lower and the higher educated about the meaning of secular ideals of individual liberty. The lower educated prove to essentialize these ideals to critique religious orthodoxy and reject Muslims and Islam, whereas the higher educated do not do so and hence relativize these same ideals. The post-Christian ideals of individual liberty that have become widespread in the Netherlands since the 1960s are hence nowadays used by the lower educated as a basis for social exclusion.

Chapter 2

Agony of Choice?: The Social Embeddedness of Consumer Decisions

With Sebastiaan van Doorn and Jochem Verheul

'Agony of Choice'

The recent privatization of telecommunication, health care insurance and domestic power supply in the Netherlands has made the 'agony of choice' a widely debated phenomenon, evoking images of consumers suffering from stress, doubts and anxiety due to the virtually infinite maze of options and opportunities they face up to. Next to prophets of doom from psychology, such as Schwartz (2004), many a contemporary sociologist also maintains that present-day freedom of choice has become a major problem. Now that the influence and legitimacy of institutions like the church, the state and the family has declined, individuals are allegedly 'condemned to individualization' (Beck and Beck-Gernsheim 1996), continuously struggling to make the correct choices in the absence of clearly defined and pre-given guidelines for thinking, feeling, and acting: 'In post-traditional contexts, we have no choice but to choose how to be and how to act' (Giddens 1994: 75, see also Bauman 2001a: 46-7). Because the variety of options to choose from has increased dramatically (Bauman 1998), and because the process of choice-making is understood as a strictly individual endeavor (Beck 1992), Beck and Beck-Gernsheim (1996) have even maintained that the West has witnessed the emergence of a new social type, *homo optionis*.

These sociological theorists of individualization maintain that the need to make a wide range of diverse and complex choices has come to dominate everyday life (Giddens 1991: 80); that this entails a proliferation of new personal risks, because people only have themselves to blame if they make the wrong choices (Beck 1992); and that they experience the ensuing insecurity as burdensome, stressful and frustrating (Bauman 2000, 2001a, Beck and Beck-Gernsheim 1996). Given sociology's markedly increased attention to these issues, it is striking to find that as yet little empirical research is available (Brannen and Nilsen 2005: 422). We will therefore explore how individuals cope with the vast number of complex choices they nowadays face up to. Consistent with the argument that the matter at hand pertains to 'small decisions' in 'day-to-day life' (Giddens 1991: 80-81, see also 1994: 74-6), we focus our study on these choices rather than on those relating to more fundamental and existential questions.

Method

We have conducted interviews with a sample of 30 students based in the Dutch city of Rotterdam, because morally traditionalist discourses that may impede the making of free choices is more firmly rejected in the Netherlands than anywhere else (Duyvendak 2004), particularly among well-educated young people, and especially so in artistic, cultural, social and hence non-economic, non-administrative and non-technical fields of education (Houtman 1996, 2003). We have therefore sampled students who pursue their studies at the Academy of Art besides students in economics and marketing at Erasmus University. If agony of choice is really the pressing problem contemporary theorists of individualization take it to be, we should hence certainly find it in this sample, particularly so within the former group of students. The students have been approached for an interview in their natural environment, that is, at the Art Academy and at Erasmus University Rotterdam. They have been interviewed at various places about how they make their choices as consumers, focusing on whether, when and why they do and do not experience these choices as difficult, burdensome or stressful, probing for examples of both types of cases.

Choice without Stress?

When asked about the stressfulness of consumer choices in everyday life, some respondents do indeed report stressful experiences, complaining without exception about the vast array of alternatives that defies all attempts at systematical and meaningful comparison. When we asked Judith to explain her difficulties in selecting a health insurance, she stated quite resolutely: 'The transparency of the choice was very poor.' Other respondents experience a similar unease when they do their daily groceries: 'Sometimes I think, "why so much and so unstructured?" Especially when I stroll around the supermarket it is hard to see the wood for the trees' (Luciana). These experiences of unease are, however, the exception rather than the rule. The majority of our respondents do not experience feelings of discomfort when they make their day-to-day consumer choices. Strikingly, neither students in economics or marketing nor the presumed stress-susceptible students at the Academy of Arts suffer from agony of choice. Apparently, then, in the real world the necessity and freedom to make selections from wide ranges of available consumer options does hardly lead to cognitive overload and stress. This is because of three different mechanisms that ward off these psychological problems, with the salience of the choice to be made for one's personal identity determining which of the three actually comes into play.

Firstly, if the choices at stake are considered trivial and unimportant, because there are no major benefits to be reaped and because there are no major implications for the presentation of self-identity, no need to make an optimal decision is experienced, so that a strategy of 'satisficing' is opted for, which basically comes down to avoiding the efforts of making deliberate and optimal choices. Secondly, if there are significant benefits and costs at stake, even though the decision has no major implications for the presentation of self, people choose to rely on the advice of experienced, trustworthy and knowledgeable members of their social networks. Thirdly and finally, consumer choices that could naïvely be expected to have the highest potential of invoking stress, doubts and anxiety, because they are considered of significance identity-wise, are in fact made virtually effortlessly. In such cases, people simply know what they want, due to taste preferences that are firmly inscribed in their cultural habitus (Bourdieu 1984), even though they rely strongly on a cultural discourse of individualism and personal authenticity.

Avoiding the Choice Process

If there are no major benefits at stake, the choice process is simply avoided, because even the 'best' choice can offer no benefits that could offset the efforts needed to find out which choice that actually is. Respondents hence decide not to choose in these instances. Examples of decisions typically mentioned in this context relate to health insurance and domestic power supply. In these cases, people simply prefer to stick to the provider they already have a contract with, to continue the contract with the power supplier of the previous tenant, or to simply accept the first option that comes up. Lisa, for example, recounts that she has not even bothered to check out all the new possibilities that have come into being with the liberalization reforms and that this has saved her a lot of mental efforts and stress: 'I could not make out the differences, stopped searching and thought "I don't care".' Dennis also considers the selection of a health insurance a mere necessary evil, and his attitude exemplifies the general aversion to the making of complex yet almost inconsequential choices like this in the first place: 'I did not look into it. First of all I have more important things to do. And second, the difference between the different providers is only a few euros at most. I just remained with my old provider.' Following the same reasoning, the choice for a power supplier did not present any problems for Luciana: 'My current provider is fine. As long as I can do what I want, such as cooking and watching television, I do not bother myself with this issue.' As long as the differences between the products offered by the various health insurance providers are negligible, and as long as the service of the current provider is not too bad, our respondents hence do not want to waste their precious time on choices such as these. They do not press themselves to arrive at an optimal outcome and are satisfied with an option they consider 'good enough.'

The same strategy of avoiding stress by deciding not to really choose at all can be observed with respect to consumer goods. Talking about her selection of a new camera, Mickey explains that she does not keep searching until she is certain that she has made the optimal choice: 'No, I do not look for the best, because I know I will not find it. As long as it works properly, I am satisfied. If I have to take into account all information out there it would cost me too much time and too much effort.' As soon as an acceptable option is found, respondents stop taking other alternatives into account and the selection process ends.

Massive and unprecedented freedom of choice does not necessarily lead to stress, then: if the selections to be made are considered unimportant, people simply refuse to waste their precious time and energy on them. What our interviewees experience is hence clearly not 'agony of choice', but at most 'fatigue of choice' (Hurenkamp and Kremer 2005). This fatigue stimulates them to avoid decision-making altogether, as we have seen, but this only applies to choices they consider unimportant. If there are considerable benefits and costs at stake, they do push for better results, increasing the potential for stress. In these instances, we do not find agony of choice either, however, because an alternative mechanism of stress prevention comes into play.

Relying on One's Social Network

If there are clear benefits at stake, our respondents consider it more important to evaluate the alternatives with respect to price and quality. Although this inevitably complicates the selection process and increases the risk of stress, the latter is contained by reliance on advice by experienced, trustworthy and knowledgeable external sources. Occasionally the Internet is consulted, especially product-comparison sites, but only to collect a limited amount of information, so as not to risk swamping themselves by a vast array of alternatives. Far more typically than relying on the Internet, however, our interviewees rely on advice provided by friends and relatives who have previously made the decisions they now face up to themselves. Marc, for instance, fully trusts the judgments of his friends in selecting a mobile phone subscription, a decision he considers too important to be made just like that: 'I want quality, but for the best price. With this choice I follow the advice of some of my friends. If they tell me they are sometimes hard to reach with provider [X] than I know that next time I get a new subscription provider [X] is off my list.' We find the same strategy with Eric, who similarly relies on advice from knowledgeable others in his personal network: 'I ask some people around me what kind of insurance they have and I check some sites. Afterwards I take the first good deal I can get.' Somewhat like the strategy of avoiding the making of choices altogether discussed above, respondents make sure that they do not involve too many different opinions into their choice process, as this would only complicate matters. They restrict themselves to one or two self-assigned 'specialists' and trust their judgment, as Justin explains: 'when choosing a mobile phone subscription, I just check what my friends have and then if it is not some obscure company it's fine by me.' This second mechanism hence has a more explicitly social character than the strategy of avoiding the choice process altogether that we have discussed above.

Lifestyle, Habitus and Personal Authenticity

Thirdly, choices that pertain to respondents' identities and are therefore seen as meaningful and important are made effortlessly, precisely because such choices are considered a direct outcome of who they are. Although the large majority of our respondents considers the selection of a health insurance unimportant, for instance, it is in fact quite meaningful and important to Sophie because it is closely associated with her lifestyle and self-image: 'This is an important choice, indeed: alternative medicine is an important part of who I am and what I believe in.' Precisely because the choice she needs to make touches upon her identity, she explains that she knows very well what to choose, making this choice an easy one, taken without any difficulty. Identity-related choices such as these are in fact not merely understood as easy and unproblematic, but even embraced as fun, interesting and vital to one's self-presentation. Chris, for example, recounts how pleasant he finds decision-making about his upcoming holiday: 'The selection of my holiday is fun. I always enjoy this, not only because the topic is pleasant, but also because with this choice I know very well what I want.'

These identity-related choices center around issues like cultural participation, vacation and clothing. Friends and relatives are hardly asked for advice here, because our interviewees know very well what they want and consider their choices highly personal and unique to themselves. They understand these choices as providing an opportunity to distinguish themselves from others and believe that originality plays a major role in making these choices. Ignacio, for instance, claims: 'Originality is important, especially with clothing, my car and my girlfriend. These choices say something about who I am. If I would choose something that everybody in my environment already has, it would not be original and that is not much fun.' Likewise, Elina explains: 'I really dislike all this boring uniformity. I am very much aware of the fact that a lot of people choose and dress alike. In that way they are all the same. I try to make an effort not to be like that.' When respondents make statements such as these, they continuously refer to their personal identity and their longing for personal authenticity, as Bernardo exemplifies: 'Clothing should fit with my identity. It enables me to be different from everybody else.'

Dreams of individualism and personal authenticity hence play a major role in containing the alleged stress that contemporary theorists of individualization attribute to consumers' need to continuously make selections from wide ranges of options, and even serve to make these choices a pleasurable and meaningful source of fun. Obviously, this effortlessness in making 'personal' choices stems from clear-cut preferences and dislikes that are firmly rooted in a pre-given cultural habitus that enables them to dismiss most of the available options as 'unacceptable' for people like themselves without further reflection (Bourdieu 1984). Marc, a business student, knows, for instance, very well what kind of holiday he wants: 'Holidays at the beach are real holidays to me, that fits me perfectly.' Marc, again referring to his authenticity, also knows quite well what he does not like: 'Cultural holidays, or too much action like picking grapes, are not my cup of tea. That is no holiday to me. It just does not suit me.' Because of this clear preference, he does not experience the need to assess the whole range of available options. Just like all other business students, Mariano is similarly outspoken about his preference for a holiday at the beach: 'To me, holiday is sun, sea, beautiful women and a nice pint on the table next to my lawn chair. ... A cultural holiday is not my kind of holiday.'

We also find major similarities amongst the respondents from the Art Academy, although their 'individual' preferences are strikingly different from those of the business and economics students. Steve, for example, does much to underscore his longing for personal authenticity when he explains his preference for a cultural holiday: 'I normally choose for a city trip to Barcelona, New York or Tokyo. I am extremely interested in modern as well as ancient architecture and the modern art that can be found in the museums in these cities. That is my idea of a perfect holiday.' He furthermore explains that a holiday at the beach, so eagerly pursued by the business students, does not at all appeal to him. The other art students use basically identical discourse, as exemplified by Mickey: 'Lloret de Mar [a popular beach resort in Spain] or something like that does not appeal to me. I would not dream of going there. I like the country [Spain], but the kind of holiday that seems inextricably bound up with Lloret does not suit me. The people who go there are not my kind of people, and I would like to do more than just partying.'

The unmistakable similarities in preferences and dislikes within the two groups of students stem from their unacknowledged need to make choices that are consistent with the preferences of their peers. Even though their preferences and decisions closely resemble those of others within the same lifestyle group, because they are firmly inscribed in the habitus, our interviewees interpret these preferences as constituting nothing less than a strictly personal self-identity that guides their consumptive decision-making. It is this dream of liberty, agency and personal authenticity that not merely protects them from agony of choice, but that also enables them to celebrate a most meaningful sense of personal authenticity through which they imagine they can distinguish themselves from others.

Conclusion

Even though the young and well-educated people from one of the most detraditionalized countries in the world should, according to contemporary individualization theory, be particularly vulnerable to agony of choice, we hardly find such a thing. This is all the more striking, because individualization theorists particularly hold choices related to identity to be an inescapable 'task' (Bauman 2001a: 144), that gives rise to 'a bunch of problems' (Bauman 2004: 12) and leads to acute insecurity and frustration (Bauman 2001a: 151). This is, however, not at all what we find. More than that: next to strategies of avoiding trivial and unimportant choices altogether and relying on advice from experienced, trustworthy and knowledgeable friends and relatives, we find that our interviewees consider the making of consumer choices through which they can set themselves apart from others a major source of meaning, fun and pleasure.

The fact that agony of choice is nonetheless discussed abundantly throughout contemporary sociology and psychology and the popular press alike hence suggests a massive blind spot for the social embeddedness of consumer behavior. Clearly, claims to the effect that 'it has become questionable to assume that collective units of meaning and action exist' (Beck and Beck-Gernsheim 1996: 40) stem from such a blind spot. Such claims grossly exaggerate and misrepresent individualization and fail to appreciate the major social significance of shared ideals of individualism and personal authenticity. Nonetheless, our findings are basically compatible with Giddens's (1991: 82) notion that lifestyles are helpful in making consumer and other choices, although he wrongly neglects how firmly these lifestyles are themselves rooted in the habitus, that firmly internalized structuring structure that subconsciously determines taste and lifestyle (Atkinson 2007, Bourdieu 1984).

Although we have only considered 'the small decisions a person makes every day' (Giddens 1991: 81) in this chapter, there are no strong grounds for believing that choices related to more fundamental and existential issues yield a different picture. Examples would be the religion to uphold or whether to believe in a God at all, decisions about marriage or partnerships, about whether to have children or not, or about the political party to vote for. Indeed, the rest of this book does much to demonstrate that such more fundamental and existential choices are equally strongly driven by a collective obsession with individualism, agency and personal authenticity that is itself firmly rooted in and structured by social forces that transcend the self.

Chapter 3
Beyond the Spiritual Supermarket: Why New Age Spirituality is Less Privatized Than They Say It Is

Introduction

In most of the social-scientific literature, New Age—or 'spirituality', as increasingly seems the preferred term—is used to refer to an apparently incoherent collection of spiritual ideas and practices. Most participants in the spiritual milieu, it is generally argued, draw upon multiple traditions, styles and ideas simultaneously, combining them into idiosyncratic packages. New Age is thus referred to as 'do-it-yourself-religion' (Baerveldt 1996), 'pick-and-mix religion' (Hamilton 2000), 'religious consumption à la carte' (Possamai 2003) or a 'spiritual supermarket' (Lyon 2000). In their book *Beyond New Age: Exploring Alternative Spirituality*, Sutcliffe and Bowman even go so far as to argue that 'New Age turns out to be merely a particular code word in a larger field of modern religious experimentation' (2000: 1), while Possamai states that we are dealing with an 'eclectic—if not kleptomaniac—process ... with no clear reference to an external or "deeper" reality' (2003: 40).

This dominant discourse about New Age basically reiterates sociologist of religion Thomas Luckmann's influential analysis, published almost half a century ago in *The Invisible Religion* (1967). Structural differentiation in modern society, or so Luckmann argues, results in erosion of the Christian monopoly and the concomitant emergence of a 'market of ultimate significance.' On such a market, religious consumers construct strictly personal packages of meaning, based on individual tastes and preferences. Indeed, in a more recent publication, Luckmann notes that New Age exemplifies this tendency of individual 'bricolage': 'It collects abundant psychological, therapeutic, magic, marginally scientific, and older esoteric material, repackages them, and offers them for individual consumption and further private syncretism' (1996: 75).

Luckmann emphasizes that those personal meaning systems remain strictly private affairs: by their very nature, and unlike traditional church-based Christian religion in the past, they lack a wider social significance and play no public role whatsoever. Writing thirty years ago, the late Bryan Wilson has made a similar claim about the post-Christian cults, stating that those 'represent, in the American phrase, "the religion of your choice," the highly privatized preference that reduces religion to the significance of pushpin, poetry, or popcorns' (1976: 96). And more recently, Steve Bruce characterized New Age as a 'diffuse religion', observing that

'There is no ... power in the cultic milieu to override individual preferences' (2002: 99).

Accounts such as those are found over and over again in the sociological literature, as Besecke rightly observes: 'Luckmann's characterization of contemporary religion as privatized is pivotal in the sociology of religion; it has been picked up by just about everyone and challenged by almost no one' (2005: 186). Work done in anthropology and the history of religion nonetheless suggests that this orthodoxy is deeply problematic (Hammer 2001, 2004, Hanegraaff 1996, 2001, Luhrmann 1989). And indeed, from within sociology itself, Heelas (1996a) has demonstrated convincingly that New Age spirituality is remarkably less eclectic and incoherent than typically assumed. Our aim in the current chapter is to elaborate on those dissenting voices and demonstrate that this sociological orthodoxy is not much more than an institutionalized intellectual misconstruction. More specifically, we criticize three related arguments that together constitute the privatization thesis: 1) that New Age boils down to mere individual 'bricolage', 2) that it is socially insignificant, because 'the transmission of diffuse beliefs is unnecessary and it is impossible' (Bruce 2002: 99), and 3) that it does not play a role in the public domain. We summarize our findings and briefly elaborate on their theoretical significance in the final section.

We base ourselves on data from a variety of sources, collected during Aupers' (2004) PhD research in the period 1999-2003. Besides literature on New Age and a variety of flyers and websites of Dutch New Age centers, we especially draw on in-depth interviews with two samples of New Age teachers. Focusing on this 'spiritual elite' rather than on people who only vaguely identify with labels such as 'spirituality' or 'New Age' enables us to study the worldview of the spiritual milieu in its most crystallized and 'pure' form. Besides, these are of course the very people who communicate this worldview to those who participate in their courses, trainings and workshops. The first sample consists of spiritual trainers who work for Dutch New Age centers in the urbanized western part of the country.[1] The centers have been randomly sampled from a national directory of nature-oriented medicine and consciousness-raising (Van Hoog 2001) and the respondents have next been randomly sampled from those centers' websites. Eleven of those initially contacted—a very large majority—agreed to be interviewed.[2] The second sample consists of trainers at Dutch New Age centers that specialize in spiritual courses for business life. Apart from this theoretically imposed restriction, the sampling procedure was identical to the one just described. Nine in-depth interviews were completed with, again, almost no refusals. Finally, we rely on data from a

---

1   This is the so-called 'Randstad', which is where most Dutch New Age centers are situated anyway.

2   This first round of interviews has been conducted by Inge van der Tak, our research assistant at the time (2002), carefully supervised by ourselves, of course. The interviews lasted about 90 minutes on average and were tape-recorded and typed out verbatim in all three rounds (see Aupers et al. 2003 for a report of the findings).

theoretically instructive case study of the Dutch company Morca that has embraced New Age capitalism. Within the context of this case study, Aupers has conducted in-depth interviews with Morca's president-director, his spiritual coach, four employees who had participated in the company's spiritual courses, and three employees who had not. Unless indicated otherwise, we draw on data from the first sample of spiritual trainers in the next section, on those from the second one in the section after that, and on those from the case study in the final empirical section.

The Ethic of Self-Spirituality

As the sociological orthodoxy suggests, teachers of Dutch New Age centers indeed prove to combine various traditions in their courses. One may use tarot cards in combination with crystal-healing and Hindu ideas about chakras; another may combine traditional Chinese medicine, Western psychotherapy and Taoism into another idiosyncratic concoction. There is, in short, no reason to deny the prominence of 'bricolage' in the spiritual milieu.

What is a problem, however, is that whereas scholars on New Age typically assume that this 'bricolage' or 'eclecticism' is the principal characteristic of New Age, *none* of the interviewees feels that the traditions on which they base their courses are at the heart of their worldview. As the Dutch New Age center 'Centrum voor Spirituele Wegen' argues in one of its flyers, 'There are many paths, but just one truth.' This *philosophia perennis* or 'perennial philosophy' derives from esotericism—and especially from Blavatsky's New Theosophy (Hanegraaff 1996)—and has influenced the first generation of New Agers in the 1970s through the work of Daisetz Teitaro Suzuki and Aldous Huxley. According to this perennialism, all religious traditions are equally valid, because they all essentially worship the same divine source. Perennialism's virtual omnipresence in the spiritual milieu can be illustrated by means of the following explanations by three of the interviewed New Age teachers:[3]

> I feel connected with the person of Jesus Christ, not with Catholicism. But I also feel touched by the person of Buddha. I am also very much interested in shamanism. So my belief has nothing to do with a particular religious tradition. For me, all religions are manifestations of god, of the divine. If you look beyond the surface, then all religions tell the same story.

> That is important: you can find spirituality in every religion ... In Christianity you'll find Gnosticism, in Hinduism it is the philosophy of Tantra, in the Jewish

---

3   Unlike those in the remainder of this section, these three quotes are taken from the interviews with the second rather than the first sample of spiritual trainers. It should be emphasized, however, that all respondents from both samples adhere to this type of perennialism.

tradition it is the Kabbalah. The fundamentalist versions of religion are divided: only Allah, only Jesus Christ. But the esoterical undercurrent is almost the same!

For me it is easy to step into any tradition. I can do it with Buddhism from Tibet, with Hinduism, and I can point out what is the essence of every religion ... I am dealing with almost every world religion … There is not one truth. Of course there is one truth, but there are various ways of finding it.

More fundamental than 'bricolage', in short, is perennialism: the belief that the diversity of religious traditions essentially refers to the same underlying spiritual truth. Accepting this doctrine, people become motivated to experiment freely with various traditions to explore 'what works for them personally.' As already briefly indicated above, Heelas (1996a: 2) has done path-breaking work in laying bare the precise nature of this underlying spiritual truth, pointing out the primacy of the doctrine of self-spirituality:

Beneath much of the heterogeneity, there is remarkable constancy. Again and again, turning from practice to practice, from publication to publication, indeed from country to country, one encounters the same (or very similar) *lingua franca* ... This is the language of what shall henceforth be called 'Self-spirituality' ... And these assumptions of Self-spirituality ensure that the New Age Movement is far from being a mish-mash, significantly eclectic, or fundamentally incoherent. (his emphasis)

In the spiritual milieu, Heelas explains, modern people are essentially seen as 'gods and goddesses in exile' (1996a: 19): 'The great refrain, running throughout the New Age, is that we malfunction because we have been indoctrinated … by mainstream society and culture' (idem: 18). The latter are thus conceived of as basically alienating forces, estranging one from one's 'authentic', 'natural' or 'real' self—from who one 'really' or 'at deepest' is:

[T]he most pervasive and significant aspect of the *lingua franca* of the New Age is that the person is, in essence, spiritual. To experience the 'Self' itself is to experience 'God', 'the Goddess', the 'Source', 'Christ Consciousness', the 'inner child', the 'way of the heart', or, most simply and … most frequently, 'inner spirituality'. (idem: 19)

This, then, is the binding doctrine in the spiritual milieu: the belief that in the deeper layers of the self one finds a true, authentic and sacred kernel, basically 'unpolluted' by culture, history and society, that informs evaluations of what is good, true and meaningful. Those evaluations, it is held, cannot be made by relying on external authorities or experts, but only by listening to one's 'inner voice': 'What lies within—experienced by way of "intuition," "alignment" or an "inner voice"—

serves to inform the judgments, decisions and choices required for everyday life' (idem: 23).

Like traditional forms of religion, the idea of self-spirituality consists of a well-defined doctrine of 'being and well-being' (Goudsblom 1985) or a 'theodicy of good and evil' (Weber 1963 [1922]). A 'mundane', 'conventional' or 'socialized' self—often referred to as the 'ego'—, demonized as the 'false' or 'unreal' product of society and its institutions, is contrasted with a 'higher', 'deeper', 'true' or 'authentic' self that is sacralized and can be found in the self's deeper layers. In the words of our respondents:

> I experience god, the divine, as something within me. I feel it as being present in myself. I connect with it as I focus my attention on my inner self, when I meditate. … It's all about self-knowledge, being conscious about yourself. … It has nothing to do with something that's outside of you that solves things for you.

> I think spirituality is something that lives inside of you. It has a lot to do with becoming the essence of who you are and being as natural as possible.

> I am god. I don't want to insult the Christian church or anything, but I decide what I'm doing with my life. … There is no 'super-dad' in heaven that can tell me 'You have to do this and that, or else….' I am going to feel!

This sacralization of the self is logically tied to an understanding of social institutions as evil. Modern bureaucracies, for instance, are generally regarded as 'alienating', 'nonsensical', 'inhumane', and 'without soul', while excessive identification with career, status and pre-structured work roles is regarded as a major source of personal problems. More generally, the subordination of the self to pre-given life orders is held to inescapably result in frustration, bitterness, unhappiness, mental disorder, depression, disease, violence, sick forms of sexuality, etcetera. The sacralization of the self, in short, goes hand in hand with a demonization of social institutions to produce a clear-cut dualistic worldview (Aupers and Houtman 2003):

> If you cannot find yourself in your work ... If you don't have pleasure in your work, then you start to think about yourself negatively and that's a bad thing. Then you become physically and mentally ill.

> It can make people really ill. You should know how many people have psychological and psychosomatic complaints because they are imprisoned in a role, a role where they are not at home. I meet many of these people in this center.

> 'I am my work.' I hear that a lot. When people retire they fall into this black hole. 'I do not exist anymore.' Because 'I am my work, my status. I am the director.' ... That's hard! Things go wrong then. They will become bitter and unhappy. Sometimes they die soon.

This dualistic worldview constitutes the heart of the doctrine of self-spirituality. Motivated by perennialist philosophy, participants in the spiritual milieu freely use various concepts to describe the spiritual essence of human beings and 'follow their personal paths' towards their deeper selves by delving into various religious traditions. They may speak, for instance, about the 'higher self' of Theosophy, the 'divine spark' of Gnosticism, the 'soul' of Christianity, the 'Buddha nature' of Buddhism or the 'inner child' of humanistic psychology. Notwithstanding those essentially trivial differences, the underlying doctrine of self-spirituality is uncontested.

The emergence of a pluralistic spiritual supermarket confirms Luckmann's classical prediction, in short, but has simultaneously blinded many observers to the commonly held doctrine of self-spirituality—the belief that the self itself is sacred. It is this doctrine that paradoxically accounts for the staggering diversity at the surface of the spiritual milieu—an inevitable outcome when people feel that they need to follow their personal paths and explore what works for them personally— and simultaneously provides it with ideological unity and coherence at a deeper level. The common characterization of New Age as 'pick-and-mix-religion' or 'diffuse religion' is not plainly wrong, then, but rather superficial. If it is believed that the sacred resides in the deeper layers of the self, after all, what else to expect than people following their personal paths, experimenting freely with a range of traditions in a highly heterogeneous spiritual milieu? The diversity of the spiritual milieu *results from* rather than *contradicts* the existence of a coherent doctrine of being and wellbeing.

The Social Construction of Self-Spirituality

As we have seen, the spiritual milieu is in fact more doctrinally coherent and hence less diffuse than typically assumed. It remains to be seen, therefore, whether 'spiritual socialization' really is an oxymoron, because 'the transmission of diffuse beliefs is unnecessary and it is impossible' as Bruce (2002: 99) claims. To study this, we analyze the biographies of the spiritual trainers of our second sample. They have been strategically selected because they specialize in spiritual courses for business life and in fact all prove to have started their own careers there. How and why did they make this remarkable shift from 'normal' jobs, such as clerk, president-director or manager, to the spiritual world of shamanism, aura reading, Tantra and channeling? More specifically: what, if any, was the role played by socialization?

Alienation as the Key: Who am I, Really?

In obvious contrast to the way Christian identities are typically adopted, only one of those nine respondents developed an affinity with spirituality due to parental socialization during his formative period. Contrary to Bruce's suggestion, however, this does not mean that socialization plays no role at all, although this process only started after they got motivated to get involved due to the experience of identity problems. Through excessive identification with the goals set by the companies they worked for, with their pre-structured work roles and well-defined task descriptions, they increasingly felt alienated. This raised questions of meaning and identity: 'What is it that I really want?', 'Is this really the sort of life I want to live?', 'What sort of person am I, really?'

The case of Chantal, who now works in the New Age center Soulstation, is exemplary. She studied economics, rapidly made a career in the business world and, she explains, completely identified with her work. Looking back she states that she was 'marched along the paths set out by society' and adds: 'I studied marketing and sales, but had never learned to look in the mirror.' Like most others, she points out that her identity crisis began with an 'intruding conversation' with a consultant:

> I was working at MCR, a computer company, and I was the commercial director. A big team, a big market, and a big responsibility for the profits. Much too young for what I did. But that was my situation: You did what you had to do. Then I was invited by a business partner to visit a consultant. I sat there talking for two hours with that man. It was an inspiring visit and suddenly he looked at me intrudingly and said: 'I hear your story. It sounds perfect, looking at it from the outside, but where are you?' In other words: 'The story is not yours. It is the standard "format" of the company you are presenting, but where is your passion? What makes you Chantal instead of Miss MCR?'

The latter question marks the beginning of an identity crisis and an enduring quest for meaning. She adds:

> I thought: 'Shit, I have no answer to this question and I have to do something with that.' The result of this conversation was a burnout that lasted almost a year. That's a crisis, you know! In the evening hours I started to do coaching sessions, I started thinking about the question: 'Who am I, really?' You start to look in the mirror. And then, at a certain moment, you can no longer unite your private life with your position at work. It's like your skis are suddenly moving in opposite directions. And that's definitely not a comfortable position: before you realize, you're standing in a split.

The suggestive metaphor of 'standing in a split' between the demands of business life and private life applies to most of the respondents. The more they become involved in 'soul searching', the more they alienate from their working environments. 'Being true to oneself' becomes an imperative and, in the end, becomes incompatible with the demands of business life. This cognitive dissonance is the main reason why respondents eventually resign from their regular jobs. Marco, founder of New Age center Merlin, specialized in Enneagram trainings (the Enneagram is a psycho-spiritual model to increase self-knowledge) and shamanistic courses, states in this respect:

> That is why I left business life. When I felt that I had to work on the basis of my intuition, or my feelings, this became a problem. ... It was just not accepted that such a thing as intuition existed. I had to base my accounts on numbers and figures. I couldn't bear that any longer. Now I want to do work that feels right.

Yet another respondent, Marie-José, worked for 19 years as a consultant, a manager and, finally, a director. She started working on 'intuitive development' in her personal life but felt increasingly that she could not reconcile these private practices with her public task as a director. These were, she explains, 'two incompatible languages':

> Finally I ended up in a sort of dull routine and realized that the organization was only interested in its own survival. ... The only thing that counted was that one could legitimate one's decisions to the outside world. I severely began to disconnect from the company. ... It became clear to me that I performed a certain role that fitted the formal position I had in that company. Like 'This is my role, so this is the way I act and what I feel is something I let out when I am at home.' Then I thought: 'I have to leave this company, because I can't stand it no longer to act as if I feel nothing, while in fact I am overwhelmed by my emotions.' ... I figured: 'What will happen when I express my feelings in the office? Should I cry?'

The process of 'soul searching' that follows should not be misconstrued as a strictly personal quest for meaning. Although a latent sense of unease or discomfort may well have been present beforehand, it is indeed quite telling that it typically became manifest only after a conversation with a consultant or coach. Remarks like 'He touched something within me', 'Something opened up' or 'The light went on' indicate that due to this contact latent discomfort becomes manifest and triggers a process of searching the depths of one's soul.

What follows is a process of socialization, in which three mechanisms validate and reinforce one another: 1) acquiring a new cognitive frame of interpretation, 2) having new experiences, and 3) legitimating one's newly acquired worldview. These mechanisms, Tanya Luhrmann (1989: 312) demonstrates in her study on neopaganism, are the pushing powers behind an 'interpretive drift': 'the slow, often unacknowledged shift in someone's manner of interpreting events as they become involved with a particular activity.'

Spiritual Careers: Knowledge and Experience Shifting in Tandem

Initially, the process of soul searching has a secular character. Motivated by their identity crises, respondents start describing their selves in vocabularies derived from humanistic psychology. Emotions are permitted and valued positively, but are not yet defined as higher, spiritual or sacred. Although they generally start out with humanistic psychological self-help books and courses, they eventually end up doing more esoteric types of trainings, such as shamanism, aura reading and the like.

Daan comments on his relentless participation in various courses as 'a sort of hunger that emerges in yourself. You start to nourish and feed it. And so you hop from course to course.' By satisfying their 'hunger' on the New Age market, the respondents acquire alternative frames of interpretation, new vocabularies and symbols to interpret their experiences. They learn to label weird, out-of-the-ordinary experiences as spiritual. Vice versa, these experiences validate the acquired frame of interpretation. In the words of Luhrmann: 'Intellectual and experiential changes shift in tandem, a ragged co-evolution of intellectual habits and phenomenological involvement' (1989: 315). The story of Marie-José provides a good illustration:

> We were walking on a mountain. ... And I was just observing, thinking what a beautiful mountain this was and suddenly everything started to flow within me. This was my first spiritual experience. ... I felt like: 'Now I understand what they mean when they say that the earth is alive.' I began to make contact and understood that I am like the earth, a part of nature, and that my body is alive.

The formulation 'Now I understand what they mean when they say' illustrates that knowledge precedes experience and, perhaps, shapes its specific content. A similar story is told by Chantal. During her stay at Findhorn she learned about the existence of auras, chakras and streams of energy inside and just outside the body. This resulted, she recounts, in 'spiritual experiences':

> When I was there, someone said: 'You have a healing energy around you and you should do something with that.' Well, I had never heard of these two words, 'healing' and 'energy.' So I was like: 'What do you mean?' She said: 'I'll give you an instruction.' After that I started practicing with a friend of mine. I moved my hand over her body and I indeed felt warm and cold places. And I felt sensations, stimulation. Then I became curious.

Chantal began to delve deeper in the matter of healing and increasingly felt streams of energy around people. After a while she started to actually see these fields of energy:

> After this I began to see auras, colors around people. At that time I still worked at this computer company and – after three months (at Findhorn) – I returned to the office. During meetings I was really staring at people; like, 'I have to look at you, because you have all these colors around you.'

Respondents voluntarily internalize a spiritual conception of the self in the process and radically re-interpret their personal identities in conformity with it. On the one hand, a new image of the self in the present emerges: undefined emotions and experiences are now understood in spiritual terms and the new identity is understood as profoundly spiritual. On the other hand, they start to re-write their biographies: they break with their past identities, now understood as 'one-dimensional', 'alienated' or 'unhappy.' As one respondent explains: 'I now know that I was structurally depressed without being aware of it.' Statements such as those exemplify the cultural logic of conversion: they have 'seen the light' and now re-interpret their past lives as 'living in sin.' As with classical conversions, they follow the logic of 'Then I thought ..., but now I know.' The more our respondents became immersed in the spiritual milieu, the more these considerations were reinforced, to eventually reach the point of successful socialization, 'the establishment of a high degree of symmetry between objective and subjective reality' (Berger and Luckmann 1966: 183).

Legitimations

Having left their regular jobs and having started new careers as trainers and teachers in the spiritual milieu, it is hardly surprising that our respondents regularly encounter resistance and critique. They are well aware that they are seen by many as 'irrational', 'softies', or 'dreamers' and that their way of life is perceived by many as 'something for people with problems.' How do they deal with these and other forms of resistance? A core element in their legitimation strategy is a radical reversal of moral positions: they argue that it is not themselves, but the critical outsider who has a problem, although he or she may not be aware of this. Following the doctrine of self-spirituality, resistance, critique and moral opposition are taken as symptoms of a deeply felt anxiety that cannot (yet) be directly experienced. Critics, our respondents argue, project an unresolved 'inner problem' on the outside world. In the words of Marie-José:

> People who have such strong resistance secretly have a strong affinity with spirituality. Otherwise they wouldn't be so angry. They just can't break through their resistance. Obviously they have a problem. Why else would you make such a fuzz about something that doesn't concern you?

Daan tells a similar story:

> People are projecting it on the outside world: they get angry. There is obviously something in themselves they are not satisfied with. And then it's easier to get angry with others than to say: 'This is jealousy in me' or 'This is greed.' 'No, let's not take a look at that, let's project it on the outside world.' To handle these problems takes loads of strength and efforts. ... To enter a process of spiritual growth, you have to be very strong. As we can read in the Vedic literature: it is much easier to conquer seven cities than to conquer yourself.

Marco, who, among other things, works with the Enneagram, explains his strategy in dealing with resistance and critique during his courses as follows:

Of course, in my trainings, I regularly meet people who show resistance but I can easily trace that back to their personality. Then I say: 'You see, this is your mechanism of resistance that is now emerging.' ... Then I say: 'I can fully understand you, I know the reasons why you are saying this.' Then they say: 'It is useless debating with you!' I say: 'But what can I do about it? ... It is part of the type of person you are, as explained by the Enneagram.'

Our interviewees normalize their positions and pathologize criticism by outsiders by 'reading' the latter as a symptom of psychological fear, anxiety or insecurity, in short. As a consequence, the 'inside' group is portrayed as courageous and free (because they choose to face their 'demons'), while the 'outsiders' are labeled as alienated because they are disconnected from their deeper selves.

The process of socialization unfolds as follows, then. Firstly, latent feelings of alienation become manifest after a conversation with a consultant, raising problems of meaning and identity—'What is it that I really want?', 'Is this really the sort of life I want to live?', 'What sort of person am I, really?' Secondly, during the process of soul searching that follows, people are socialized into the ethic of self-spirituality, with knowledge and experience shifting in tandem. Thirdly, after successful socialization, standardized legitimations are deployed, further reinforcing the ethic of self-spirituality. Those findings are strikingly consistent with those of Hammer (2001), based on a content analysis of a sample of New Age texts in his case. In his book *Claiming Knowledge: Strategies of Epistemology from Theosophy to the New Age*, Hammer (2001: 366-7) also demonstrates that several cognitive and social mechanisms are operative so as to make New Agers conform to a set of unwritten norms (see Hammer 2004 for a brief summary of the argument as well as Hanegraaff 2001 for a similar type of analysis):

> Labeled spiritual rather than religious, experiences are presented in numerous New Age texts as self-validating and primary. Thus, attention is turned away from the fact that the frame of interpretation is culturally constituted, and that ritual forms and collective practices fundamentally shape individual experience.

This process of socialization into a spiritual discourse about the self reveals that participants in the spiritual milieu are less authentic than they typically believe they are. After all: how authentic are those concerned, when they have in fact been socialized into a shared emphasis on the primacy of personal authenticity? New Agers' self-claimed authenticity rather reminds one of the classical scene in Monty Python's *Life of Brian*, in which a crowd of followers enthusiastically and literally repeats Brian's words with one voice when he desperately attempts to convince them to go home and leave him alone: 'We are all individuals!', they shout, with only one astonished dissenter muttering 'I'm not...'

It is striking to note that, apart from the latent feelings of alienation that trigger it, the process of socialization into a spiritual discourse about the self is basically identical to that revealed by Howard Becker in his classical study of marihuana users. In that case, too, acquired knowledge underlies the recognition and positive evaluation of experiences, just as in both cases 'deviant groups tend ... to be pushed into rationalizing their position' by means of standardized legitimations (1966: 38) so as to neutralize critique from outsiders and reinforce the adopted way of life to insiders.

Self-Spirituality's Public Significance: Bringing 'Soul' Back to Work

'Sociologists rarely study spirituality in the workplace', Grant et al. (2004: 267) observe. Although some substantial studies have been done in this field (for example, Goldschmidt Salamon 2001, Heelas 1996a, Mitroff and Denton 1999a, Nadesan 1999, Roberts 1994),[4] this blind spot is probably due to the received wisdom that spirituality lacks public significance, remaining confined to 'the life-space that is not directly touched by institutional control' (Luckmann 1996: 73) and failing to 'generate powerful social innovations and experimental social institutions' (Bruce 2002: 97). But obviously, the very rarity of studies of spirituality in the workplace precludes any premature conclusions to the effect that spirituality fails to affect our 'primary institutions', modern work organizations. '[I]f it appears to sociologists that spirituality cannot take root within secular bureaucracies, it may be because their theories have not yet allowed it', as Grant et al. (2004: 281) rightly note. And indeed, notwithstanding common claims to the contrary, it is difficult to deny that spirituality has in fact entered the public domain of work organizations.

New Age Incorporated

In the 1980s, business organizations became interested in the worldviews and practices of the New Age and, *vice versa*, New Age began to turn towards business life (Heelas 1996a, Nadesan 1999). Renowned management magazines such as *People Management*, *Industry Week* and *Sloan Management Review* publish articles on the opportunities of spirituality for business life on a regular basis (for example, Baber 1999, Berman 1999, Braham 1999, Hayes 1999, Mitroff and Denton 1999b, Neal 1999, Traynor 1999, Turner 1999, Welch 1998). Indeed, on a basis of 131 in-depth interviews and 2,000 questionnaires in American companies, Mitroff and Denton demonstrate that employees and managers feel a great need to integrate spirituality in business life. In *A Spiritual Audit of Corporate America* (1999a: 14) they conclude:

> This age calls for a new 'spirit of management.' For us, the concepts of spirituality
> and soul are not merely add-on elements of a new philosophy or policy. ... No
> management effort can survive without them. We refuse to accept that whole

---

4   Substantial fieldwork on New Age and business organizations has also been done in Denmark, published in Danish, by Kirsten Marie Bovbjerg (2001).

organizations cannot learn ways to foster soul and spirituality in the workplace. We believe not only that they can, but also that they must.

Most of the spiritual ideas, initiatives and practices that are applied in business life can be labeled as self-spirituality: 'The inner-individual orientation is what most people, including the majority of our respondents, mean by spirituality' (idem: 26).

Examples of large companies that have become interested in New Age trainings are Guinness, General Dynamics, and Boeing Aerospace—even the US Army has adopted them (Heelas 1996a). It is hard to tell to what extent New Age affects American business life, but there are some indications. Naisbitt and Aburdene (1990: 273) refer to a survey held among five hundred American companies, at least half of which had at one time or another offered 'consciousness-raising techniques' to their employees. They estimate that companies in the US spend at least four billion dollars on New Age consultants annually, which is more than ten percent of the total of thirty billion spent on company trainings every year (see Barker 1994, Nadesan 1999, Swets and Bjork 1990: 95).

Since the 1990s, the shift of New Age towards business life has become clearly visible in the Netherlands, too (see Aupers 2005 for more details about the history of New Age in the Netherlands). A prime example is Oibibio in Amsterdam, founded in 1993. Oibibio's business department offered trainings in spiritual management, such as 'Team management and the soul' and 'Management in astrological perspective', to keep companies 'ready for battle' in times in which 'dynamic streams of production, services and information increasingly put pressure on organizations and managers.' They make the following claim in their flyer: 'Our trainers are builders of bridges: they speak the language of business life and pragmatically know how to implant the spiritual philosophy in your organization; they do so in cooperation with your employees.'

Oibibio's bankruptcy in the late 1990s did not trigger a decline of New Age capitalism in the Netherlands. Instead it marked the birth of many other, more successful New Age centers such as Metavisie, Soulstation, Being in Business and Firmament. Metavisie, probably one of the largest players in this field, claims to have offered in-company trainings to 75 of the 100 most renowned companies in the Netherlands.[5] The list of clients on their website comprises more than two hundred national and international companies and institutions, among them many of the major Dutch banks and insurance companies (ABN Amro, ING, Generale, Rabobank, Aegon, Amev, De Amersfoortse, Centraal Beheer, Interpolis, Zwitserleven and Delta Lloyd) and IT-companies (Cap Gemini, CMG, Compaq, Getronics Software, High Tech Automation, IBM Nederland, Oracle and Baan Software). Internationally renowned Dutch multinationals such as Ahold,

---

5   These claims were published on the website of Metavisie, available at: www. metavisie.com [accessed: November 24, 2005]. We have not contacted the companies mentioned on the website to validate whether they indeed contracted Metavisie to provide in-company trainings.

Heineken and telecom company KPN are also on the list, as well as remarkably many government-sponsored institutions such as the national welfare organization UWV-GAK and the University of Amsterdam, and the Ministries of Finance, the Interior, Trade and Industry, Justice, Agriculture and Fisheries, Transport and Public Works, Welfare, Health and Cultural Affairs, and Housing, Regional Development and the Environment. This is, indeed, convincing evidence that New Age is penetrating the public sphere. More than that, the list indicates that especially organizations producing immaterial services rather than material products provide their employees with spiritual in-company trainings. Especially the post-industrial service sector seems hospitable towards New Age, then. What is the goal of the spiritual in-company trainings in all of these organizations?

The interviews with trainers of New Age centers that specialize in spirituality in business life and those centers' websites reveal that their courses aim primarily at deconstructing the typically modern separation between the private and public realms, by trying to impose the logic of the former upon the latter. This complies, of course, with the ethic of self-spirituality: the centers aim to make the rationalized environments less alienating and more open to 'authenticity' and 'spirituality.' By doing so, it is argued, they seek for a win-win situation or, in the terms of Heelas (1996a) 'the best of both worlds.' In the following accounts, derived from the websites of Metavisie, Soulstation, Being in Business and Firmament respectively, 'authenticity' is held to result in both well-being *and* efficiency and 'spirituality' in happiness *and* profit, while 'soulful organizations' are portrayed as successful:

> Organizations are in movement. The pressure increases. People want dedication. There is a call for a new sort of leader. A leader that takes business results and human potential into account. ... Metavisie helps to create these leaders of the future. Together we cause a paradigm shift in society. A society that is not primarily obsessed with money and profit but a society that celebrates the quality of human life. Where it is the highest goal to be your most authentic self.[6]

> The mission of Being in Business is to build a bridge between organizations and spirituality to make businesses more successful. Success, then, is not primarily defined as making more profit, but also as increasing well-being for you and your employees. Being in Business shapes this spiritual dimension in your organization by providing services that will increase consciousness, vitality, fun, pleasure and energy. Spirituality is profit. Because profit is nothing more than materialized energy. The more energy your organization generates, the higher the profit. And spirituality in your organization is of course much more.[7]

> People who develop personal mastership steadily become more capable to live their authenticity. In such a situation, one can put all one's natural talents in

---

6   Available at: www.metavisie.com [accessed: November 24, 2005].
7   Available at: www.beinginbusiness.nl [accessed: November 24, 2005].

the world and do what one is really good at. The more authentically one lives, the more effective one's actions. Authenticity therefore has a large impact on productivity within organizations.[8]

Firmament strives towards unlocking, developing and reinforcing the unique potential and inspiration of individuals. By doing so, they bring back the soul into your organization. It is our experience that vital and soulful organizations, where employees recognize their personal goals in the goals of the organization, operate powerfully on the economic market.[9]

Although bureaucratization may pose all sorts of practical obstacles to the introduction of spiritual practices in the workplace (Grant et al. 2004), this should not blind us to the fact that it also paradoxically underlies attempts to bring 'soul' back to work—to break with 'alienating' bureaucratic organizational structures and pre-given work roles. As we have seen, this seems to apply especially to organizations in the post-industrial service sector, probably because the highly skilled and specialized work in this sector is much more difficult to rationalize and control from without, and because attempts to nevertheless do so are likely to meet with fierce professional resistance.

Indeed, the 'best of both worlds' approach that dominates the concomitant discourse suggests that tensions between bureaucratic demands on the one hand and opportunities for spiritual practices on the other may in fact be less severe than typically assumed. Organizational goals are typically taken for granted and remain strictly instrumental, after all, while the 'inner lives' of employees are considered valuable assets that enable firms and organizations to strengthen their positions in highly competitive and demanding environments. Although it is hard to deny that spirituality has entered the public realm of work, then, what is badly needed is good ethnographic research into whether and how tensions between bureaucratic demands and spiritual practices emerge and, if so, how those are dealt with on an everyday basis.

Self-Spirituality in Action: 'Grow or I'll Shoot!'

We finally present the findings of a case study of a company that has to a large extent institutionalized the ethic of self-spirituality. This case is not typical of contemporary business life, but is theoretically instructive. Whereas people enter the spiritual milieu freely and voluntarily, driven by problems of identity caused by alienation, as we have seen, the employees of this particular company find themselves in a setting in which the ethic of self-spirituality is more or less imposed upon them. Its functioning as a binding social norm—as a 'social fact' in the classical sense of Emile Durkheim—thereby becomes more visible and easier

---

8 Available at: www.soulstation.nl [accessed: November 24, 2005].
9 Available at: www.firmamentbv.com [accessed: November 24, 2005].

to study, precisely because not all employees are equally enthusiastic about such an imposition of a spiritual regime. As such, this case study enables us to further illustrate the claims made above about the existence and nature of a coherent spiritual doctrine of being and wellbeing and about the dynamics of socialization into such a spiritual discourse about the self.

The company in case is Morca, a producer of bathroom equipment with branches in various countries in Western Europe.[10] Geert, its president-director, is deeply involved in New Age and provides in-company trainings for his employees. On a personal level, Geert is motivated to implement spirituality in business life because of his own biography. The development he went through exactly matches the analysis in the previous section: he went through an 'enormous personal crisis', made contact with his current spiritual coach, followed various New Age courses and increasingly embraced the ethic of self-spirituality. He discovered—in his own words—that he is both 'the question and the answer' and 'the painter and the canvass.'

Marcel, his coach and spiritual mentor, takes care of the courses at Morca. Marcel works with various religious traditions (Christianity, Taoism, Buddhism), embraces the 'perennial philosophy' and emphasizes the primacy of self-spirituality: 'The spiritual leader knows that self-knowledge is the source of all wisdom.' Three questions are at the heart of his courses: 'Who am I?', 'What do I want?', and: 'How do I get it?' The president-director explains the goal of the courses as follows:

> I want to provide the opportunity for employees to find themselves in their jobs. And it is my conviction that if you 'follow that path', you'll end up encountering your inner spirituality. And when people get inspired they are inclined to make beautiful things. And we all profit from that.

Like the New Age centers, then, Morca aims for the 'best of both worlds.' It aims to transform the public realm of the organization into a private sphere where employees can express themselves fully because 'authenticity is the most important thing in the world.' By doing so, Morca expects its employees to be more happy and, hence, more effective, so as to increase productivity and profits.

It is important to note that participation in the courses is *formally* a free choice. Geert claims to have abandoned his former missionary attitude 'Grow or I'll shoot.' Having learned that people cannot be forced into a spiritual lifestyle he now argues (like his coach): 'Pulling the grass will not make it grow faster.' As we will see, however, employees in Morca are in fact subject to social pressure to participate in the in-company trainings, producing mutual distrust, critique and a divide between participants and non-participants.

---

10   To safeguard anonymity, the actual name of the company and names of the president-director, the spiritual trainer and the employees interviewed have been replaced with pseudonyms.

Participants: 'It Takes Guts!'

All of the interviewed who have participated in the trainings are people in mid- to top-level management positions. They are extremely positive about the trainings, because those have given them the opportunity to solve personal problems ('stones in your backpack') and to grow spiritually. They emphasize the influence of Geert and Marcel in making them participate. In the words of Mark, an assistant group controller: 'I am doing it because someone gave me a kick in the butt to participate. That's how it feels. That one is Geert.' The latter's influence is perceived as stimulating. Originally, they were skeptics and thought it was all 'vague' and 'irrational.' In compliance with the analysis in the previous section, they now label these forms of skepticism as 'psychological resistance' or 'fear of growth.' Beforehand, they were just not aware of their problems in private and working life, thinking 'Private is private, don't bother me about that!' This attitude changed while participating. Arthur was the first to 'break through his resistance' during the courses. He explains:

> A lot of shit from the past entered my consciousness. When you become emotional and start to cry in front of the group – and not just a little bit, but letting loose completely... That takes guts! You need that guts. If you don't have those, well, then it gets tough. Everybody thought: 'I am sitting here with my colleagues, I have to work with them tomorrow, I am not going to cry!' So there was this mechanism of resistance: 'I don't want this.' I was one of the first who dealt with a serious emotional problem. ... Once I did it, others showed the courage to follow.

This statement exemplifies the legitimations discussed in the preceding section. 'Opening up' to colleagues and showing emotions is now understood as a sign of 'guts', while defending the boundary between private and working life is understood as a symptom of fear. Frank is another participant who entered the world of self-spirituality through the courses:

> I am very rational and before I started the course I told Marcel this: 'What I know about myself is that I have the feeling that I don't really have emotions.' However, the first session we did, I was filled with tears, overwhelmed by emotions. In a certain situation Marcel told me: 'I thought you had no emotions?' Then I thought: 'Well, I obviously have them but they are normally hidden somewhere where I cannot reach them.'

In short, the stories of these employees exemplify the breakdown of the modern separation between private and public life produced by the shift towards self-spirituality in the organization. They are convinced that this approach works: it helps them to solve personal problems and to be more open and expressive at the office. This in turn, they argue, stimulates a sense of fellowship and community:

'We have become much more open towards one another. We have become a group. We really trust each other.' Under the influence of the president-director and his coach, then, self-spirituality has become an organizational asset. But how do those who did not participate in the courses evaluate all of this?

Non-Participants: 'I Don't Feel Like Doing That!'

The interviewed who have not participated in the trainings are mainly people who occupy lower positions in the organizational hierarchy (production, administration and the like). Moreover, they are supervised by the participants discussed above. Their accounts mirror those of the managers who have participated and who have become involved in spirituality in the process. They experience the influence of the president-director not as stimulating, but as pressure. Taking a more conventional stance, they reject the privatization and spiritualization of public organizational life and wish to preserve the divide between private and public. Personal issues, Johan argues, are out of place in a working environment:

> I think courses like this are disturbing. I mean: I am not against it, but I would never do such a thing with colleagues. I've heard that it revolves around showing your personal feelings and emotions. That frightens me. ... To really let yourself go, you need to know people very well. You need to trust people. ... In this respect, I really want to keep my private life private.

Martijn tells a similar story:

> At a certain moment it was explained what the course was all about. How you had to act, what you had to do and how you had to open yourself up to others. Then I thought: 'Do you really have to do that in front of your fellow-workers?' Actually, I don't feel like doing that. It's not that I have to keep everything as a secret, but it 'runs deeper', they say. And then I think: 'Do I want that?'

These employees paint a completely different picture of spirituality in business life: they defend the modern boundary between private and public and perceive the sharing of emotions with co-workers (especially superiors) not as courageous, but as frightening; the influence of the president-director not as stimulating, but as pressure. Moreover, they disagree with the participants that the courses result in a stronger sense of unity. On the contrary:

> In a company like this you get two camps, because there are people who participate and those who do not. And, to be honest, I think that the people who participated have changed. How do you say that? These were people who already had high self-esteem. That became stronger during the course. Maybe that is the power of the course: 'Believing in yourself.' But it's not nice to feel better than others and treat them that way.

The other interviews confirm that there are two camps in the company. The spiritual group argues that the others would better join in, because otherwise 'They will miss the connection.' The secular group 'feel(s) less than the others', feels that they 'don't fit in' and 'are not respected.' These quotes nicely illustrate the tension that has built up around the courses and, more generally, around spirituality in the organization. In her critical study on 'New Age spiritualism' in business life, Nadesan (1999: 19) claims: 'Those who reject the (spiritual) discourse or those who fail to achieve success get labeled as unwilling to take care of themselves or, worse, as reaping their karmic rewards.'

As we have demonstrated, spirituality is widespread in Dutch business life and is considered a valuable asset to enhance both meaning *and* effectiveness. We are not dealing with a mere hype or the latest management fashion. After all, the discussed developments began already in the late 1980s, blossomed in the 1990s and have remained salient ever since. More substantially, our data indicate that especially organizations in the post-industrial service sector are hospitable towards self-spirituality. Highly educated professionals working typically in mid- to top-level management are, in comparison with production workers, more oriented towards intrinsic motivations, goals and rewards. They give priority, Mitroff and Denton (1999a: 212) demonstrate on the basis of their survey, to 'interesting work' and realizing their 'full potential as a person.' Indeed, from an organizational perspective, this makes it profitable to break with alienating bureaucratic structures and incorporate issues like self-understanding, identity and self-spirituality in corporate culture. This elective affinity between the post-industrial service sector and New Age spirituality further strengthens our conviction that spirituality in public organizational life cannot be dismissed as a mere hype or the latest management fashion.

The case of Morca, again, is not typical of spirituality in the public realm, but it does demonstrate convincingly that substantially more is at stake than individuals exploring their own spirituality. More specifically, it demonstrates that self-spirituality is a well-defined doctrine with a strong potential for socialization: people at this company learn the importance of rejecting external authorities and making contact with their 'deeper selves.' Although exactly the same occurs in the spiritual milieu, as we have seen above, it easily remains unnoticed there. This is because participants who enter voluntarily to work on their personal problems are likely to experience this process of socialization as a strictly personal and authentic delving in the self's deeper layers.

Conclusion

In his defense of secularization theory, Steve Bruce (2002) criticizes authors such as Rodney Stark (1999, see also Stark and Bainbridge 1985) and Grace Davie (1994), who argue that secularization is *by definition* accompanied by religious innovation. Stark, Bruce explains, makes *a priori* assumptions about religion as a universal human need, while Davie argues from a similar perspective that there will always remain a 'believing without belonging.' We agree with Bruce that such claims about humans as 'essentially' religious beings are 'nonsociological' (2002: 104). More than that: they are metaphysical, we would argue.

We also agree with Bruce that much research into spirituality is sociologically naïve and immature. This not only applies to the research of those who are overly sympathetic to spirituality and hence cannot resist the temptation of 'going native', as our colleagues from anthropology say. Perhaps surprisingly, it equally applies to the work of those who are highly critical of it (see Woodhead 2010 for examples). Because of his own tendency to criticize other people's ideas about spirituality as 'nonsociological' (2002: 104) or 'bad sociology' (1998), Bruce himself perhaps provides the best example. Attempting to hammer home the radical individualism of the spiritual milieu, he writes (2002: 83):

> Findhorn, one of Europe's oldest centres of New Age thought and teaching, *requires* of those who take part in its various forms of group work that they confine their talk to 'I statements.' The point of this is to establish that, while each participant has a right to say how he or she feels or thinks, *no-one has a right* to claim some extra-personal authority for his or her views (our emphasis).

To be sure, those observations do much to underscore the radical individualism of the spiritual milieu. But simultaneously, and ironically, they do more than that. They also demonstrate how this very individualism operates as a socially sanctioned obligation of personal authenticity, revealing precisely the social significance of spirituality that Bruce denies. Arguing that allegedly 'diffuse beliefs' such as those cannot and need not be transmitted (2002: 99), Bruce's failure to capture and satisfactorily theorize this ambiguity of the spiritual milieu's 'individualism' causes him to overlook that people are socialized into compliance to the doctrine of self-spirituality.

What Bruce has on offer, then, is a mere sociologically naïve reproduction of New Age rhetoric about the primacy of personal authenticity rather than a mature and critical sociological analysis. The assumption that people all by themselves develop their strictly personal and authentic spiritualities is obviously sociologically naïve, since 'as good sociologists, we all know that there is no such thing as an isolated individual' (Besecke 2005: 194). Besecke also criticizes the received conception of 'privatized religion', arguing that it results in a conception of religion 'as almost an exclusively psychological phenomenon, with very limited and indirect social consequence' (idem: 187). As we have demonstrated, spirituality is in fact less unambiguously individualistic and less privatized than most sociologists hold it to be.

The conception of spirituality as embraced by Bruce (and, to be sure, most other sociologists of religion) inevitably coincides largely with the self-image of the spiritual milieu. It is hardly surprising, after all, that the spiritual practitioners interviewed by Heelas et al. (2005: 27) also deny in every possible way that the doctrine of self-spirituality is socially constructed, transmitted and reinforced: 'Time and time again, we hear practitioners rejecting the idea that their relationships with their group members or clients have anything to do with pre-packaged ... ways of transmitting the sacred.' But even if spiritual practitioners do not '[tell] their group members or clients what to think, do, believe or feel' (idem: 28), they do tell them that they should take their personal feelings seriously, that a one-sided reliance on thinking at the cost of feeling is detrimental and that one should follow one's heart.

The task to be taken up in the years that lie ahead, in short, is a radical sociologization of research into New Age and spirituality. What we need is research that critically and systematically deconstructs emic rhetoric to document how precisely spirituality is socially constructed, transmitted and reinforced in the spiritual milieu and how, why, and with what consequences it is introduced at the workplace.[11]

---

11   Obviously, it is important to study whether normal participants in the spiritual milieu, just like the spiritual elite studied here, also adhere to the doctrine of self-spirituality. Furthermore, it is preferable to study the process of socialization by means of participant observation. An obvious drawback of the methodology used for the current chapter—that is, interviewing those who have completed the full process after the fact—is that biographical data thus obtained are inevitably coloured by the newly acquired spiritual identity. It should be noted, however, that given the nature of this identity (self-spirituality, primacy of authenticity, anti-institutionalism, etcetera), the approach used here seems biased *against* the finding that processes of socialization do occur. Another drawback of our approach here, and hence another advantage of participant observation, is that only the latter enables one to study the role of resistance to socialization into a spiritual discourse as a reason for abandoning a course.

Chapter 4
'Be Who You Want to Be'?: Commodified Agency in Online Computer Games

Introduction

*You*Tube, *My*Space and *i*Pad—contemporary media culture is rife with discourses tapping into and expressing individualism. Particularly Web 2.0 applications invite individuals to put user-generated content online, to join social network sites like Facebook, to express themselves on blogs and to 'broadcast themselves' in personal movies on YouTube. Agency, personal autonomy and (inter)active control over media content are at the heart of new media's 'participatory culture' (Jenkins 2006, Schäfer 2009, Taylor 2006). Media theorists like Jenkins argue that we are in the midst of a paradigm shift since 'audiences, empowered by these new technologies, occupying a space at the intersection between old and new media, are demanding the right to participate within the culture' (Jenkins 2006: 24). New digital media culture, it is held, is not so much anymore about the omnipotence of a 'culture industry' (Horkheimer and Adorno 2002 [1944]), its dominant-hegemonic ideology and media texts that may or may not be 'decoded', negotiated or opposed by the audience (for example, Fiske 1998, Hall 1980). It is primarily about handing over the means of production to an emancipated, critical audience and facilitating self-expression for the individual.

According to media theorists, computer games exemplify this turn to interactivity, agency and self-expression online (for example, Bartle 2004, Jenkins 2006, Rushkoff 1999, Turkle 1995). 'Digital games', Kline et al. (2003: 14, 16) argue, 'are interactive media *par excellence*' and are in fact 'celebrated for creating a new caste of media audience: an active subject, parting with the tyranny of mass media for the freedom of joysticks.' And indeed: every new generation of games has more technical options, choices and interactivity, featuring unlimited freedom for players as the 'holy grail' of game design. Game psychologists suggest that 'the intrinsic need for autonomy is what fuels the player's hunger for more freedom in games, and why games that provide freedom and open-ended game play are so highly valued' (Rigby and Ryan 2007: 3). The paradigm example of game worlds providing sheer unlimited agency for players, are popular Massively Multiplayer Online Role-Playing Games (MMORPGs or MMOs), also referred to as 'virtual worlds' (Bartle 2004) or 'synthetic worlds' (Castronova 2005). These are persistent three-dimensional environments on the Internet played worldwide by millions of players simultaneously boasting emergent cultures, social structures, economies and ecologies. They are interactive—players can have a profound influence on the structure of the game world—and in these environments players are held to express themselves, live out their fantasies and dreams. As Castronova puts it: 'We are no longer stuck with the game of life as we receive it. We can make a new one, almost however we like' (2005: 70).

But can we? Discourses about expressive individualism and experiences of freedom in computer games are, of course, not born in a vacuum: they are mediated by and constructed in a commercial, technological and social context that is by and large ignored in recent studies on 'participatory culture' (Jenkins 2006). In the 1990s, game environments on the Internet, like so-called Multi-User Dungeons (MUDs)—textual role-playing games on the Internet developed by Roy Trubshaw and Richard Bartle in the early 1980s—were still anarchistic free-zones in commercial, legal and technical terms. Nowadays, online gaming has, however, become a major industry: according to figures of the Entertainment Software Association (ESA), computer game sales in the U.S. steadily grew from $2.6 billion in 1996 to $11.7 billion in 2008,[1] while online computer worlds are currently produced, owned and governed by major multinationals like Sony, Microsoft, Sega and Blizzard Entertainment (for example, Humphreys 2008, Noveck and Balkin 2006, Taylor 2006). Against this background of massive commodification of computer gaming, typically ignored in game studies, this chapter addresses not only in-game experiences of agency, but also relates the latter to their production and commodification.

The analysis focuses on the online computer game *World of Warcraft*, launched in 2004 and followed by three extensions, *The Burning Crusade* (2007), *The Wrath of the Leach King* (2008) and *Cataclysm* (2010). *World of Warcraft* is by far the most popular MMO; it is inhabited by about 12 million players worldwide. The first part of the study is based on in-depth, qualitative interviews with 20 Dutch players of *World of Warcraft* and analyzes their in-game experiences of freedom and the meaning such experiences have in the context of their offline lives. The second part of the study contextualizes these experiences by analyzing how the latter have been shaped, produced and invoked by game designers. We do so by means of a content analysis of seven books on game design and online advertisements for 51 popular online games.

Self-Expression in Online Computer Games

The Role-Playing Paradox

Ever since its emergence and widespread application in the 1990s, the Internet has been associated with individual liberty. Motivated by cyberpunk novels

---

1   See ESA reports *2010: Sales, Demographics and Usage Data: Essential Facts about the Computer and Video Game Industry* and *Video Games in the 21st Century: The 2010 Report*, both available at: http://www.theesa.com.

from Vernor Vinge, Neal Stephenson and William Gibson—emphasizing the otherworldly, disembodied and free essence of 'cyberspace'—the Internet was imagined as a space beyond the alienating forces of modern society, a realm where individuals—literally—could be who they want to be and express themselves fully. In 1993, John Perry Barlow published his famous *Declaration of the Independence of Cyberspace* against the 'giants of flesh and steel' of the 'industrial world', who should not be allowed to bar or interfere with people's right to access 'the new home of the mind.'

In conformity with this distinctly 'counter-cultural' (Dery 1996) and 'techno-libertarian' (Borsook 2000) spirit of the 1990s, the precursors of online computer games were heralded in existential terms as spaces where one could experiment with identity and develop human potential. In MUDs people were thought to live out their fantasies, perform 'gender-bending' and develop their human potential (for example, Dibbell 2001, King and Borland 2003). The most vocal academic expression of this perspective was articulated by MIT psychologist and sociologist Sherry Turkle. Based on an extensive study of youngsters playing in MUDs she theorized that '[t]he anonymity of MUDs gives people the chance to express multiple and often unexplored aspects of the self, to play with their identity and to try out new ones' (Turkle 1995: 241). In open-ended online games like MUDs, Turkle theorized, people choose to play desired roles, and by doing so they paradoxically come closer to 'who they are' or 'who they want to be.' Richard Bartle (2004), developer of MUDs and designer of virtual worlds, calls this the 'role-playing paradox.' Through the mediation of role-playing, that is, playing a self-chosen character, a brave knight, an assertive thief or a powerful wizard, he argues, people can express themselves more than in real life:

> You're not role-playing as a being, you *are* that being; you're not assuming an identity, you are that identity; you're not projecting a self, you are that self. If you're killed in a fight, you don't feel that your character has died, you feel that you have died. There's no level of indirection, no filtering, no question: you are there ... When player and character merge to become a personae, that's immersion; that's what people get from virtual worlds that they can't get from anywhere else; that's when they stop playing the world and start living it. (Bartle 2004: 155-6)

According to this perspective, online role-playing games enhance human potential since they encourage players to express sides of themselves that are suppressed in real social life. This reasoning remains quite prominent in theories about Massively Multiplayer Online Role-Playing Games such as *Ultima Online* (1997), *Everquest* (2002), *Dark Age of Camelot* (2004) and *World of Warcraft* (2004). Bartle states, for instance, that '[t]he celebration of identity is the fundamental, critical, absolutely core point of virtual worlds', adding that 'players play virtual worlds to be themselves' (idem: 159, 162). MMOs, other authors insist, invite players to 'follow a personal path' (Yee 2007), invoke strong 'emotional involvement' and a 'sense of authenticity' (Turkle 1995, see also Jansz 2005) and even encourage 'a kind of spiritual development' through the act of online role-playing (Kelly 2004: 85). The question, then, is whether players of *World of Warcraft* do indeed enjoy experiences of in-game agency and, if so, how these experiences can be characterized.

The Quest for Supernatural Agency

> You are there – living the fantasy. ... You are the wizard and can do extra-ordinary things. And you can actually do that together with other people. (Hendrik)

Individual choice is at the heart of the game of *World of Warcraft*. Once players enter the world in the 'starter zone', they have to choose a character—an 'avatar' that functions as a digital representation of their identity. Given the main 'fantasy' narrative of the game world of *World of Warcraft*, the imagined history and legendary war between the Horde and the Alliance that has been at the core of the Warcraft mythos for years, it is imperative to make (moral) choices between 'good' (Alliance) and 'evil' (Horde); to choose between races (that is, dwarf, gnome, human, night elf, orc, tauren, etcetera), class (for example, sorcerer, druid, wizard, summoner, healer or shaman) and a variety of professions (alchemism, fishing, leatherworking and the like).

This construction of an avatar through multiple choices is a first step for players in their personalization and privatization of the game space. Through this process of selection they, after all, construct a character that is potentially unique and authentic in the game world. Moreover, because their choices are informed by their own subjective taste and idiosyncratic motivations, they rapidly experience their character as an extension of themselves. In line with Bartle's role-playing paradox, they emphasize that the character is not an Other, but an expression of the self. This personalization is, our respondents argue, a unique and appealing feature of MMOs like *World of Warcraft*. As Ronald puts it: 'Everybody can play Pac-Man ... But in this game you make a unique choice about who you are. ... And you are you, you are yourself in that world.' It is, as Peter states, an extension of one's 'ego' and from this perspective it is not surprising that they talk about their character in the first person and not in the third person: 'It' [the digital character on the screen] is not so much experienced as a '(S)He' but as an 'I' that actually 'exists' in the online world. Steven illustrates his point by arguing: 'When I talk with other people in the game about places were we have been or fights that we had, I never say my character was there. I say: "I was there." It's just you in that world ... Your character is an extension of yourself.'

Although identification with the character is already part of its construction at the beginning of the game, most respondents insist that this increases and intensifies in time, since they invest much personal energy, work, money and a lot of playing time in it. In the words of Tom:

It becomes a bit of 'you' because – I think – you invest a lot of time in it. You progress, because you gain gear and equipment ... And your power is increasing. It's like you're creating a character in a novel – all those stories and all those memories you have...

While Tom is still hesitant in arguing that he is actually becoming his in-game avatar, Dave is not: 'At a certain moment you become your character in the game.' Because the heroic roles they are playing—as a warrior, healer or magician—are not easily available in real life, they experience their in-game identities as a version of themselves that is better than in real life. Through role-playing, in other words, they access different parts of their identities, idealized parts, which cannot come to the surface in real life (or so they argue). This opportunity for self-expression, in short, invokes strong feelings of in-game freedom. As Ronald puts it:

> People choose a character because they like it and – in part – because they can express themselves through it. Like, this is who I am or this is how I really want to be. It says something about your dreams: you play the person that you cannot be in real life but would like to be.

Individual gamers thus construct a fitting character and, while playing, they project 'dreams', and ideal images of themselves on it. These dreams and images differ. Some gamers are 'achievers' (for example, Bartle 2004, Yee 2007), involved in 'instrumental play' (Taylor 2006). They often play out their personal dreams of being materially wealthy, powerful and search for in-game status through the possession of virtual items and high-standing outfits.

Most gamers in my sample, however, fall in the category of, what can be called, romantic 'explorers' (Yee 2007). They are not so much interested in in-game material status or power, but are mainly fascinated by the online world and their own subjective 'inner world.' They particularly play out personal fantasies about being a charismatic hero with special magical powers. As one gamer summarizes this collectively shared ideal of supernatural agency in the game world: 'Everybody wants to be a superhero.' The online world, they feel, provides such opportunities. Brandon, Danny and Hendrik respectively, claim from this perspective:

> When I look at myself – the way I am at the university, at work and at home – then I must say that I am very different compared to who I am in the game. ... When I read fantasy books or watch movies, I can identify mostly with mysterious, dark and tough types. ... I think I have chosen to become a 'warlock' in the game because these are a bit dark and mysterious characters – and that's what I find most interesting.

> What I would like most, of course, is for my character to be the greatest hero. A hero that follows his own path and does his own thing – that's the way I have

designed him. And I like playing with the idea that I am him. He is like a part of me, something that I would like to be.

You can be someone else. I think it is a beautiful world full of fantasy – a world that you encounter only in books. Unlike in real life, you can become a real hero.

Like Brandon (first quote), Michael is influenced by (fantasy) literature, television series and Hollywood movies in the way he perceives his own, heroic role in *World of Warcraft*:

In the game, I always say I am Indiana Jones. So everybody calls me that way. He is a bit of a cowboy. Indiana Jones knows exactly what he is doing and is really cool. ... It is how you really want to be.

The freedom of the in-game identity goes hand in hand with freedom in behavior. The respondents emphasize that they can act out private, violent and magical fantasies through their characters in the game world. Expressing those fantasies, they argue, is impossible in real life since they are simply physically impossible (for example, flying, 'transforming' or practicing magic) or considered 'deviant' or 'uncivilized' in a social-cultural sense. In the online world, they agree: 'you can do what you want—without consequences' (Danny) and 'in real life you can't practice magic or throw a fire ball' (Bram). Hendrik comments about his sometimes violent behavior in the game world: 'Is there anything nicer than doing things that you can not do in real life. I can take my sword and decapitate people. It is indeed a different world.' More than anything else, however, gamers embrace the supernatural agency provided by MMOs. As Richard states:

The impossible becomes possible. In *City of Heroes* you are a superhero with supernatural powers; you can do there what you can not do in real life. I can't lift things with my thoughts, but I can do this in *City of Heroes*. Just like *Spiderman* and the *X-Men*. And that is really cool!

Escaping the 'System'?

Respondents enjoy their in-game freedom because it enables them to escape the limitations and imperfections of ordinary offline life. For one thing, they appreciate the opportunity to experience the transcendence of the limits imposed by the natural world. Although Newtonian laws do generally apply in the game world (Bartle 2004), they can in most games be temporarily bent or broken, so as to enable flying, practicing magic or 'teleporting' from one place to another. Much more important, however, is players' appreciation of the escape from the social constraints and obligations of their everyday lives. Many interviewees complain about the everyday oppression exerted by social institutions like school, work and the family, which are experienced as limiting freedom and standing in the way of self-expression:

> In real life you are bound by rules, rules you are forced to obey. ... There are many things you have to do, like work, going to school, keeping contact with your friends, your relationships. You have to do it otherwise you will not achieve anything. And even if you want to game a lot, you have to work for the money – especially when you play *World of Warcraft*. ... That's the main difference between real life and the game: in the game you can do what you want and there are no obligations. (Ronald)

> In this [the real] world you have to work, you age, die and see suffering all around you. In the virtual world everything is perfect. You can do what you want. (Hendrik)

> You are thrown into a corner and forced to do things you do not want to do. Off course, I am quite pessimistic (there are some nice things) but I think the system is not good. I prefer running around naked through the fields. It's better than working. It's like 'you have to do this', 'you have to do that.' There are many obligations forced upon you and there is no way to escape. In the game there are no obligations. (Michael)

> I have a problem with authorities. The best way to make me leave is to tell me to stay or to force me to do so ... One of the most awful inventions ever invented is the clock. People work from 9 to 5, Sunday is a resting day. I hate these things. People are forced into straitjackets. (Peter)

Most respondents, in short, identify institutions they are dealing with on a day-to-day basis as the source of the felt limitations on freedom in real life: school, work and family generate (social) obligations. In most cases, however, they are also quite cynical about developments in society in general: 'politicians are just babbling without solving problems', Tom comments, while others critique the influence and omnipresence of media, relentless consumerism and technology. Michael and Peter go further than the other interviewees in critiquing 'the system', expressing stronger feelings of alienation and powerlessness, as well as stronger desires of escapism. Michael, for instance, talks as follows about 9/11, the War in Iraq and the opacity of US politics:

> This [the real] world sucks! ... Look at 9/11 for instance. They [the United States] want revenge, but if you hear the theories about what is really happening, you think ... Of course these may be rumors. For me: the truth will never be known. For that I am too small a person in this world. It's a pity. In the game world you are not so powerless.

Peter recounts:

> I think we are killing the world because everything is all about the money, the
> economy and we are developing technologies that we do not comprehend. We
> can not see the consequences of what we are doing and these consequences will,
> I think, be dramatic for us. ... Why should I invest in a world that will come to an
> end in the nearby future? ... In the game you don't have these kinds of problems.
> You escape in a world where it's good, where actions have no consequences and
> you don't have to think about 'what you will be doing within 20 years.' So, in a
> sense, gaming is the ultimate escape from reality ... And it's better than drugs:
> you don't get a hangover.

Critiquing the economy and its relentless quest for new technology in contemporary
society, he ironically suggests that 'in the game you don't have these kinds of
problems.' He is no exception in this, as others make similar claims:

> In the old days everything was better, I think. I really like the country side, rural
> life and sunny summers; this makes everybody happy. When you walk through
> the world of *World of Warcraft*, these things are all just there. And...*you are not
> continuously confronted with high-tech.* (Mark, our emphasis)

Producing Self-Expression in Online Computer Games

Having analyzed the dreams and experiences of agency in the online environment
of *World of Warcraft*, it is clear that its players collectively celebrate the
opportunity to express their human potential online through role-playing. They
act out what they consider to be a better, more heroic or even supernatural version
of themselves that does not easily surface in modern life. Paradoxically, however,
these experiences of escaping the 'system' are shaped, produced and invoked by
capitalist corporations like Sony, Microsoft and Blizzard Entertainment. Indeed,
our analysis of advertisements for 51 online games demonstrates exactly how
promises of a romantic escape route from modern society have become the main
selling points of the gaming industry.[2]

---

2   The advertisements are displayed on the websites of the following 51 games:
*2moons, 9Dragons, Active Worlds, Anarchy Online, Asheron's Call, Auto Assault, City
of Heroes/Villains, Cybertown, Dark Age of Camelot, Dark Ages, Dungeons & Dragons
Online, Entropia Universe, Era of Eidolon, Eve Online, Everquest, Everquest II, Final
Fantasy XI, Fury, Guild Wars, Helbreath, Horizons, Kal Online, Knight Online World,
Lineage, Lineage II, Lord of the Rings Online, Majestic, Mankind, Matrix Online, Mu
Online, Perfect World, Planetside, Prison Tale, Ragnarok Online, Ran Online, Rappelz,
Realm Online, RF Online, RunScape, Second Life, Silkroad Online, Sims Online, Star Trek*

Marketing Agency

Although the first MMOs in the 1990s, *Realm Online*, *Neverwinter Nights* and *Meridian 59*, were fairly successful, Origin Systems ('We Create Worlds') made a big leap with the launch of *Ultima Online* in 1997. Within 6 months it was played by about 100,000 people and the text from the advertisement exemplifies the genre that has been developed ever since:

> If you've ever felt like you wanted to step out of yourself, your life, into one that was full of fantasy and adventure – virtual worlds offer you this opportunity. ... You choose your own virtual life and immerse yourself into the mystical, medieval world of Britannia ... Ultima Online is the place where you can be whatever you want to be. (*Ultima Online*)

MMO advertisements promise a romantic escape to a world full of limitless agency, freedom and self-expression. They do so by articulating a dichotomy between a dull, prosaic and disenchanted real life and an adventurous, exciting life in the virtual world where 'one can be whoever one wants to be.' In most cases, such virtual worlds are constructed as mystical and medieval, that is, like the worlds that preceded modernity—untouched by rationalization and what Max Weber called the 'disenchantment of the world.' Such advertisements, Kimberly Lau (2008: 9) has argued, 'circle back to an imagined past existing prior to industrialization, a past epitomized by references to more integrated relationships and the interconnectedness of all living things.' By incorporating these values and perspectives, she adds, companies 'exploit ... anxieties about risk society and the diseases of modernity.'

Promises of real and absolute freedom, in other words, are generally articulated within the context of narratives of enchantment (Aupers 2007). Indeed, looking at the history of MMOs, it is clear that they have been strongly influenced by the work of J.R.R. Tolkien and that no less than 90 percent of the current examples are based on the fantasy genre (Woodcock 2008). Unencumbered by historical accuracy, the game designers cut and paste in various historical cultures, popular myths and legends to construct an otherworldly setting and facilitate an enchanting liberation from modernity. This narrative is used in advertisements to seduce consumers to engage in the freedom of the online world. Examples are *Dark Ages*—an 'online role-playing game set in a fantasy world of faeries and magic', *Realm Online*—'an exciting, adventurous land of monsters, magic, and medieval society' and *World of Warcraft*: 'A world awaits ... Descend into the World of Warcraft and join thousands of mighty heroes in an online world of myth, magic and limitless adventure ... An infinity of experiences await.'

Online, Star Wars Galaxies, Supreme Destiny, Sword of the New World, Tale in the Desert, Tibia, Ultima Online, Vanguard: Saga of Heroes and *World of Warcraft*.

Other romantic flights from modernity are situated in worlds that are particularly informed by Anglo-Saxon legend (*Ultima Online*), 'ancient Egypt' (*Tale in the Desert*), 'Norse mythology' (*Dark Age of Camelot*) or oriental culture (*Kal Online*). Even the much smaller proportion of futuristic science fiction worlds, like *Matrix Online*, *Star Wars Galaxies*, *Asheron's Call* or *Anarchy Online* promise the players other-worldliness and enchantment since, as science fiction writer Arthur C. Clarke correctly stated, 'sufficiently advanced technology can no longer be distinguished from magic.' And indeed: mysterious events and magical transformations happen in the world of *Anarchy Online*: 'Step almost 30,000 years into the future, to an age where common surgical implants and microscopic nano-bots can relieve most forms of human suffering... or transform any normal being into a weapon of destructive force.'

Having set the context of a re-enchanted world in an imagined past or future, the game companies promise consumers sheer unlimited choice, agency and self-expression. The pinnacle of this dominant theme in the advertisements is the choice players have to construct a character. By making selections of race, class, profession, gender, color of hair, eyes, clothing, etcetera, players can construct their own unique, personalized characters in the game world. This promise of authenticity and uniqueness is boasted in almost every advertisement, as the following examples illustrate:

> Create a unique character: Adventure as a Man, Elf, Dwarf or Hobbit. After choosing where your character hails from, select region-appropriate colour palettes for skin, hair, eye color, and more. Equip yourself with items like sturdy Dwarven armor, intricate Elven mail, or weapons created with the knowledge of past Ages. (*Lord of the Rings Online*)

> The first step in your adventure is to create your character's traits, including race, gender, face, hair color, body size, job, and nationality. This will become your on-screen 'alter ego' in the world of FINAL FANTASY XI. (*Final Fantasy XI*)

> When choosing a character to create in World of Warcraft, there are many choices before you. There are ten races and nine classes available, but the game's primary choice when it comes to character creation is the faction you wish to fight for. You can join the Horde or the Alliance, and your choice here has an impact on what you can and cannot accomplish in the world. (*World of Warcraft*)

> Players of Dark Age of Camelot are greeted with not only 15 races to choose from, but also 44 character classes providing players with numerous gameplay styles. This will give an immersive gameplay experience to the realms the players choose to play in. (*Dark Age of Camelot*)

This theme of personalization plays a major role in driving competition between game producers, with new games always promising more options and more agency than older, competing games:

> Enjoy *unparalleled* character customization, including 80 character skills, hundreds of special attacks, thousands of items and a wide range of clothes, weapons and armour. *No other online game* delivers more character customization and depth. (*Anarchy Online*, our emphasis)

Asheron's Call even promises 'millions of possible combinations … to make your character truly unique' and to 'create your personal saga', while others pursue the quest for unlimited freedom by adding new features to surpass their competitors. *Sword of the New World*, for instance, boasts the opportunity to play with multiple personalities simultaneously, thus broadening the notion of agency from the construction of a single unique in-game identity to that of a 'fragmented identity' or a 'distributed self' (Turkle 1995):

> Sword of the New World gives players more options, variety … and challenges than any other MMORPG can by virtue of its unique design features. With multi-character control (MCC), players are able to command up to three characters simultaneously. No longer limited to playing one character at a time, players can instantly switch between their favourite character classes or control them all at once. … With an entire family of such characters to develop, players will finally get to experience the sort of MMORPG game play they have been craving for years. (*Sword of the New World*)

The *Era of Eidolon*, on the other hand, promises the opportunity to use one unique character in different games:

> The Era of Eidolon game series is based on our unique game concept that allows you to use the same Hero in a whole range of different games and game types for your mobile phone. You can play the EoE games everywhere and you will get countless hours of game play against people from all over the world. (*Era of Eidolon*)

And finally, *Mankind* states that the player's 'alter ego' will remain active in the world even when the player is not online:

> Unlike most MMOGs, Mankind boasts a truly persistent universe. Things keep going even when you're offline. So, your forces keep doing what you've instructed them to do - guard a base, patrol a sector of space, or continue to mine resources to fuel your empire. (*Mankind*)

Online game worlds, in short, aim to avoid structure and to provide as many 'free' choices as possible, as epitomized by a *Runescape* ad: 'What a player does in RuneScape is entirely their decision: nothing is predetermined.' The ultimate goal is self-expression by enabling players to become what they *really* want to be in the game world—wizards, warriors or true heroes, as ads for *Asheron's Call* ('a new and heroic identity awaits you!'), *World of Warcraft* ('players assume the roles of Warcraft heroes as they explore, adventure, and quest across a vast world') or *City of Heroes* ('where you and thousands of other players take on the roles of super powered heroes') make clear. *Guild War* is characteristically marketed in the following fashion:

> In a world torn by conflict, where human kingdoms are all but destroyed and guilds sacrifice all for a chance to control the Hall of Heroes, a champion must rise from the ruins of a once-proud land to lead refugees from the ashes and fulfill an ancient prophecy. Will that hero be you? (*Guild War*)

Online games based on movies and TV-series, like *Star Wars Galaxies*, *Star Trek Online* and the *Matrix Online*, emphasize that the heroes that one could once just watch in a more or less passive manner, can now actually become alive, with players becoming them rather than just passively identifying with them.

> You've enjoyed watching the Star Wars universe for years—now's your chance to live in it! Fight alongside Han Solo and Chewbacca, smuggle goods for Jabba the Hutt, defend Imperial stations from the ravages of the Rebels, and more. (*Star Wars Galaxies*)

> The matrix online is the future of the Matrix, picking up right where the trilogy left off ... Be ANYONE you want to be. Matrix online is a game that features a rich storyline that you can choose to become intimately involved with, and a deep, everchanging world in which you can create your own adventures and join with others as well. (*Matrix Online*)

The producers of *Ultima Online* hold that '[t]here are limitless possibilities with only your imagination to bridle them—so take hold of the reins and choose your own destiny!' *Mankind* explains that '[y]ou are the master of your fate and you alone will choose your inclinations, there's no limit except the one you'll have set', while *Dungeons and Dragons Online* in a similar vein contends that '[a] character can try to do anything you can imagine.' And *Entropia* promises that 'the universe is yours to enjoy as entertainment.'

Engineering Agency

The message of game companies like Blizzard Entertainment, Sony and Microsoft is loud and clear: we facilitate unlimited agency in our game worlds and opportunities for self-expression that can not be compared with those in the real world. This message is, however, overly selective and strategic, since it leaves aside the technological and commercial context that mediates such experiences of freedom, as Kline et al. (2003: 245) have rightly emphasized: 'The paradox of information capitalism is that even as it encourages an expanded enclave of freedom and self-development of "pure play", it begins to undermine that enclave by commodifying it.' This is in itself almost a truism, because it is of course obvious that game companies have commercial goals. Blizzard Entertainment, for instance, has made 1.3 billion euros in 2004, its production team for *World of Warcraft* consists of 2,700 employees, and the game has about 12 million active subscribers who each pay 13 euros a month. Agency and freedom have hence in effect become commodities and game designers do indeed, as we will demonstrate below, actively inscribe agency and freedom in games in such a way as to seduce players to—in the words of one of them—'play forever' (Hopson 2001).

To accomplish its goal of keeping gamers playing, the game industry directs much of its production budget and its technical expertise towards the engineering of experiences of 'immersion' (for example, Bartle 2004, Freeman 2004, Newman 2004). Immersion entails amnesia: it makes gamers forget the offline social, technological and commodified environment of the game and makes them identify with the game world. In the words of one game designer:

> One of the goals of good game design is that the user becomes completely immersed into the experience so that they are not thinking that they are interacting with a computer, they are not thinking that they are fiddling with a joystick. The technology is so seamless, the design is so seamless, that they get into the character, and they completely lose sight of their surroundings and everything. In order to convince the person that they are immersed in an experience, the technology has to be so good that it makes itself invisible. (quoted in Kline et al. 2003: 19)

David Freeman, another designer, puts it this way:

> If you do your work well, the gamers will be drawn emotionally into the game, but they will have no idea why. They'll have no idea that you did tremendous work over countless hours to cause that effect. So, oddly, their thinking you did almost nothing will be your greatest reward. (Freeman 2004: 38)

The experiences of players of *World of Warcraft* discussed above illustrate how immersion works. They have experiences of *being* in the virtual world, *living* their virtual lives as heroes, whereas they forget about real life and the technological, commodified nature of the game. Exemplary is the remark of one of the gamers that in *World of Warcraft* 'you are not confronted with high tech.' Such strategies of 'naturalization' (Barthes 1986)—making the artificial world feel natural, intuitive and self-evident—is not just a matter of technological skills (making technology 'seamless', 'invisible' and avoid 'lagging'), but also a matter of good and clever narration: the narrative of a medieval, natural and pre-technological world untouched by the juggernaut of modernity helps in naturalizing the technological infrastructure. Game designers even argue in an online discussion that the use of technological artifacts in the narrative of the online world itself should be avoided since, they argue, 'technology is an immersion breaker in most fantasy realms' and 'immersion is easier with magic than technology.'[3]

As game designer Richard Bartle notes in his book *Designing Virtual Worlds*, engineering a strong sense of agency is a good way of stimulating immersion: 'Self-expression is another way to promote immersion. By giving players freeform ways to communicate themselves, designers can draw them more deeply into the world—they feel more part of it' (2004: 244). Starting from this assumption, game designers construct online worlds as brimming with multiple choices, possibilities to interact with the environment, chat with Non Playing Characters (NPCs), connect with other players and create idiosyncratic outfits, unique gear and, ultimately, 'authentic' characters and personalities in the game word. This is paradoxical: agency is ultimately the result of design and game designers are the 'coding authorities' (Castronova 2005)—even in matters of choice and agency. It is from this perspective that Kline et al. (2003: 19) argue that '[g]aming choice usually remains a matter of tactical decisions executed within predefined scenarios whose strategic parameters are preordained by the designers.' And indeed: many books on game design develop and formulate strategies on how to construct feelings of agency. In *Character Development and Storytelling for Games*, Lee Sheldon, for instance, argues about in-game characters:

> Stereotypes diminish the overall gaming experience. They limit the sophistication of our stories. And as a result, limit our audience. ... We want men and women to play our games, to live out their fantasies, but unless we turn these fantasies into living, breathing individuals, the experience will be hollow. (2004: 57)

According to Marks:

> Players must be able to build character, making them more powerful over time through developing skill and finding or creating magical items or increasing power; without this there is no sense of accomplishment. To a degree, it is the fact that the players have actually built a character that they can be proud of that keeps them coming back for more. (2003: 69)

Like Marks and Sheldon, Freeman emphasizes that a feeling of agency is the most important thing in game design and gaming experience. He comments:

---

3   Available at: http://terranova.blogs.com/terra_nova/2005/09/magic.html [accessed: March 29, 2011].

'Who's in charge, the game designer or the gamer? Making the player *feel* like he or she is impacting, or even shaping the story is sometimes called "giving the player a 'sense of agency'"' (2004: 327). In his book titled *Creating Emotion in Games: The Craft and Art of Emotioneering*, Freeman distinguishes no less than 32 categories of 'emotioneering techniques' to enhance an individual feeling of agency and authenticity in computer games. Emotions, he argues, can be stimulated by injecting emotion into games' story elements, exciting plots in the game world, relationships between players, relationships between players and NPCs, using symbols, creating complex situations and characters etcetera. In summary:

> The goal of Emotioneering is to move the player through an interlocking sequence of emotional experiences (…) Emotioneering is the vast body of techniques (…) that can create, for a player or participant, breadth and depth of emotions in a game or other interactive experience, or that can immerse a player in a world or a role. (Freeman 2004: 7)

A sense of agency in the online game should not just be a short-lived moment—a temporary experience—but should also be strengthened over time. A programming strategy to actively produce such feelings of 'personal growth' and character development and, at the same time, keep the player as long in the game as possible, is 'behavioral game design' (Bartle 2004: 254-7, Hopson 2001). This technique, based on the behavioral psychology of B.F. Skinner, implements a reward system in the game world based on a carefully considered 'variable ratio reinforcement schedule.' In the beginning of the game, players will find instant gratification (through the rapid gain of experience points, material items or new levels) whereas such gratifications are systematically and rationally delayed as the game unfolds. Studying these underlying mechanics of the online game *Everquest*, Yee (2001) writes about the MMO as a 'Virtual Skinner Box', a sort of human treadmill for youngsters who endlessly seek rewards.

In short, players' individual decisions are by and large pre-scripted by designers; in-game emotions and experiences of personal freedom and self-expression are technically engineered; and in-game character evolution is reinforced by behavioral programming. Indeed, Marks (2003: 76) asks about in-game agency and ownership: '[W]ho owns a player's creation inside a game? When a player spends months on end creating the perfect Everquest character, does the character belong to Sony or to the player? The short answer is, it belongs to Sony.' And indeed: notwithstanding players' feelings of becoming 'who they are' or 'who they want to be', the companies that produce *Everquest*, *Dark Age of Camelot* and *World of Warcraft* are ultimately in charge and the game world remains their intellectual property: they own all content, including players' characters. And as noted in the End User License Agreement of *World of Warcraft*: 'Blizzard may suspend, terminate, modify, or delete the account at any time with any reason or no reason, with or without notice.'

Conclusion

The debate about new media is nowadays dominated by conceptions of a 'participatory culture' (Jenkins 2006), informed by 'users claiming their cultural freedom from the culture industries' (Schäfer 2009: 148) and based on a conception of consumers as holding power over the means of production and of new media as facilitating rather than determining agency. Online computer games like *World of Warcraft* are held to exemplify this development. This contemporary academic discourse, we conclude on the basis of our analysis in this chapter, has a blind spot for the social forces that are operative in the game world—forces that shape practices of in-game self-expression as much as they shape discourse about unlimited agency. This blind spot is in itself not surprising, because, as Althusser has argued, '... one of the effects of ideology is the practical denegation of the ideological character of ideology by ideology: ideology never says, "I am ideological"' (2006 [1971]: 79).

Nonetheless, notions of agency, freedom and self-expression in online computer games are elements of a well-crafted, carefully preserved and powerful myth, or an ideology in the sense of neo-Marxist theories about the construction of 'false consciousness' by economic powers that control the means of production (for example, Horkheimer and Adorno 2002 [1944], Marcuse 1964). Notwithstanding the moral biases and empirical shortcomings of such neo-Marxist theories (for example, Gans 1999 [1972]: 27-77), they do apply seamlessly to our findings. Game producers, after all, actively and consciously construct a sense of agency through marketing discourse, game narrative and game design, while the characters people play remain ultimately commodities that are controlled, governed and owned by the company. This myth of agency online is hence similar to the 'pseudo-individualism' (2002 [1944]: 63) discussed by Horkheimer and Adorno. On the one hand, it exploits the cultural ideal of expressive individualism and in doing so provides players with 'real' meaning, that is, makes them feel unique, authentic and special. On the other hand, however, it is precisely this experience that mystifies the commodified character of the game and the bare economic interests of the industry. It is, after all, a clear interest of the game industry to get people thinking of themselves as becoming more like 'who they really are' through online role-playing when, in fact, they start to identify more and more with the commodified game world. One can take this paradox even further: at the moment gamers are totally immersed in the virtual world, fully identify with their in-game character and experience ultimate freedom, they have actually come under the spell of the 'culture industry' that can, according to Horkheimer and Adorno, 'do as it chooses with the needs of consumers—producing, controlling, disciplining them' (idem: 115), so that immersive online games do in fact reduce 'the individual to a standardized commodity' (idem: 94).

Such 'commodity fetishism new style' (Aupers 2011) actively veils how the game is produced and enhances the enchanting appeal of the product by tapping into Western cultural ideals of being a completely autonomous and free individual.

But this cultural myth of agency also constitutes a powerful new mode of social control of customers, because it seduces players to remain actively involved in the game world and, ultimately, in the game of capitalism. 'More gaming by more people', McGonigal (2011: 43) has recently noted, 'is the primary goal of the industry' and 'the industry wants to create lifelong gamers.' MMOs like *World of Warcraft* are on average played about 23 hours a week, and a small percentage of gamers is actually addicted, that is, neglecting relations, school and work (Yee 2007). Much of the latter is doubtlessly due to the accurately crafted, constructed and designed experiences of agency discussed above—especially, as the interviewed gamers themselves recount, because in-game feelings of personal freedom and empowerment are atypical in their offline lives.

'Stormfront is like a Second Home to Me': Social Exclusion of Right-Wing Extremists

Online Right-Wing Extremism

Academic interest in right-wing extremism on the Internet has increased significantly since roughly the year 2000. Its strong focus on the role of the Internet in disseminating right-wing extremism has yielded insights into the ideological contents and structure of online networks (see Adams and Roscigno 2005, Caiani and Wagemann 2009, Duffy 2003, Gerstenfeld et al. 2003, Levin 2002, Schafer 2002, Tateo 2005, Thiesmeyer 1999, Whine 2000), but despite widespread claims about the existence of virtual communities, the social significance of online extremist forums for those involved is still far from clear.

Although many scholars assume a sense of community on right-wing extremist online venues, this has not yet been systematically studied. In her analysis of the features of online neo-Nazi rhetoric, Thiesmeyer (1999), for instance, asserts that a sense of community is present among members of extreme right-wing websites. However, this is neither demonstrated nor analyzed. And examining the rhetorical content of extremist sites, Duffy (2003) presumes a virtual sense of community as well, although this is not part of her analysis.

A common problem affecting this literature is that scholars do not take the perspectives of the participants in online venues into account. As a result, no theoretical understanding of the sense of community sought or constructed by right-wing extremists has been obtained. Scholars, for instance, simply infer a sense of community from the presence of certain features of a website, such as 'imagery and icons' (Hara and Estrada 2005: 508, see also Thompson 2001). Others suggest that the mere presence of interactive features on online venues provides evidence for the existence of virtual communities, irrespective of the actual use of these features (Reid and Chen 2007, Zhou et al. 2005). Scholars also rely on network analyses of extreme right-wing online venues to 'identify communities' (Chau and Xu 2007: 59, see also Reid and Chen 2007, Zhou et al. 2005), even though they do not scrutinize the meanings the structural ties they uncover have for the participants involved (see De Koster 2010: 32-3 for a critical discussion). Moreover, if contents of right-wing extremist websites are analyzed, attention is usually paid to those created by the administrators of these sites (for example, Hara and Estrada 2005, Reid and Chen 2007, Thiesmeyer 1999). Because the communications of individual users are clearly of most importance for the study of an online sense of community, this is not a satisfactory approach either. And, ironically, in the exceptional case that participants in right-wing extremist web forums are interviewed (Glaser et al. 2002), this does not concern their online experiences: the Internet is merely used for contacting right-wing extremists in order to study their ideas about interracial violence.[1]

Therefore, it is unsurprising that there has recently been a call for 'more systematic studies (…) to explore [extremist] groups' utilization of the web to form virtual communities' (Reid and Chen 2007: 178). This 'fundamental question' (idem: 178) has been open since it was put on the research agenda as 'a worthwhile subject for further research' by Burris et al. (2000: 232) quite some time ago. Since systematic studies on this subject have not been carried out yet, the existence, background, and function of online communities of right-wing extremists—the latter two vitally important from a theoretical point of view—remain obscure. Aiming to contribute to filling this void, we study virtual community formation on the Dutch branch of the international 'Stormfront White Nationalist Community'—the best-known online forum for right-wing extremists of the world (Burris et al. 2000, Reid and Chen 2007, Wojcieszak 2010, Zhou et al. 2005). In order to develop a framework for such a research, we first present a concise overview of virtual community studies.

Research on Virtual Communities

In Internet studies it is widely held that online groups cannot be termed 'communities' just like that, because 'there are many aggregations of people that do not qualify as communities' (Etzioni and Etzioni 1999: 241, see also Fernback 1999: 216, Papadakis 2003: vii). Although 'community' is a hotly debated concept of which no universally agreed conceptualization exists (Driskell and Lyon 2002, Komito 1998, Yang 2000), there seems to be agreement that 'commonality' lies at its core (Fernback 1999: 204, Wilbur 1997: 8). More specifically, it is widely held that members of a community have a shared culture and display mutual commitment (see for example, Etzioni 2004, Etzioni and Etzioni 1999, Komito 1998).

When it comes to the question of online community, claims cannot be made about the Internet as a whole, as the first wave of utopian and dystopian Internet studies of the 1990s did (see for example, Wellman 1997 for an overview). This 'totalizing' tendency has not completely disappeared since, as is indicated by studies that rely on a dichotomous distinction between 'real' and 'false' community to discuss

---

1   The only example of a study in which a sense of community is discussed by addressing the perspectives of right-wing extremists themselves is a thorough ethnographic analysis by Simi and Futrell (2006). However, their broad study of right-wing extremists' activities on a wide variety of online venues is not primarily focused on the subject of virtual community and as such does not yield the theoretical insights we strive for.

whether virtual communities *in general* are 'true communities' (see for example, Driskell and Lyon 2002, see De Koster 2010: 2-4 for an overview). Opposing this practice, Fernback has rightly argued it is more fruitful to pay attention to the meaning users attach to their online interactions than to ask in general terms 'whether or not cybercommunity is or isn't real community' (2007: 63, see also Bakardjieva 2005: 168-9). Because it is often used in a 'totalizing' way, Fernback declares the concept of virtual community 'inadequate and inappropriate' (idem: 62), stating that scholars are 'burdened by the community label' (idem: 64). However, in the interpretive approach she herself advocates, it can be theoretically productive to find out under which circumstances people *experience* their online interactions as a community. In such an approach, an 'aggregation only becomes a community if [the participants] perceive it to be so, and experience the spirit of community' (Ward 1999: 96). Thus, it is important to study which meanings members of an online venue attach to it. Do they feel they have a shared culture and do they display mutual commitment? This line of thought is also followed by Blanchard and Markus (2004), who add that to warrant labeling an online group as a community such an 'experienced sense of community' should be supported by 'community behaviors', that is, offering support, practices of inclusion and exclusion, and social control (Watson 1997: 110).

From a theoretical point of view, it is obviously not so much important to *describe* whether a particular group qualifies as a community (for example, Blanchard and Markus 2004, Nieckarz 2005, Roberts et al. 2002), but rather to *explain* or *understand* experiences of online community. For this purpose 'it is vital we understand those physical-world needs fuelling online social relations' (Campbell 2004: 192). To overcome a common problem in studies on social interactions on the Internet it is important 'to re-locate virtual culture in the real world' (Robins 2000: 92), since 'nobody lives only in cyberspace' (Kendall 1999: 70). All too often, attention to the motives and experiences of Internet users rooted in offline life is lacking. 'Most of the existing research ... [has treated] online group phenomena in isolation from the actual daily life experiences of the subjects involved' (Bakardjieva 2005: 167). Although it is frequently stressed that the interrelationship between online and offline phenomena should be taken into account, in common research practice this is hardly done (Hardey 2002: 571, Nip 2004: 409). This lack of attention for offline life is especially visible in the literature on online right-wing extremism, which is characterized by a strong bias toward the virtual: predominantly employing content and network analyses of websites, such studies focus almost exclusively on the online context. In this way, the social backgrounds and functions of potential virtual communities remain obscure, thus hampering the development of explanatory theory.

In short, there is a need for systematic empirical research taking the online and offline experiences and understandings of those involved into account. Taking this need seriously, we start our study of the Dutch branch of 'Stormfront White Nationalist Community'—referred to as *Stormfront* for the sake of brevity—with an overview of the identities presented online. Then we pay attention to participants' experiences in offline social life. Subsequently, their reasons for participation as well as their online experiences are analyzed in relation to those offline. In the final section we discuss our findings and formulate hypotheses for further research. Before all this, we present our data and methods.

Data and Methods

Stormfront

Stormfront is the largest right-wing extremist Internet forum in the Netherlands.[2] Next to the forum, members can interact through Internet Relay Chat, but this option is hardly used. In order to become a member and be able to post to the forum, one has to register under a self-chosen username.

Apart from 'Stormfront Britain', the Dutch section is the most intensively-used branch. Since August 2001, when the message archive was lost due to the introduction of new software, approximately 19,000 threads have been created, in which over 224,000 messages have been posted. During our data collection, the number of users online was always high, averaging at about one hundred. The lowest number of visitors we witnessed online is 56, the highest 268. Many participants have been members for several years and posted hundreds or even thousands of messages.

Qualitative Content Analysis

The first part of our study consists of an interpretative analysis (Hijmans 1996) of the messages on the forum. We have selected messages by means of relevance sampling (Krippendorff 2004): instead of addressing all postings (which would be practically impossible) or drawing a random sample from these, we have studied forum messages in which members address their extreme right identity, their offline experiences and actions relating to this identity, their motives for participation in *Stormfront*, and the way they experience *Stormfront*.

Naturally, harm to individual users and the group as a whole should be avoided when collecting data on online forums (Eysenbach and Till 2001, King 1996). However, obtaining informed consent for the use of this type of data is under debate. Some argue that messages posted on an Internet forum are 'public acts deliberately intended for public consumption' (Paccagnella 1997), whereas others find it difficult to determine whether communications on online forums are to be regarded as private or public (see Eysenbach and Till 2001).

King (1996) distinguishes two aspects of online groups that are vital in determining the need for informed consent. The first is 'group accessibility', indicating 'the degree with which the existence of and access to a particular Internet

---

2   This forum is available at: http://www.stormfront.org/forum/forumdisplay.php?f=22.

forum or community is publicly available information.' Group accessibility is lower—and the need for informed consent higher—if procedures like registration are required to gain access to the messages on a forum (Eysenbach and Till 2001).

The second aspect of importance is 'perceived privacy', denoting 'the degree to which group members perceive their messages to be private to that group' (King 1996). Attention has to be paid to indications for perceived privacy in the content of the forum messages. Besides, the number of users of a forum is important: if ten people use a forum, the perceived privacy, and therefore the need for informed consent, is higher than in the case of hundred or thousand users (Eysenbach and Till 2001: 1104).

Stormfront is characterized by a high level of accessibility: the forum is well-known, the messages can be read by anyone—including non-members—and are indexed by search engines like Google. The perceived privacy on the forum is very low: the users explicitly indicate they are aware that non-members with diverse backgrounds read the postings on the forum. Furthermore, the number of users online is high at any moment. Therefore, we did not regard it necessary to obtain informed consent for the use of forum messages in our qualitative content analysis.

Synchronous Online Interviews

Contrary to common practice, our qualitative content analysis is supplemented with semi-structured interviews with members of *Stormfront*. During these interviews, respondents were encouraged to speak freely, while it was ascertained that the above-mentioned topics were addressed—we inquired after their ideology and identity, their related experiences and actions in offline life, their motives for their online participation, and their experiences on the forum and the meanings they attach to it. In order to recruit respondents, we posted a request at a prominent part of the forum after consulting one of the moderators.

Having overcome severe skepticism about our promise to safeguard their privacy, eleven members agreed to be interviewed online. These interviews have been conducted using software for synchronous communication, since this is most apt for non-standardized online interviews (Wenjing 2005). It is to be preferred above asynchronous communication for methodological reasons, especially because asynchronous interviews tend to become structured around interviewer's questions and to become too formal (Hodkinson, quoted in Mann and Stewart 2000: 76-7).

A practical objection to online interviews is that people might give relatively short answers because typing takes much more effort than speaking. Besides, it can be difficult to respond to unforeseen turns in the interview (see for many examples Markham 1998). Unsurprisingly, the experiences of other researchers using online methods are mixed (compare, for example, Kivits 2005 with Sanders 2005). Because in our study all respondents cooperated greatly, these practical problems could be overcome and all of the themes mentioned above could be addressed extensively. The shortest interview lasted no less than almost two hours, while various respondents spent much more time during several sessions. Moreover, because respondents were reluctant to participate in this study at first, an important advantage of online interviews is that people tend to reveal more about themselves if they use computer-mediated-communication, especially when dealing with sensitive information (Joinson 2005).

Seven of our 11 respondents are between 16 and 20 years of age, two between 20 and 30, and two older than 30. *Stormfront* seems to be used mainly by men, but women participate on the forum as well. Nevertheless, all respondents are male. To protect the privacy of the respondents, we use fictitious names. In the analysis these names are distinguished from the usernames relating to data retrieved from the forum by italicizing the latter. We have translated all quotations below from Dutch.

Identities Presented Online

The postings on the forum as well as the interviews point out that members of *Stormfront* have great troubles with contemporary Western society. They all abhor its lack of shared moral guidelines and the individualism and cultural disorder that arise from this condition. On the forum, *Ridder in de Orde van Cicero* summarizes the members' common view as follows:

> Since ... the nineteen sixties our leftist 'comrades' have brutally disrupted our cultural traditions. These 'liberal leftists' ridiculed family life and made many assaults on European traditions and customs. ... We West Europeans have become alienated from our magnificent age-old cultural customs and traditional values. Instead, we were forced to deal with demo-liberalism, feminism, homosexuality, capitalism, paedophilia, multiculturalism and multiracialism.

'Thanks to the social democrats, who have been in power for ages, anything goes. The Netherlands have become a giant mess since the nineteen seventies' states *Siegheiligman*, and *d0gZ* experiences cultural disorder in the Netherlands today too: 'I do not hate races because they are lower. I hate them because they kill my culture.' This diagnosis of culture is inextricably intertwined with the extreme-right identity of those involved. Six of the respondents describe themselves primarily as 'nationalist', one as 'extreme right', and four as 'national socialist.' This is in line with the characterization of *Stormfront* by moderator *Heidens Bloed* as 'a Nationalist or National-Socialist site.'

The members of *Stormfront* are strongly attached to the ideology that lies at the core of their identity. As Herman states it: 'My vision is reflected in every aspect of my daily life. It is not something I can set aside just like that, it is a feeling like the deepest and greatest love.' This idea is shared by many others, like Joop: 'My outlook on society is a very important part of my personality. And

I act according to it.' For this reason, they are primarily active on *Stormfront* and not on other well-known right-wing forums. *Stormfront* is frequently characterized as a 'serious' forum that features profound discussions, whereas other popular Dutch extreme right forums are perceived as more childish and merely provocative. Dedicated members of *Stormfront* are even offended when they are not distinguished from visitors of the latter forums: '[these people] deprive nationalist right of any chance of being taken seriously because of their absurdly childish behavior' (Herman). They are considered 'brainless and stupid' (Dirk): '[they] don't know what they are talking about ... and their ignorance harms our image' (Arjan). In line with this opinion, members of *Stormfront* who do visit other forums seem to prefer small and deeply ideological forums, among which the national-socialist 'Großdeutsches Vaterland' is referred to most frequently.

Members of *Stormfront* express their attachment to their extreme-right ideology in several ways online. Firstly, usernames are chosen to reflect their views. Telling examples are *AryanMaster*, *KaKaKa* (a phonetic acronym of Ku Klux Klan), *HHakenKKKruiSS* (meaning *Swastika* and containing acronyms of 'Heil Hitler', 'Ku Klux Klan', and 'Schutzstaffel'), *Moslimhater* (meaning '*Hater of Muslims*'), and *Zyklon_B*. Others bear names provided with a numerical code—'88', which stands for 'Heil Hitler', is especially popular. Examples are *Devil88lady* and *skinhead-88*. Many other members are active under less extreme names, but nevertheless use these to express the ideology they adhere to. Especially if the context is taken into account, names like *dutchNLpride*, *NationalistNL*, *WhiteDutchman*, and *white and proud of it* leave little to the imagination. Members of *Stormfront* obviously acknowledge themselves, too, that usernames like these express an extreme right identity. *Dux Bellorum* writes 'You can choose that name ... yourself, it CONVEYS something about you', while *HHakenKKKruiSS* explains his choice for this name by stating 'It makes immediately clear what I stand for, doesn't it?'

Members have the opportunity to place 'avatars' next to their usernames. These, too, are used to express an extreme right-wing identity, as a rule by means of historical nationalist or national-socialist symbols. As Alfred Rosenberg remarks: 'it goes without saying that [members] often have avatars of people or things that mean much to their ideology.' Many of these consist of the Dutch national flag and references to national-socialist Germany, the 'white power' movement, and the Dutch National-Socialist Movement. Many members also emphasize their ideology by means of a 'signature', a text placed automatically underneath all of one's messages. Signatures consist of quotes of Hitler, praise for the political leaders of national-socialist Germany, or slogans such as 'Own people first!! Down with multiculturalism!!!' and 'WHITE POWER!!!'

In short, members of *Stormfront* are characterized by a deeply entrenched extreme right-wing ideology which they display online. What are participants' experiences relating to their extremist identity in offline social life? This will be discussed below.

'We Are a Threatened Species, and the Hunt Is Open': Offline Stigmatization

'Why Are You a Dirty Nazi?': Negative Reactions in Everyday Life

Many contributors to the forum indicate that their right-wing extremist identities are met with strong condemnation by people in their social surroundings. For several members, this even applies to their small family circle:

> My family from my mother's side, which I meet daily, is left or extreme left. Of course, you understand that these people look upon me askance. At every family party people come to ask me: 'Why are you a dirty Nazi?' (*EInherjar88(vl)*)

Members of *Stormfront* who still attend school are confronted with negative reactions there, too:

> A friend of mine and I, who are in the same class, are constantly punished and abused by teachers when we make no secret of our rightist ideas, whereas we always express ourselves quietly and politely. We should not be punished, for it is our right to express our opinions, and schools ought to be neutral. (*Dorien_14*)[3]

Members who have a paid job experience the same difficulties, but often with more serious consequences: 'I was very probably fired because I am too rightist!!! After I had spoken with colleagues who share my ideas, someone has informed the floor manager ... As you see, the leftist rats are everywhere' (*j.boere*). Adverse reactions outside school and the workplace are frequently reported on the forum as well:

> [Outside a group of close friends] I often encounter people who do not agree with me in class, at my soccer club and in the rest of my social surroundings. They think I am a Nazi, frequently without knowing the actual meaning of this word. ... When my more extremist opinion arises, and I say I feel some sympathy for Hitler and that as far as I am concerned all non-whites should leave (so, not only the riff-raff), people often become suspicious and the insulting and stigmatizing starts again. (*Tha man*)

Fiuv uses an epigrammatic summary of those experiences as his signature: 'We are a threatened species, and the hunt is open.'

The interviews confirm the importance of experiences of social rejection. No fewer than eight of the eleven respondents experience negative reactions in

---

3 The number 14 in this username most likely does not refer to the age of this forum member, but to a fourteen-word slogan that is popular in right-wing extremist circles: 'We must secure the existence of our people and a future for white children.'

their social surroundings. These are discussed in what follows, while we will pay attention to the three members who do not struggle with social rejection in the final part of our analysis.

For Dirk, Ferdinand, Herman, and Ron, the negative reactions to their right-wing extremist identity they encounter are no reason to hide their deviant ideas. Dirk, for example, says:

> The headmaster has so often called me to account. ... When I just told him why it was like that and why I had such an opinion, he had just one word to say: 'Absurd.' After that, he said: 'I do not want to hear anything about it. When from this time on people ask for your view, you should shut up. None of that for me.' He also said: 'if you did not have such good grades, you would have been removed from school already.'

Besides, Dirk says he is called 'racist' everyday when he 'just walks down the street' in his jacket with a small Dutch flag attached. Although he considers himself 'quite deviant' as a result of these experiences, this is no reason for him to conceal his ideology.

When asked whether people try to impose their ideas upon him, Herman responds: 'Some (unfortunately the majority) do so.' They do so by 'ignoring you, denying you your opinion because "you are just a Nazi", [and by] banning certain ideas like [right-wing extremist] music and revisionism.' He, too, indicates that it is not possible for him to express his ideology at school without getting into trouble.

> I am not allowed to join in political discussions at school because of my views ... I am 'too extreme' and 'affect my fellow students in a negative way.' Sometimes one is not even permitted to enter class at all, sometimes one is sent out, sometimes one has to stay in the corridor, and so on.

Unlike Herman, Dirk, Ferdinand, and Ron, the anticipation of such negative reactions is a reason for Arjan, Barend, Joop, and Peter—the other respondents who experience negative reactions in everyday life—to conceal their deviant ideology as much as they can. Outside his family, for instance, Joop hides his ideas. Expecting great trouble, he does not even consider disclosing these at his workplace:

> If people at work ... know that you are a right-wing extremist, this would greatly disturb the atmosphere. Cooperation with others would be much more difficult, many more tensions between colleagues would arise. If you have an opinion like mine, you cannot express it at a place like that.

Arjan, too, does not inform people about his ideology, since he would have 'a lot of problems' if he did. He finds this really frustrating: 'I think it is disgusting that you can be fired or expelled from school if you express your opinion.'

What Joop, Arjan, Peter, and Barend, nevertheless, have in common with Dirk, Ferdinand, Herman, and Ron is that they do not feel free to express their ideas in Dutch society. Asked whether they experience freedom of expression, Herman answers 'Anything but', Dirk says 'Absolutely not!', and Peter states: 'Freedom of expression and democracy are an illusion.'

Stigmatization and Fatalism

Summing up the foregoing, many members of *Stormfront* experience stigmatization in the classical sense of Erving Goffman (1986 [1963]), aptly paraphrased by Manzo (2004: 401) as 'an expectation of a discrediting judgment of oneself by others in a particular context.' They have, in other words, a 'spoiled identity' (Goffman 1986 [1963]). This leads not only to 'felt stigma', but also to status loss and discrimination (Green et al. 2005: 198, see also Link and Phelan 2001). Naturally, the latter only holds for people whose stigma is known to others, the so-called 'discredited' (Goffman 1986 [1963]: 4). The 'discreditable' members of *Stormfront*, on the other hand, hide their stigma and try to 'pass' as 'normals' (Page 1984: 20).

The experience of stigmatization creates feelings of dissociation or disattachment (Rotenstreich 1989). Some respondents emphasize this vehemently, explaining that they feel attached neither to those with whom they deal on a personal basis, nor to the Dutch population at large: 'On the one hand, I feel attached to them because of national consanguinity. But I do not feel anything but loathing for leftist treasonable people and I have no personal commitment to them' (Herman).[4]

These widespread feelings of disattachment prove to go hand in hand with aversion to political action: 'Frankly, I do not feel at all like devoting myself to a people of social democrats who hate me because of my anti-Jewish and anti-multiculturalist opinions. I prefer to be devoted to myself; let the Jew-blowing multiculturalist *hoi polloi* eat shit' (*De-botte-bijl*). The messages on the forum indicate that many members of *Stormfront* hold a fatalistic worldview. *Phrea|k*, for instance, does not think demonstrations are of any use, and *Parsifal* states: 'It is clear that "the extreme right" won't have any success under the current conditions. Demonstrations, discussion programs, and political parties are all useless ... It is quite naïve to believe that these might work.' These views are reflected by our

4   Such feelings are not confined to the members who are open about their identity. The strategy of passing of those concealing their identity does not indicate in any way that they endorse the social norms underlying their stigmatization. Passing is just applied to avoid status loss. So, although implied by some authors (for example, Carnevale 2007: 11-12), passing does not preclude strong feelings of disattachment from the prevailing cultural codes (see Simi and Futrell 2009 for a similar argument).

respondents. None of them is or would like to be a member of a political party, and only one of them is occasionally involved in political actions. Barend, for instance, does not dedicate himself to spreading his ideology: 'that would be pointless ... it gets you nowhere.' Herman conveys as well that the implications of his ideology are usually limited to his thoughts: 'I do not want to provoke. I do not feel like ruining my life because of a criminal record this early.'

In short, for many members of *Stormfront* the great meaning they attach to their ideology does not lead to political action. It proves to function merely as a guideline for everyday life—respondents, for instance, indicate that they would always avoid 'racial mixture.' Joop explains: 'It is a signal. I believe many people ... will not understand it, but what can I do? I do not have the power to change the law, so I have to make my contribution in another way.'

The common offline experience of the members of *Stormfront* discussed so far is, in short, stigmatization leading to dissociation and fatalism. Many members who experience stigmatization have not only turned away from society at large, but they also believe that little can be done to change the world according to their ideology. Now, how does this relate to their online experiences?

'A Place Where I Have Many Comrades': The Social Significance of *Stormfront*

'A Safe Place to Express Your Opinion': Freedom of Expression in Anonymity

The lack of freedom of expression experienced offline is a reason for their membership in *Stormfront* for all respondents who struggle with stigmatization. For Ferdinand, it is even the most important motive: '*Stormfront* really is an exhaust valve for ideas that can be discussed hardly or not at all in daily life.' This motive is mentioned on the forum, too: 'I became a member because I am fed up with disclosing my feelings and thoughts' (*remco*). And Dirk says about his first activities on *Stormfront*: 'I had, as it were, finally found a place where I could express my opinion.' Moreover, he remarks: 'Nowhere did I have such a place where I could talk like that.' He feels free to express himself on *Stormfront*: 'There, I can just talk about my feelings and about the way I see things.' He, therefore, refers to *Stormfront* as 'a safe place to express your opinion.' Like many other forum members, Herman shares this thought. According to him *Stormfront* is 'a free port for nationalists where we can talk about our vision without being punished for it.'

Since this is possible because of the anonymity that is perceived on the Internet, the respondents who experience stigmatization declare without exception that they attach strongly to their online anonymity.[5] Therefore, they

---

5   Of course, it would be more precise to speak of 'pseudonymity' instead of the widely used concept of 'anonymity', since members know each other through their usernames

constantly warn one another not to disclose too many personal details. A new member who reveals details on his place of residence, family situation and the school he attends is, for instance, immediately lectured by an established member: 'If I were you, I would not openly mention your personal information and remove it quickly. We do not live in a country in which every conviction is approved of' (*Tiwazz*).

'We Are an Oppressed Species, This Creates a Bond': A Virtual Community

The freedom of expression they perceive online is not the only motive underlying the participation of the members of *Stormfront* who experience stigmatization—it is closely intertwined with urgent social reasons. These members greatly enjoy the company of like-minded spirits. One of Ron's reasons for being a member of *Stormfront*, for example, is that he 'feels more at ease' with like-minded people, and for Peter meeting virtually with 'people with a comparable opinion' is a prominent motive for participation in *Stormfront*, because 'this is not easy [offline].' Postings on the forum tell the same story. *Vlaming13* writes: 'I am extremely happy that there are so many people who share my opinion on the whole multiculturalist issue. This site is really amazing.' Because of their similarities, the stigmatized members feel at home on *Stormfront* and display clear feelings of belonging, stating that '*Stormfront* is like a second home to me' (*Farkasfarsang*). Because members largely share each other's views, they can express themselves freely and generally feel accepted by the others.

Moreover, almost all respondents who feel stigmatized offline, experience solidarity and comradeship online. Mainly because of this, *Martinborman* is very excited about *Stormfront*: 'At last, I have found a place where I can talk with comrades who think likewise.' Herman says: '*Stormfront* provides me with a place where I have many comrades', and Dirk observes:

> [Comradeship] is really something that exists in this group, that is really true. Mainly because most of us have many problems expressing their opinions, since they experience a lot of resistance. People insult them and [they experience] everything I already told. Because of that, people feel more connected to each other: because they are, as it were, a cornered group.

Another social aspect of *Stormfront* is the prominent thread in which members congratulate one another on their birthdays. All respondents who experience stigmatization consider this thread—with many messages enriched with toasting, dancing, and laughing 'smileys'—a source of sociability.

(Roberts et al. 2002: 227). What counts for the stigmatized members of *Stormfront*, however, is that information by means of which they could be identified in offline life remains unknown to others.

In short, it is clear that *Stormfront* is more than a mere collection of individuals: according to its stigmatized members, it reflects the key characteristics of community. The members experiencing offline stigmatization unmistakably display shared values, norms and meanings on the forum (Etzioni 2004: 225, see also Komito 1998: 99): they feel safe as they 'understand each other well' and are 'hardly ever puzzled or taken aback' (Bauman 2001b: 2). And the material presented above indicates that this goes hand in hand not only with sociability (Wellman and Hampton 1999: 648), but also with 'communal solidarity' (Komito 1998: 98) and 'affect-laden relationships' (Etzioni 2004: 225) that underlie a deeply felt sense of belonging (Foster 1997: 29, Kelemen and Smith 2001: 372, McMillan and Chavis 1986, Nieckarz 2005). It is important to observe that *Stormfront's* members who struggle with stigmatization in offline social life are strongly attached to this virtual community, whether they hide their right-wing extremist identity in offline life or not. Some of them actively reflect on this themselves: 'We have a cohesive factor: love for our people and fatherland, incomprehension by outsiders, and loyalty. [A community exists] because we are an oppressed species, this creates a bond' (Herman).

In addition, various 'community behaviors' (Blanchard and Markus 2004, see also Watson 1997) are displayed on the forum. Consistent with their affect-laden relationships, members offer one another support in case of unpleasant events in their offline lives—mostly in the form of comforting words and compassion. All respondents who experience stigmatization acknowledge the existence of such support, and they all appreciate it. Moreover, conformity to common rules (Feenberg and Bakardjieva 2004: 5, Papadakis 2003: 9) is enforced by means of social control: 'conduct-policing' (Watson 1997: 111) takes place to ensure the members live up to common rules. The moderators play an important role in this by constantly scanning the forum for deviant postings. Besides minor violations like sloppy usage of the Dutch language, quarrelling is strongly condemned: moderators see to it that members do not insult *each other*. One of the guidelines for posting is: 'No attacks on other White nationalists.' This adds to the feeling of safety the forum's stigmatized members value online. Arjan, for instance, thinks it is a great benefit that 'there are people in command, so that you do not get abused just like that'.

These internal practices of control go hand in hand with inclusion and exclusion. New members are, for instance, included as they are expected to introduce themselves in a prominently placed thread that has been created for this very purpose, usually to be given a warm welcome. Furthermore, the fact that 'leaving a community is emotionally traumatic' (Fernback and Thompson 1995) is reflected on the forum as well. The departure of a dedicated member evoked many 'sad' emoticons and expressions of grief. He was not only wished good luck—the loss for the other participants was stressed as well: 'I and many others will miss you', 'come back!' (*Thulean Knight* and *DutchSkinNL*). Exclusion of those labeled as 'outsiders' is common, too. For example, moderators attempt to keep out people who endanger *Stormfront's* unity, and new members' contributions are screened before being posted 'because this forum is unfortunately visited a little too often by fools, opponents, and troublemakers' (*Full of Pride*). Of great importance as well are indications of disloyalty to nationalism or national socialism. Dissidents are either confined to a special part of the forum called 'the lion's den' or banned from *Stormfront* altogether. Moreover, those who set aside their extreme-right ideology and leave the forum voluntarily provoke adverse reactions and are labeled traitors.

Having demonstrated that the importance attached to a virtual community on *Stormfront* can be understood from members' experiences of stigmatization in offline social life, we will now discuss the question of how their online participation relates to their offline interactions.

'I Stay Safely Behind my PC': Stormfront *as a Virtual Refuge*

For the greater part, the virtual community exists exclusively online: many participants seem to be solely acquainted with one another through their online communications and have never met in person. This is noted by our respondents as well: 'Many members do not know each other in [offline] life' (Arjan). Moreover, the contacts of those members who do meet offline are also largely online—they meet only occasionally offline, whereas they are active on the forum on a daily basis.

If members do meet offline, this generally takes place at so-called 'drinks', which are organized irregularly by individual members. According to *Hatecore_ Rudolf*, a drink is 'an informal meeting for members of the forum to get acquainted with each other' and 'the perfect chance to meet like-minded people.' Although announcements and evaluations of these meetings are posted in the forum's sub-section on 'activism and politics', political action is not intended. The drinks are all about comradeship and sociability, and 'not in any way associated with an organization or political party' (*Nordfront*): 'it is no demonstration, and there will be no parade' (*NordCore*). When asked why these apolitical meetings are discussed in a section on activism, moderator *Full of Pride* replies: 'After all, it is an activity [smiley].' And after one of the gatherings *orion1980* writes: 'We were not there to express our opinion. This day was solely intended to promote comradeship, and I believe this was a great success.' Messages on the forum indicate that these drinks are principally organized in support of the virtual community on *Stormfront*, which is considered to be of primary importance. The goal is 'to see who you are talking with on the forum' (*Hatecore_Rudolf*): 'The purpose is to have a nice chat and to get to know the face that exists behind the *Stormfront* username. Often, this stimulates the atmosphere on the forum' (*Full of Pride*).

Whereas these social meetings are supportive of the virtual community which these members consider to be most important, some other members differently conceive of the relationship between online and offline social life. Unsurprisingly, a major right-wing extremist forum like *Stormfront* is also visited by people who are active in extreme-right political parties. Contrary to the greater part of *Stormfront's* members, their online participation is instrumentally motivated, instead of aimed at constructing a virtual community: their contributions to the forum focus on the dissemination of information on extreme-right party matters and offline political actions. One party whose members make such an instrumental use of the forum is the Dutch right-wing extremist fringe party NVU.[6] A member called *nvu-ombudsman*, who—just like other NVU members active on the forum—has adopted the NVU party logo as an avatar, has, for instance, started a thread called 'News from the NVU headquarters', in which information on the party is provided and in which demonstrations are announced. Other threads on offline activism are generally started by people affiliated with political organizations as well, and they are by far the most active contributors to these discussions. Indicative of the fact that the motives for online participation of *Stormfront's* members who struggle with stigmatization differ from the instrumental ones of this group of participants, these political activists seem to hold a marginal position on *Stormfront*. After demonstrations announced on *Stormfront*, the latter frequently complain about low levels of participation: 'It is a great pity that so few of us were present' (*dietschland_jeugd*). The low levels of activism of most forum members are reflected upon by activists. *Tatts32*, for instance, laments: 'Probably no one will come. People talk much, but actions are often omitted.' And *Cherryl* cries out: 'Fair words butter no parsnips. I have read quite a few pieces around the forum, and it strikes me that a great fuss is made, whereas little happens. The section activism/politics itself is plainly ridiculous. … Not to mention the assemblies where just four people turn up.'

From time to time, anger is expressed by means of variations on the pejorative term 'keyboard warrior.' As NVU-member *Sander* states: 'There are too many keyboard warriors who all think they know better, but stay home and do nothing.' In reaction to such remarks, members not affiliated with political parties clearly indicate they prefer to participate solely in *Stormfront*. *Sonne* argues: 'Surely, I am entitled to have an opinion without actively carrying it out. … I do not attend demonstrations and I neither join a political party, but how I think and act… that says enough. If this makes me a keyboard warrior, that is all right. I feel good this way. … I am not ashamed of it.' And *WhiteDutchman* writes: 'So I stand behind my ideology, and I stay safely behind my PC indeed.' This focus on online interactions is in line with the fatalistic worldview observed before: 'I will not waste time and energy. I wipe my keyboard clean once again to express my opinion on the net' (*Oi*).

In short, all evidence suggests that the virtual community constructed by *Stormfront's* members who struggle with stigmatization in offline social life functions as a 'second home' in which they find refuge. Their interactions largely take place online, and the offline meetings that do take place are secondary to the community online. The virtual community valued by these members does not function as a basis for offline collective action. Whereas people connected to extreme right-wing parties make instrumental use of the forum, a large part of the

---

6   NVU stands for *Nederlandse Volks-Unie*, which translates as *Dutch People's Union*.

members of *Stormfront* value it as an online refuge, which can be understood from their experiences of stigmatization and fatalistic worldviews. They are disattached from society at large, believing nothing can be done to alter their position, and in the virtual community found on *Stormfront*, they turn away from people thought to hold different views as much as possible. This conclusion is validated by the numerous adverse reactions to outsiders who are perceived as threats to the virtual community: 'We are comrades, brothers, and sisters, this is our home. Leave us alone, we do not force you to read these messages, do we?!' (*The Trooper*). And the observation that online and offline social lives are understood as strictly separated by the forum members who struggle with offline stigmatization is underlined by members who are of the opinion that their online participation has a seamy side as well:

> I do think [participation in *Stormfront*] makes [offline life] somewhat harder, because I see it like this: what one does not know causes no woe. So, if it would not be there, I would not miss it either. But since I know there are places where I can express my opinion, it is harder to accept that this is impossible in normal life. Then I feel somewhat trapped. (Dirk)

Since the findings up to this point indicate that offline and online experiences should be understood in relation to one another, we will conclude our analysis by discussing the three respondents who have different offline experiences.

Members without Offline Stigmatization

Evert, Steve, and Wouter are the respondents who do not experience stigmatization in offline social life. For Wouter and Steve this is the case because their political views are more moderate than those of the forum members who do struggle with stigmatization because of their extremist identity. Wouter conveys he is under the impression that his vision is accepted on the whole: 'I am not hampered to express my real opinion …, because I am not as extreme as some others.' Steve has 'never felt hampered' in the expression of his opinion either, which he does not consider deviant: 'Leftists can easily agree with me. … And I can associate well with immigrants; many of them even share my opinion. They are not happy with particular things either.' For Evert, in contrast, offline stigmatization of his extreme-right identity is no issue at all because he associates, privately as well as professionally, mainly with people who share his political outlook.

Not surprisingly, those three respondents have other reasons for participation in *Stormfront* than those who do experience stigmatization. They do not seek refuge online and value the forum for instrumental reasons instead. Wouter visits *Stormfront* primarily for the information that is available on the forum, whereas Steve has a broad interest in politics and therefore uses *Stormfront* as an instrument to support his diverse political activities and to share his knowledge. Evert participates because he likes the political issues discussed on *Stormfront*, and because he thinks the medium offers a specific advantage: he indicates he simply is more of a writer than a talker.

Unlike members who struggle with stigmatization in offline life, Evert, Steve, and Wouter are not part of the virtual community that provides refuge, and they do not display attachment to its social and supportive role. Wouter says: 'No, I do not think it is cozy. … To be honest, I think it is somewhat pathetic to have to look for sociability on the Internet.' Steve even thinks it is 'strange' to ask whether *Stormfront* could offer something extra over offline life. None of them experiences online solidarity or comradeship. Evert writes his postings 'mainly for [himself]', and 'does not care about' what other members think of him. Steve conveys that members he does not know personally offline are 'just numbers' to him. He considers online social contacts to be of minor importance, and he characterizes *Stormfront* as 'a database of knowledge' rather than as a virtual community. And whereas anonymity is very important for the members who struggle with stigmatization, Evert could not care less: his real identity can very easily be deduced from his username.

Because Evert, Wouter, and Steve do not experience offline stigmatization, they are not part of the virtual community providing refuge. This adds validity to the finding that the value *Stormfront's* other members attach to a virtual refuge can be understood as a reaction to stigmatization in offline social life.

Conclusion

For many members of *Stormfront*, participation in the forum can be understood as a reaction to negative experiences because of a 'spoiled identity'—as a reaction to stigmatization. This is in line with Erving Goffman's (1986 [1963]) classical analysis, according to which the stigmatized seek moral support, acceptance, and comfort with people who share their stigma. Many members are active on *Stormfront* for this very reason: they consider themselves 'a threatened species' and experience *Stormfront* as a virtual community providing refuge.

The mechanism of offline stigmatization leading to online community formation demonstrated here resonates with a suggestion made by other scholars. Although '[t]here is much anecdotal evidence that the Internet provides significant benefits to people with unusual identities or concerns' (DiMaggio et al. 2001: 318, see also Adler and Adler 2008, Blevins and Holt 2009, Deshotels and Forsyth 2007, Mehra et al. 2004, Tanis 2007), this theoretically vital issue has hardly been studied systematically yet. As our study suggests that offline contexts generating stigmatization are of vital importance in understanding online community formation, it has provided fresh theoretical insight, which is all the more important as scholars have observed that 'exceptionally little' is known about the backgrounds of online community formation (Blanchard and Horan 2000: 13) and have argued that this subject should therefore 'remain high on the agenda for research in the virtual communities tradition' (Blanchard and Markus 2004: 77).

At a more general theoretical level, our case study of Dutch right-wing extremists reveals the social significance of contemporary individualism. It demonstrates that a strong emphasis on cultural ideals of tolerance and individual liberty—a discourse more deeply entrenched in the Netherlands than anywhere else (Duyvendak 2004)—does not simply mean that all people have obtained the liberty to do and say whatever they want. This sociologically-naïve argument that in contemporary modernity 'anything goes' (Gergen 1991) is frequently made—remarkably enough by sociologists too. Beck and Beck-Gernsheim (2002) and Kellner (1992), for instance, claim that people are free to choose their lifestyle or identity these days, while Bauman (2004: 29, see also Bauman 1995: 238) maintains that nowadays all identities are considered equal and cultural hierarchies no longer exist. Dutch sociologists Halman and De Moor (1994: 58) even assert that 'in the Netherlands the highest value seems to be to let everyone do what he likes.' Our analysis indicates, however, that the dominance of a progressive discourse does not mean that social behavior is no longer subject to moral regulation. It rather means that these ideals come to operate as a coercive regime themselves. Just like any other discourse, then, such a discourse generates its own social exclusion of specific social groups. As we have seen, many of *Stormfront's* members actively flee offline social life because they experience stigmatization in the morally progressive Netherlands. This exclusionary aspect of the Dutch discourse is underlined by the fact that only few members do not long for a virtual refuge because they are able to retreat in offline social networks of likeminded people.

All in all, our finding that the Dutch branch of *Stormfront* provides the extreme right with a virtual refuge can only be understood by taking the progressive Dutch context into account. Exclusion of deviant identities proves not to be limited to 'traditional' societies and cultures: in a 'post-traditional' society like the Netherlands, where people widely share progressive values of individual freedom and tolerance, precisely those individuals that do not subscribe to these ideals of liberty are stigmatized and excluded.

Chapter 6

Contesting Individualism Online: Catholic, Protestant and Holistic Spiritual Appropriations of the World Wide Web

With Ineke Noomen

Introduction

The notion that modern technology and religion are incompatible, because—in sociologist of religion Bryan Wilson's words—'technology is itself the encapsulation of human rationality' and because 'the instrumentalism of rational thinking is powerfully embodied in machines' (1976: 88), have long been a social-scientific mainstay. The implication of this notion that religion will inevitably suffer from encounters with technology has meanwhile been challenged by historical studies demonstrating that the two have in fact often developed in tandem (for example, Davis 1998, Noble 1997). Their potential for peaceful coexistence has become even more evident since the emergence and widespread religious use of the Internet since the 1990s.

Religion and the Internet has become a hotly debated field in academia. The earliest studies still breathed utopian views of cyberspace, which got imputed with all kinds of spiritual and liberating qualities (Aupers and Houtman 2005, Bittarello 2008, Brasher 2001, Davis 1998, Dery 1996, Karaflogka 2003, O'Leary 2004, Turkle 1995, Wertheim 1999). It was often portrayed as an otherworldly realm in and of itself—as 'metaphysical' (Heim 1993), a 'paradise' (Stenger 1991: 52), 'new Jerusalem' (Benedikt 1991: 14), or a 'technological substitute of the Christian space of heaven' (Wertheim 1999: 16).

Contemporary studies, however, do not so much address the Internet as a religious source in and of itself, or how it contributes to the transformation of religion, but focus instead on how existing religious traditions shape, appropriate and colonize the Internet (Barzilai-Nahon and Barzilai 2005, Campbell 2010). They address how well-established religious traditions like Roman Catholicism, Protestantism, Buddhism, Hinduism and Islam communicate their messages online, just like neo-pagans, witches and others who identify with the field of holistic spirituality do (for example, Dawson and Cowan 2004, Ess et al. 2007, Højsgaard and Warburg 2005). Going online to 'spiritualize the Internet' (Campbell 2005) is, however, by no means an automatic thing to do for religious groups and it is moreover unlikely that the Internet means the same to all of them, irrespective of their historical particularities, national backgrounds and other offline features. Therefore, we study in this chapter how the Internet is dealt with in the Dutch Catholic, Protestant and spiritual holistic milieus and, more specifically, what dilemmas and struggles each of these traditions encounters in appropriating this radically decentralized and individualized medium.

The Internet: An Individualized Medium

The mass media, as the term already implies, have for a long time been monopolized by the nation state and major corporations, with broadcasting aimed at a more or less generalized audience. Film, radio and television, Horkheimer and Adorno (2002 [1944]) famously claimed, together constitute a 'culture industry' that produces pre-packaged, commodified and standardized messages for the 'masses' and colonizes the life-world of individuals. Notwithstanding the well-known and empirically sound critique that these allegedly passive consumers at the receiving end of the mass media actually 'decode', 'negotiate' or even 'subvert' the mass-mediated messages of the culture industry (for example, Fiske 1998, Hall 1980), the point remains that the mass media are monopolized, top-down organized and oriented towards a generalized, relatively passive audience. Individuals have limited control over media content, let alone over the means of communication.

This changed with the emergence and widespread application of the Internet in the beginning of the 1990s. The Internet is, after all, not a medium that is organized top-down and monopolized, but is essentially an open, transnational and decentralized network of interconnected websites—'a flexible network of networks … where institutions, businesses, associations, and individuals create their own "sites", on the basis of which everybody with access can produce her/his/its "home page", made of a variable collage of text and images' (Castells 2000: 383). The Internet can thus be understood as a medium that enhances the liberal principle of an open market, providing space for ideological pluralism and individual autonomy. From the 'supply side', anyone with access can create a new virtual space and add information or new content. From the 'demand side', Internet users can freely switch from one piece of hypertext to the next by clicking hyperlinks. Through the web, consumers hence obtain an active role in creating the final text or message (De Mul 2002: 117-8), which marks the interactive character of the net and blurs the distinction between production and consumption (De Mul 2002: 120, Castells 2000: 365-8): unlike consumers of mass media, Internet users are 'prosumers' (Ritzer and Jurgenson 2010). With the introduction of typical Web 2.0 applications like social network sites, online computer games, YouTube, MySpace, Hyves, Facebook and the like, this interactive, personalized and individualized character of the Internet has become only more pronounced over the last five years (for example, Jenkins 2006).

With regard to religion, this decentralized structure of the web fosters religious pluralism or, in the words of De Mul (2002), 'virtual polytheism', because it invites the multiple gods and worldviews of Buddhists, Hindus, Christians, Gnostics, occultists and countless other religious groups, sects and cults to compete with one another online. More than anything else, religion on the Internet hence exemplifies Thomas Luckmann's (1967) modern 'market of ultimate significance', in which the widest possible range of religious and spiritual traditions is on offer and in which religious consumers actively construct their own personal, idiosyncratic forms of religiosity.

As a decentralized and individualized medium, in short, the Internet is distinctly different from the traditional mass media: it manifests itself as a worldwide open market with competing parties, groups and ideas and this encourages individuals to search, compare, pick, mix, cut and paste different religious traditions. Online, one may even say, individualism is no longer a choice but a technologically induced social fact. Given the open structure of the web, after all, it is sheer impossible to remain safely enclosed within the boundaries of a particular tradition, social or religious group. This feature of the Internet raises the question what dilemmas and struggles representatives of the Dutch Catholic, Protestant and spiritual holistic milieus experience in appropriating this radically individualized medium.

Research Design and Data Collection

We base ourselves in this chapter on an analysis of in-depth qualitative interviews with 21 web designers who—either professionally or on a voluntary basis—work in the Dutch Catholic, Protestant or holistic spiritual milieus. Since we aim to unravel how the Internet as an individualized medium is received and dealt with in these milieus, we have strategically chosen to focus our study on religious web designers, because they work at the junctions of these religious milieus and the Internet. They are, as it were, mediators, who typically work in organizational contexts in which they find themselves faced with competing ideas and demands regarding the purposes, contents, functionalities and visual outlooks of the websites they are working on. As such, they provide us with an excellent source of data for our study of religious appropriations of the Internet: these processes most decisively take place in the minds and hands of the people who build the religious websites that Internet users eventually find themselves confronted with.

Nine of our interviewees are engaged with the Catholic field. Three of these are directly professionally affiliated with the Catholic Church in the Netherlands (Hendrikjan, Jeroen and Sanne) and two are priests involved with Internet projects (Martijn and Stephan). Two others work for the broadcasting organization that accommodates the Dutch Catholic Church's official website, KRO/RKK (Alex and Bas). Richard was formerly involved with KRO/RKK as well, but is now preoccupied with an ecumenical web project of Catholic and Protestant churches. This leaves one web designer who is professionally unaffiliated with the church and hosts one of the largest and most successful Dutch websites on Catholicism (Jan).

Because Protestantism emphasizes believers' individual relationships with God, and because this almost inevitably results in conflicts and schisms motivated by theological disputes, the Dutch Protestant milieu is fragmented to the extreme, featuring a broad range of religious and media organizations. Compared to Catholics, the six web designers in this field are hence less easy to pin down. Connie works for the PKN, (Protestant Church in the Netherlands), which is a coalition of Reformed (Dutch: *Hervormd*), Dutch Reformed (Dutch: *Gereformeerd*) and Lutheran (Dutch: *Luthers*) churches, comprising about eighteen hundred congregations with liberal, mainline as well as conservative outlooks. Klaas is involved in a Protestant website initiated by a cluster of Protestant organizations, Emma is professionally affiliated with the liberal Protestant broadcasting organization IKON and Mark is involved with a foundation that closely relates to the Liberal Protestants in the Netherlands. Two interviewees in this field do not work for Protestant organizations: one used to host the website of a large Protestant church in Utrecht (Henry) and another works for a small-scale media company that builds websites for non-profit religious, cultural and ideological organizations (Dirk). The latter has worked with organizations from different religious currents, but is now involved with a large Protestant web project for PKN.

Finally, our six interviewees in the field of holistic spirituality (Annemarie, Caroline, Daan, Erwin, Patrick, and Ronald) own small businesses in what has been dubbed the 'cultic milieu' (Campbell 2002 [1972], Luckmann 1996)—the non-institutionalized network that comprises all kinds of small spiritual organizations and single-person businesses that provide holistic workshops, courses, therapies, books and art in the Netherlands. Most of them host multiple websites for the different spiritual projects they are involved in.

The interviews had an open character and addressed general ideas about the meaning of the Internet for (the future of) religion and spirituality, the aims and aspirations that made the various religious groups decide to go online, the main objectives and target groups of the websites, and considerations about functional and visual design. In addition, respondents' websites were thoroughly explored before the interview, so as to be able to ask detailed questions about them. All interviews (except for one, which took place by telephone) were conducted face-to-face in the period between September 2008 and April 2009. On average, the interviews lasted about an hour and a half. All interviews were recorded and transcribed verbatim and all quotations used in this chapter have been translated from Dutch. Respondents have been given fictitious names so as to safeguard their privacy.

Religious Dilemmas in Appropriating the Internet

Because going online is, of course, by no means a 'natural' thing to do, we first discuss how the changing Dutch religious and media landscapes have led the religious and spiritual groups under study to embrace the Internet in the last decades. We then explore the problems and dilemmas the interviewed web designers find themselves confronted with and how these stem from typical offline features and conflicts that characterize the respective religious fields.

The Web as a Last Media Resort

Until well into the 1960s, the Dutch system of 'pillarization', a type of societal organization peculiar to the Netherlands back then, was still firmly in place. It consisted of a handful of vertically arranged religious and political segments, or 'pillars', that existed side by side, with people identifying with only one of these throughout most of their lives. This system of pillarization has deeply affected the religious, political and media landscapes of Dutch society. Catholics and Protestants had their own newspapers and broadcasting organizations that catered to their own people and depended on the size of their constituencies for airtime and financial resources. When processes of secularization sparked 'de-pillarization' in the 1960s, new religious and non-religious competitors gained ground, which has made it more difficult for the Christian churches to cater to the religious needs of their crumbled constituencies (Dekker and Ester 1996). Moreover, the increased importance of ratings since the 1980s and the introduction of commercial television in 1989 have led to an even further decline in airtime for Catholic and Protestant broadcasting organizations.

The consequences of the process of de-pillarization are basically twofold, then. On the one hand, the Christian churches now need to compete with new, secular ideologies and with newly emerged and less institutionalized holistic spirituality. While the guaranteed mass media access that Catholics and Protestants once enjoyed has strongly declined, this same decline has ironically strengthened their felt needs to make themselves heard amongst the cacophony of secular and religious voices that has resulted. Even though holistic spirituality has, of course, never experienced the luxury of having its 'own' national newspaper or broadcasting organization, this urge is also found in the holistic milieu, as we will see.

Respondents from all three religious groups under study emphasize that they face the difficulty of insufficient television airtime and access to newspaper audiences. Richard, who works in the Catholic confines, explains that 'previously we of course had Catholic newspapers and the like ..., but well, these are practically all gone' and infers that 'right now the Internet is the only channel left through which the church can directly address an audience.' In a similar vein, holistic web designer Patrick had been striving for a program on national television, which proved very difficult to accomplish, however. For him, too, the web has become an attractive alternative for sharing his ideas, since 'through the Internet I could still reach my audience!' In this way, the Internet virtually serves as a 'last resort' to all religious groups under study—as the only viable option left to them if they want to make themselves heard.

In contrast with the traditional mass media, moreover, the Internet is quite hospitable to small groups addressing niche audiences. Broadcasts for highly specific audiences can no longer be afforded in national programming, but can easily be offered online. Hendrik-Jan explains how church topics 'that bite the dust again and again' in national programming can easily be 'transmitted through the Internet and [are] watched very well.' Bas, who works at the Internet department of the Dutch Catholic channel, gives the example of their bimonthly online broadcasts of the Pope's Wednesday's general audiences and his Angelus prayers on Sundays. '[W]e would say that it is not expedient to broadcast it on television. But there is an audience for this, and that's why we offer it through the Internet', Bas explains, concluding that this 'certainly caters for a need.' Similarly, a recent Dutch newspaper article reports a boom of orthodox Protestant radio stations on the Internet, serving groups that 'are lacking their own news, opinion and music at the national channels' (Visscher 2010). It concludes that the web enables program makers to 'make their own choices' regarding the Christian music, church news, psalms, and organ concerts they want to broadcast, '[w]ithout interference of a public net manager', and without non-Christian music or advertising 'being imposed' upon them.

The experienced lack of viable media alternatives stems, of course, from a strong motivation to make oneself heard in the cacophony of secular and religious voices that already exists online. This is because respondents from all three fields, even though they express it somewhat differently, conceive of the Internet as a stage where sometimes highly idiosyncratic or over-simplified thoughts, opinions, and dissatisfactions are disseminated. Emma, for example, speaks of 'very scary weblogs, indeed about people who tell you with red-hot flames when the end of the world is near' and Hendrik-Jan notices 'people who, well, do really weird things' online and observes 'all kinds of evil sites.' Quite similarly to these two respondents, who work in the Protestant and Catholic domains, respectively, Erwin, who works in the field of holistic spirituality, speaks of 'that negativity on the Internet ... all kinds of excesses which are there', available 'only through one mouse click.' Considerations such as these do not cause religious groups to avoid the web, but actually give them paramount reason to counterbalance these voices in the Internet 'jungle' (Bas) by providing reliable information or statements of a more positive kind. Emma argues that the church should realize that it 'needs to put a balanced answer up against this, on a site that looks professional, of which people think, "oh, this has authority…".' Martijn reasons that the Catholic Church should 'put [its] own stall' in this 'large market, where there are all kinds of stalls', because otherwise 'everyone can be found out there, except for the church.' In a similar fashion, Erwin explains that he has made a number of websites only to 'show positive messages and beautiful things: nice pictures, nice texts', 'purely to just put positive things on the Internet.' Unlike Emma and Martijn, he is part of the spiritual milieu and as such not constrained by any organizational authority structure, yet understands it as his personal responsibility to counterbalance content that contradicts his personal values and ideals.

In sum, people from distinct religious fields experience a need to provide web users with 'reliable' religious or spiritual content, because they are well aware of the everyday significance of the Internet as a source of information, communication and entertainment. As we will see, however, this consensus about the importance of the Internet does not mean that its religious appropriation is an easy process. Quite the contrary: each tradition faces its own typical dilemmas and struggles in appropriating and culturalizing the Internet through web design. These different dilemmas can, however, in all cases be related to the fact that the Internet manifests itself as an open, pluralist market where individualism prevails.

Catholic Struggles with Individual Freedom Online

The pluralism of the Dutch religious landscape and the relentless privatization on the religious market, as already envisioned by Luckmann (1967) in the 1960s, poses more of a problem *and* a challenge to Catholics than to either Protestants or those who identify with the spiritual milieu. This is because Catholicism is historically and theologically a monopolistic creed, the aim of which has always been to unite a global community of believers representing God's Kingdom on earth, which has now come to find itself in decline and facing an increase in pluralism—in the Netherlands even more so than elsewhere. Referring to this situation, priest and website maker Martijn observes that 'the church as an institute that provides meaning' is only 'one party in a competitive market', a view that is shared by independent Catholic web designer Jan, who conceives of Catholicism as 'one of the parties on the reli-market.'

The notion that the Catholic community and identity are under threat is virtually omnipresent in Dutch Catholicism, and the Internet is understood as a means that may help to counter this problem (Campbell 2005). Jeroen, initiator of a Catholic news site, wants to 'show what [is] going on in the church', intending to 'stimulate the self-awareness of Catholics.' Likewise, Alex aims to 'make people more conscious of our values' and to demonstrate that Catholicism concerns 'a tradition that ain't frozen, but one that still lives on and constantly gets reinterpreted.' Such a rejuvenation of Catholic identity is, moreover, experienced as a necessary basis for more encompassing missionary goals put forward in Pontifical documents that designate modern media like the Internet as '"gifts of God" which, in accordance with His providential design, unite men in brotherhood and so help them to cooperate with his plan for their salvation' (Second Vatican Council 1971, see also Pontifical Council for Social Communications 2002). Our respondents express a similar emphasis on the need for a shared Catholic identity. '[I]f you want to survive as a church, then you need that clear identity again', Stephan argues, and Sanne explains that the Catholic youth forum she is involved with aims to 'make [youngsters] surer of themselves' so that 'we'll get a larger group of Catholics who know how to stand their ground, and then you have people to go and face the world.'

Reaching out to a mixed audience of adherents and potential believers through the Internet, however, also demands reflection on and redefinition of 'who we are', 'what we believe in', and 'what we stand for.' Questions such as these invoke contrasting ideas about what exactly constitutes—or rather: *should* constitute—this Catholic identity nowadays and how it should be articulated on the web. On the one hand, there are quite orthodox voices that try to transpose church authority, tradition and hierarchy onto the Internet by way of regulation and control of online information, whereas on the other hand there are more progressive pleas for openness and dialogue.

One way to accomplish control over online information is the use of a strict linking policy, of which the Vatican website, which lacks any links to external websites, is a paramount example. This is a designer strategy to maintain a relatively well-defined, traditional Catholic identity online and exclude individualistic beliefs and other religious and secular voices. Hendrikjan, a Dutch Catholic Church official, recounts how this issue has caused 'quite some discussions' when starting the official website of the Catholic Church in the Netherlands. To avoid bringing in 'organizations that you're rather not associated with', they decided 'after long talks' to only link to websites 'for which we can take responsibility ourselves.' Martijn gives another example, when he tells about his participation in an ecumenical Catholic-Protestant foundation that had been registering Dutch religious domain names in the early stages of the Internet. Its aim was to avoid these domain names falling into the hands of so-called 'domain grabbers' and to assure that these web domains would only lead to 'what we judge is good information', which, however, caused major disputes with Christian organizations that wanted to use these domain names.

Contrary to these initiatives to keep control over content, doctrine and believers online, Richard, who is also active in Dutch Catholicism, rather feels that 'people [should be allowed] to exercise their personal responsibility', because it 'would really not be a good thing' if the church was in a position to control the information supply. This more progressive perspective aims to open up the Internet as an individualized medium. Jan recounts how contrasting ideas about how to handle online information have even hindered online cooperation between Dutch Catholic organizations: 'the main current was conservative' and proposed to work out 'a traffic light system to indicate the reliability of Catholic information', whereas he himself 'really was not into that.' Hence this consortium fell apart 'because there were too many different opinions on how one should manage this on the Internet.' Jan personally holds the view that the Internet 'really works democratizing' and firmly believes that 'that's the way it works: if I don't find it here, I might find it there, or elsewhere, or hold my own opinion about it.'

To sum up, the traditional dilemma of Dutch Catholicism of either 'conservatively' holding on to church authority or 'progressively' providing opportunities for dialogue, diversity and individualism is revived in the dilemmas faced by web designers who need to make decisions about the functionalities, web links and contents of Catholic websites. In Dutch Catholicism, then, more than in the other religious traditions under study, individualism on the Internet is utterly contested.

Communicating a Fragmented Protestant Belief

Unlike Roman Catholicism, Protestantism is not based on a coherent and unified— let alone monopolized—religious identity that has to be protected against overly individualistic interpretations. To the contrary: Protestantism has always been an individualistic and hence fragmented religion, since it principally emphasizes believers' individualistic relationship with God and the Bible. In the Netherlands, like many other countries, this has sparked a proliferation of competing theological interpretations and a fragmentation of Dutch Protestantism into numerous congregations and churches. The largest branch of Dutch Protestantism, the Protestant Church in the Netherlands (PKN) characterizes itself as a church 'in unity and diversity' (PKN 2005: 7) and a 'community centered on the Word' (PKN 2005: 6). Although declining church attendance and church membership are naturally a major concern to the Protestant churches, they nonetheless appear to feel less challenged by contemporary religious and ideological pluralism than the Catholic Church does, because this is very much the type of situation in which they have historically always found themselves. Religious pluralism is virtually a natural condition for Dutch Protestants.

The individualized and fragmented nature of the Dutch Protestant landscape therefore seems at first sight to fit the Internet quite well, because it provides each of its often small congregations with a means to communicate its own message to its adherents as well as to a broader audience of potential believers. Next to Evangelical Protestant groups that are quite successful in communicating their beliefs to new audiences in religiously pluralistic contexts (for example, Roeland 2009 on Evangelicalism in the Netherlands, and Smith et al. 1998 on American Evangelicalism), there are Liberal Protestants without any missionary goals who use the web primarily as an 'important informative site for materials, a range of ideas, texts, etcetera' that 'provides people within a tenth of a second with information about something they want to know' (Mark), thus using it as a tool to find and exchange information of all sorts (Campbell 2010: 26). Even orthodox Calvinist congregations that condemn media like television for its opportunities for entertainment and its role in distracting believers from more important things, have quite easily found their ways online. Through their own websites these orthodox Protestant groups serve their adherents with highly specific media menus, adapted to their respective moral standards and interests.

The Internet thus provides Protestant organizations of quite different sorts with a convenient platform to serve their specific audiences. The web also challenges Protestant groups to present themselves in a unified manner to a lay audience that is typically ignorant of this internal diversity. Several of our respondents are responsible for representing the Protestant Church in the Netherlands, or mainline Protestantism generally, online and they unanimously characterize this as a difficult task because of the differences between various Protestant churches.

Dirk, who designs websites for various religious groups and ideological organizations and is currently involved with an all-embracing PKN Protestant web project, discloses that 'it wasn't as easy as one would think to choose the words … to indeed create a sort of collective appearance', characterizing it as 'a very, very vulnerable balance that one needs to find.' Connie, an employee at PKN, also underscores the difficulties that stem from conflicting religious interests and identities. When talking about a collective representation of the Protestant Church online she states: 'that's what *we* would like, but the congregations, they couldn't care less. They have their own particular character.' Klaas, who hosts a general informative website about Dutch Protestantism and aims to represent 'the breadth of Protestantism', experiences similar difficulties with Protestantism's fragmented nature:

> It's not my point to represent 'the churches.' Because if the website were meant
> to represent *the* Protestant Church, then I could forget it! Then there would be
> quite many pulling out immediately, saying: but I won't be a party to that!

This eventually resulted in a strictly informative website, without any religious or missionary aspirations, that explains the different standpoints and views within the Dutch Protestant reach. It hence proves much easier in the broader Protestant field to offer 'clean' information or technological and organizational facilities online than to present substantial religious content, because the latter is almost inevitably contested and bound up with religious conflicts and theological disputes.

A struggle of a different kind concerns the strongly visual character of Internet culture. As principally text-based creeds, (non-Evangelical) Protestant groups appear less conscious of their visual presentation than their Catholic and holistic spiritual counterparts, yielding quite some difficulties for web designers in this field. Mark claims that for him it was a 'conscious choice' to 'immediately confront people with content' on the homepage, and in a like manner Conny confines her visual design to a 'nice picture' to go with the text, but 'nothing more.' Yet, others feel that their websites need to be visually attractive to reach an as yet not involved public. Particularly Emma and Dirk, both professional web designers who have also worked in other religious fields, stress the importance of a visually attractive website in the competitive online religious market and explain how difficult it actually is to accomplish this in a strongly text-based tradition like Protestantism.

Emma, who has previously worked for a Catholic organization, explains that it is very difficult to 'visualize' Protestantism, because it 'lacks any rituals and images, no pictures of Mary, no saints and the like.' She advocates 'visually modern' religious websites ('So, not like, "well, OK, we put an image of our church building on it, and that's it"') and Dirk holds the same view, critiquing Protestant websites that portray 'pale clergymen' or 'the interior of a church holding just four people.' Just like Emma, he thinks the Protestant Church should create a more 'modern' and 'contemporary' look of itself, a process in which it has, in his view, so far only taken the first few small steps.

Apart from this uneasiness due to lack of familiarity with the visual culture of the Internet, and in contrast with the Catholic milieu, Dutch Protestants feel remarkably at ease with the individualized and pluralist new medium. This is because of Protestantism's own marked individualism, its strong emphasis on private belief, and its history of theological dispute. It is, however, this same internal fragmentation that makes it difficult for PKN, Dutch Protestantism's largest branch, to construct a website with a coherent and unified Protestant identity.

Holistic Spirituality: Connecting on the World Wide Web

Holistic spirituality has emerged as a new competitor in the Dutch religious field in the 1960s, when the first New Age centers were established in Amsterdam (Aupers 2005). Instead of boasting loyalty to a particular religious body of thought, this type of spirituality is based on the notion that all religious traditions are man-made constructions that at bottom all refer to the same underlying spiritual core. This notion of 'perennialism' (Hanegraaff 1996, Heelas 1996a) implies a strong receptivity towards a broad range of spiritual and religious traditions, with regard to which individuals are seen as free to choose their own spiritual paths. As such, holistic spirituality is highly individualistic. More than that: participants in the spiritual milieu collectively share the assumption that the sacred is everywhere in the natural world, and is operative in and through the individual (see Chapter 3 of this book).

In the last decades of the previous century, these notions have proliferated tremendously in the Netherlands and holistic spirituality has by now become a sizable component of the Dutch religious landscape. The Internet, it has been argued, has played an important role in this (Brasher 2001, Curott 2001, Penczack 2001). And indeed: apart from typically minor hesitations relating to people's distraction from their 'natural' offline lives, or the distortion of fields of spiritual energy by computer radiation (both echoes of holistic spirituality's fears of alienation by modern technology), there are hardly contestations about the use of the Internet among our spiritual respondents, particularly in comparison with the Catholic and Protestant milieus. To the contrary: motivated by the ethic of perennialism and the imperative to actively seek and follow one's personal spiritual path, the web designers celebrate the Internet because it gives ample room to voice critique of modern society and its dominant culture, to connect with people working in multiple traditions, and to develop human potential.

The interviewed web designers thus fully embrace the individualized and open market character of the Internet. Most of them run their own spiritual businesses promoting spiritual ideas and selling spiritual products and services and, consequently, they do not have to communicate (traditional) doctrines on behalf of larger organizations or religious traditions, like most web designers in the Catholic and Protestant fields need to do. In a typically holistic fashion, they explain that promoting products online is just as much the realization of a spiritual ideal as it is a commercial endeavor; just as much a way to earn money as a way to express 'who they really are.' Annemarie, who hosts several websites on spiritual matters and sells her spiritual books through these, explains how much she enjoys that through these websites she can 'live [her] passion' and 'just disseminate the things [she wants] to share.' Similarly, Caroline uses her website as an outlet for her spiritual art work, for providing information about related joint projects and for her work as a therapist. As such, she understands her website as representing her personal spiritual identity ('at once you're showing: "this is me!"') and she realizes that 'this is what I stand for; this is what I have on offer.' Rather than expressing a shared religious identity, those involved hence use the web to channel their personal views and practices, while at the same time intending to inspire their online visitors and stimulate them in their personal development. Caroline, for instance, explains that on her website she puts forward that 'it is possible to communicate with elemental beings' and 'that the world consists of energy' in order to 'wake people up' and 'give them that nourishment.' Consistent with this, various neo-pagan authors have celebrated the web as 'an incredible resource' (Nightmare 2001: 42), 'a beautiful chaos ... where anyone can share anything' (Penczak 2001: 253), and 'an endless source of sustenance' (Curott 2001: 17).

Using the web as a platform for sharing, connecting and spiritual self-discovery, then, feels almost like a natural thing to do for those involved here, and it hardly causes the types of struggles and dilemmas faced by Catholic and Protestant web designers. They often design their online spaces in such a way as to help others share their own ideas and experiences, and sell their products and services, too. '[E]verything is aimed at this exchange', Daan claims, 'and the website is of course ideal for that, right?' Ronald likewise created 'a platform where people can respond to each other's statements', explaining that 'in this way discussions and networks will arise and things will get connected' and adding that 'that actually is what the Internet very much is intended for at the moment.'

Ronald is an example of someone who has designed what he calls a 'spiritual marketplace' on one of his websites, where spiritual providers are invited to advertise their products and services. In sharp contrast with the Catholics who try to control online information, Ronald does 'not [want] to make any judgments about soundness' with regard to all the healers, mediums, therapists and coaches who make use of this service. He does not want to 'deliver any warranty of quality' either, because 'it's not up to us to give a value judgment.' Annemarie, who is involved in an online spiritual radio station with a forum for its listeners, explains that 'we want to offer a platform, and that doesn't have to mean that we agree with it. Because exactly spirituality is just something so individual.'

All in all, the Internet is appreciated in holistic spiritual circles as a platform for sharing spiritual wisdom, connecting to others to enrich people's spiritual lives and to express 'who one really is.' Unlike the orthodox Catholics, this spiritual group thus celebrates the individualistic and pluralistic features of the world wide web—a metaphor that already indicates an affinity with the holistic spiritual worldview. What is more, the web's visual culture is in striking accordance with holistic spirituality's marked focus on intuitive knowing and spiritual experience. Ronald, for example, stresses the importance of the 'look and feel' of his websites and Patrick claims that 'images provide a much nicer way ... to take in information.' As such, and in striking contrast to typical Protestant understandings, spiritual messages need not so much be understood, but rather experienced.

Conclusion

Now that the Internet has come to pervade the lives of almost all people in the West, and now that its use increasingly appears practical and profane rather than liberating or other-worldly, the focus in Internet studies has shifted to understanding online practices as embedded in offline routines and values and it is held that offline-based aspirations need to be taken into account in order to understand online participation in virtual communities (Bakardjieva 2005, De Koster 2010, Slater 2002). In the study of religion and the Internet, these pleas have resulted in notions of 'cultured technology' (Barzilai-Nahon and Barzilai 2005) and 'spiritualizing of technology' (Campbell 2005). These notions stress that online religion is not so much determined and shaped by technology, as studies in the 1990s suggested, but rather that digital technologies are culturally and religiously appropriated.

Guided by this perspective, we have studied religious appropriations of the Internet from within the fields of Dutch Catholicism, Protestantism and the holistic milieu. Such religious appropriations, we have seen, are not simply processes in which coherent offline traditions are smoothly translated by designers to a new online context. To the contrary: these processes are suffused with struggles and dilemmas. Although it is generally felt that getting online is the only remaining viable way to reach out and make oneself heard in the radically pluralist cacophony of voices that has resulted from processes of secularization and religious change, the appropriation of the Internet is a conflict-ridden process, rife with power, negotiation and contestation. Most crucial in this is the understanding of the Internet as an individualized medium: more than anything else, it constitutes an open market place in which individualism, private (religious) consumption and personal *bricolage* prevail.

This online individualism is religiously contested, first of all, within religious tradititions, particularly in Catholicism. Conflicts among Dutch Catholics about the desirability of either following Roman orthodoxy or creating room for dialog, diversity and individual interpretation, pose major dilemmas to web designers who need to decide about the functionalities, web links and contents of the websites they are working on. Catholic websites are hence the negotiated outcome of religious conflict between progressive and orthodox forces in the church with distinctly different moral evaluations of the Internet as a highly decentralized and individualized medium.

Protestant web designers face their own dilemmas regarding individualism and pluralism on the Web. Precisely because the Protestant tradition, unlike Catholicism, is based on individualism, and because the Dutch Protestant landscape is because of that characterized by fragmentation and theological disagreement, designers are hardly able to build websites that transcend the particular religious identities of specific Protestant congregations. Designing websites that are acceptable to all, or even a majority, of the Protestant congregations demands the sacrifice of content to such an extent that the resulting websites become substantially disappointingly empty, flat and neutral. In appropriating the Internet, Protestants are hence only spared from the conflicts found in Catholicism to the extent that they are either prepared to let a thousand flowers bloom or to surrender to a shallow Protestantism.

The decentralized structure of the milieu of holistic spirituality and its perennialist-cum-holistic worldview of being open to all religious traditions to find one's own spiritual path, finally, makes the Internet an almost natural habitat to share spiritual wisdom and connect with others. Neither of the problems faced by Catholics and Protestants are experienced here, which means that holistic spiritual appropriations of the Internet are less conflict-ridden and smoother processes than their Catholic and Protestant counterparts. For this spiritual group the decentralized, individualized nature of the Internet is unambiguously a blessing and certainly not a curse.

These differences make clear that individualism online is not just contested *within* religious traditions, but also *between* them. Catholicism in particular has much more problems in coping with the individualized medium of the Internet than holistic spirituality has. In a more general sense, our study thus points out that overly general and mono-causal secularization theories, according to which technology inevitably and unambiguously undermines religion (for example, Wilson 1976) neglects this difference between religious traditions. The Internet and holistic spirituality, we conclude with Helland (2004), definitely constitute a 'match made in (cyber)heaven.'

Chapter 7

Two Lefts and Two Rights: Class Voting and Cultural Voting in the Netherlands, 2002

With Peter Achterberg

New Politics as New-Leftist Politics?

Ever since he published his book *The Silent Revolution* (1977), American political scientist Ronald Inglehart has maintained that due to increasing affluence, 'postmaterialist' values, pertaining to the primacy of individual liberty and self-attainment, have moved center stage in Western countries. This is held to have resulted in the rise of a 'new political culture', that has increasingly overshadowed the 'old political culture', central to which were issues concerning the distribution of wealth and income between society's classes (Inglehart 1977, 1990, 1997, see also Clark 1998, 2001, Dalton et al. 1984, Hechter 2004, Rempel and Clark 1997).

This new political culture has not left the political landscape unaffected either, given the emergence of new left-libertarian parties such as *Les Verts* in France, *Die Grünen* in Germany, and *GroenLinks* in the Netherlands (Inglehart 1990: 281-3, see also Hoffman-Martinot 1991).[1] Indeed, ever since the appearance of Inglehart's pathbreaking book (1977), the idea that 'there are now two Lefts, ... which are rooted in different classes' (Lipset 1981: 510) has been a mainstay in political sociology and political science alike (see also Weakliem 1991). These new left-libertarian parties are held to attract well-educated voters in particular, because these are more than others characterized by postmaterialism. These parties are thus considered to play a major role in undermining the familiar alignment of the middle class with the right (Inglehart 1997: 254).

Inglehart's influential theory has not remained uncontested for long, however. Its critics have pointed out that it is in fact quite problematical to exclude the possibility of 'rightist-authoritarian postmaterialism' by definitional fiat (Dekker et al. 1999, Flanagan 1979, 1982, 1987, Middendorp 1991: 262). This objection makes all the more sense, because new-rightist populist parties have been electorally successful all over Europe since the 1980s, constituting a veritable

---

1   With the founding of PPR and PSP the Netherlands witnessed the emergence of two new-leftist parties during the 1970s. These two parties later on merged with the former Communist Party (CPN), which had itself changed unrecognizably due to the influence of the new spirit of the time, into the new party GroenLinks in 1989. GroenLinks has ever since remained the only new-leftist party of considerable size in the Netherlands.

'silent counter-revolution' (Ignazi 1992) that flies in the face of Inglehart's claim that only left-libertarian issues are central in the new political culture (see also Ignazi 2003, Veugelers 2002).[2]

What Inglehart's critics argue, is that the theory of the new political culture needs to be broadened so as to acknowledge the existence of its rightist-authoritarian branch, too. In making this argument, they assume that voting for new-rightist parties can be explained through basically the same mechanism as voting for new-leftist ones—although working in the reverse direction, of course. It is assumed that in both cases voting is driven by 'new' cultural issues that as such tend to reverse the traditional class-party alignments as these emerge from the 'old' class-based economic interests. We study in this chapter whether Inglehart's critics are right in this and to do so, we start with a critical discussion of how so-called 'class voting' has been studied in the past and why this conventional approach mixes it up with the allegedly 'new' type of 'cultural voting' rather than systematically disentangling the two types (see also Achterberg 2006a, 2006b, Achterberg and Houtman 2006, Houtman 2001, 2003).

Class Voting and Cultural Voting: Hypotheses

Class Voting and Its Measurement: The Alford Index

Changes in levels of class voting are typically measured as changes in the tendency of the working class to vote for leftist parties and the middle class to vote for rightist ones. This has become pretty much the standard procedure in the study of class voting since Robert Alford (1967: 80) proposed in the 1960s what has since come to be known as the 'Alford index.' This index measures class voting 'by subtracting the percentage of persons in nonmanual occupations voting for "Left" parties from the percentage of manual workers voting for such parties.' So, the more frequently workers vote for leftist parties and the less frequently non-workers do so, the higher the Alford index, and the higher the level of class voting. If workers vote exactly as frequently for leftist parties as non-workers, the Alford index is zero, there is no evidence of class voting, and the class people belong to does not in any way affect how they vote. Although statistically more advanced varieties have been proposed since (for example, Hout et al. 1993), these do not affect Alford's theoretical rationale and hence tend to produce 'the same conclusions with respect to the ranking of the countries according to their levels of

---

2 Examples of electorally successful new-rightist populist parties in Europe are the FPÖ in Austria, the Schweizerische Volkspartei (SVP) in Switzerland, the Progress Party (FrP) and the Danish People's Party (DF) in Denmark, the Progress Party (FrP) in Norway, the Vlaams Blok (renamed to Vlaams Belang in 2004) in Flanders, Belgium, the Republikäner in Germany, Front National in France, and the Lijst Pim Fortuyn (LPF) and (later on) Geert Wilders's Freedom Party (PVV) in the Netherlands.

class voting, and according to the speed of declines in class voting' (Nieuwbeerta 1996: 370). The still widespread use of Alford's index can be demonstrated, for instance, by its application in many of the contributions in the edited volumes *The Breakdown of Class Politics* (Clark and Lipset 2001) and *The End of Class Politics?* (Evans 1999).

The Alford index and its contemporary offshoots are deeply problematic, however, even to such an extent that their increase or decline across time can tell us basically nothing about changes in the degree to which class drives voting (Houtman 2003: 103-20). This is because its entire neglect of voting motives obscures the extent to which a relationship of a particular strength between class and voting emerges from a class-based economic motive (that is, working-class economic egalitarianism and middle-class aversion to economic redistribution) on the one hand and from a cross-cutting cultural motive as emphasized by Inglehart (postmaterialism) and his critics (authoritarianism) on the other. This is problematic because although such a cultural motive is surely empirically related to class, it does nonetheless not stem from class-based economic interests like the economic motive for voting does. Clearly, then, we need to go beyond the simple bivariate relationship between class and voting by, firstly, actually including the class-based economic motive for voting that the Alford index merely assumes and by, secondly, adding the cross-cutting cultural motive for voting as emphasized by advocates of the emergence of a 'new political culture' (that is, Inglehart and his aforementioned critics alike). We elaborate these shortcomings of the Alford index in what follows, so as to develop an analytical distinction between what we will call 'class voting' and 'cultural voting.'

Class Voting and Cultural Voting

A large number of studies since the 1950s has pointed out that two political value domains exist in Western democracies, which are by and large independent of one another among the electorates at large. The first domain, referred to as 'economic conservatism/progressiveness' here, pertains to the degree to which one favors either *laissez-faire* liberalism or economic redistribution by the state. The second domain, referred to as 'authoritarianism/libertarianism' here, pertains to the degree to which one favors either protection of individual liberty or maintenance of social order. This second value domain has in the meantime been demonstrated to include Inglehart's notion of postmaterialism as well (Dekker et al. 1999, Flanagan 1979, 1982, 1987, Houtman 2003: 66-82, Middendorp 1991: 262). 'Thus, the distinctive claim of the postmaterialist argument is not that a second ideological dimension exists, but that it is having an increasing impact on voting', as Weakliem (1991: 1330) rightly notes.[3]

---

3   Nevertheless, Inglehart (1997: 4, 43, 47) holds that the shift towards 'postmaterialism' is somehow 'at the core' of a more general process of cultural change (see for skepticism about this claim, see Houtman 2003).

Already hinted at by Lipset in the 1950s (1959), the zero-relationship between economic conservatism/progressiveness and authoritarianism/libertarianism has been found ever since among the mass publics of Western countries (for example, De Witte 1990, Evans et al. 1996, Felling and Peters 1986, Fleishman 1988, Heath et al. 1994, Houtman 2003, Kelly and Chambliss 1966, Middendorp 1991, Mitchell 1966, O'Kane 1970, Olson and Carroll 1992, Scheepers et al. 1992). This means that without additional information (Achterberg and Houtman 2009), one cannot predict among the public at large whether, for instance, someone is for or against the death penalty (authoritarianism/libertarianism) if one knows his or her stance towards income redistribution (economic conservatism/progressiveness) (and *vice versa*, of course).

Studies into the relationship between class and political values have found over and over again since World War II that authoritarianism does not emerge from a low income, but rather from a low level of education (see Houtman 2003 for a review of the relevant studies). The latter relationship has nevertheless often been interpreted as indicating that authoritarianism, just like economic progressiveness, emerges from a weak economic position. Likewise, the well-known positive relationship between education and postmaterialism has been interpreted by Inglehart (1977, 1990) as supporting his theory that growing up under conditions of affluence produces a long-lasting commitment to individual liberty and self-attainment. For a detailed theoretical discussion and empirical critique of these 'Marxist lite' theories about authoritarianism and postmaterialism, the reader is referred to a previous book by one of us (Houtman 2003), which demonstrates that both interpretations of this educational effect are flawed: authoritarianism and postmaterialism are neither driven by one's present economic class position, nor by parental affluence during one's formative years, but are instead intimately bound up with the amount of cultural capital one has at one's disposal (compare De Graaf and Kalmijn 2001, Kalmijn 1994).

The circumstance that two separate political value domains exist and that authoritarianism/libertarianism, unlike economic conservatism/progressiveness, does not so much emerge from class in an economic sense, but rather from cultural capital, calls for a new conceptualization of the relationship between class and voting. Although there is ample reason to be skeptical about the alleged economic basis of 'postmaterialist' values (Houtman 2003), this new conceptualization nevertheless gives due to Inglehart's suggestion that voting is driven by two radically different logics. '[The] relation between class and vote cannot be described adequately by a single dimension' as Weakliem (1991: 1355) rightly notes, adding that 'the conventional model of class politics may have been inaccurate even before it attracted widespread challenge.' Besides emphasizing the decisive role of cultural capital rather than class in an economic sense as the driving force behind cultural voting, the new conceptualization also refines Inglehart's distinction between 'class voting' and 'voting according to postmaterialist values' (for example, Inglehart 1987: 1298). It acknowledges that class voting also entails 'voting according to values', although these are obviously radically different

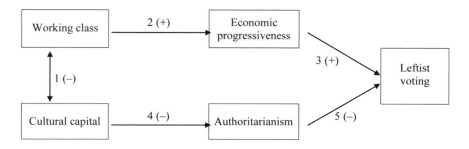

Figure 7.1   Distinguishing class voting (path 2 x path 3) from cultural voting (path 4 x path 5)

ones than those involved in cultural voting, and it replaces too narrowly defined 'postmaterialism' by the more general 'authoritarian/libertarian' value domain as the driving force behind cultural voting (for a similar conceptualization, see Middendorp 1991).

Figure 7.1 displays the new conceptualization of the relationship between class and voting. Class voting is now conceptualized as voting for a leftist party on the grounds of economically progressive political values generated by a weak class position (or, reversely, voting for a rightist political party on the grounds of economically conservative political values generated by a strong class position). Class voting as such needs to be distinguished from cultural voting, which is not driven by class-based economic interests, but rather by cultural capital and related authoritarianism/libertarianism. Cultural voting, then, is voting for a leftist political party on the grounds of libertarian values generated by ample cultural capital (or, reversely, voting for a rightist political party on the grounds of authoritarian political values generated by limited cultural capital).

Given this distinction between class voting and cultural voting, it is likely that voting for old-leftist and old-rightist parties needs to be understood as class voting, while voting for new-leftist and new-rightist ones alike rather stands out as cultural voting. This is so, because new-leftist and new-rightist parties are precisely held to differ from old-leftist and old-rightist ones, because the former emphasize cultural issues rather than issues of economic distribution—with new-leftist parties emphasizing the need to expand individual liberty and tolerance for cultural diversity and new-rightist ones emphasizing the need to maintain social order, of course.

New Left and New Right in the Netherlands

Due to the traditional Dutch way of dealing with political pluralism—the 'politics of accommodation' (Lijphart 1968), which aims for consensus and carefully avoids conflicts between minority groups—, the electoral breakthrough of new-rightist politics occurred much later in the Netherlands than elsewhere in Europe. Taboos on new-rightist and ethnocentrist political discourse were still firmly in place in this country when the late Pim Fortuyn started successfully attacking them in 2001. While rightist-populist parties had until then been marginal in the Netherlands,[4] Fortuyn's new-rightist Populist Party (LPF) won no less than 17 percent of the votes in the national elections of 2002, after having already collected no less than 35 percent of the votes in the local elections in Rotterdam in March of that same year. Fortuyn's landslide election victory has had lasting consequences for the Dutch political culture and the Dutch political landscape. The politics of accommodation and the multiculturalist discourse of the past have become increasingly contested since, resulting in a sharply polarized cultural and political climate and electoral successes of rightist-populist politicians (Houtman et al. 2008b, Houtman and Duyvendak 2009).

Because the 2002 national elections finally witnessed the historical breakthrough of new-rightist politics in the Netherlands, they offer the perfect opportunity to test our theory about the shortcomings of the Alford index due to its mixing up of class voting and cross-cutting cultural voting. The new-rightist Populist Party (LPF), just like the new-leftist Greens (GroenLinks), does after all not so much present itself through issues concerning economic distribution, but rather through cultural ones. Whereas the Greens (GroenLinks) strongly emphasize the value of individual liberty and hence the rights of traditionally-excluded cultural minority groups, the Populist Party (LPF) instead emphasizes the necessity of maintaining social order in the nation, especially by means of strict cultural assimilation of Muslim migrants. Both parties thus differ from the Labor Party (PvdA) and the Conservative Party (VVD), the two large parties that have in the Netherlands traditionally represented the economic interests of the working class and the (upper) middle class, respectively.

The assumption that 'new' political parties are principally engaged in cultural politics leads to the hypothesis that voting for the new-rightist Populist Party (LPF) rather than the new-leftist Greens (GroenLinks) during the Dutch parliamentary elections in 2002 constitutes cultural voting rather than class voting. Voting for the old-rightist Conservative Party (VVD) rather than the old-leftist Labor Party (PvdA), on the other hand, is expected to constitute class voting rather than cultural voting. If these hypotheses are confirmed, this suggests that we can indeed discern not only 'two lefts', but 'two rights', too. We hence test two additional hypotheses to find out whether such is the case. Firstly, Inglehart's arguments suggest that voting for the new-leftist Greens (GroenLinks) rather than the old-leftist Labor Party (PvdA) constitutes cultural voting by those with ample cultural capital. Secondly, we expect that voting for the new-rightist Populist Party (LPF)

---

4 Although the rightist-extremist Center Party (later on, Center Democrats) had managed to mobilize some electoral support in the Netherlands during the 1980s, this was very limited indeed.

rather than the old-rightist Conservative Party (VVD) constitutes cultural voting by those with limited cultural capital.

Data and Method

Data

To test our four hypotheses, we analyze the data of the *European Social Survey* (2002) for the Netherlands, which contains relevant information pertaining to work, income, education, voting behavior, and opinions on all sorts of moral and political issues. The Dutch fieldwork for this international survey has taken place in the period between September 2002 and February 2003, hence shortly after the historical elections of May 2002. The sample size of 2,364 (based on a response rate of 68 percent) enables us to restrict ourselves to those who voted for the four aforementioned political parties, while still retaining a sufficient number of respondents. This restriction leaves us with 990 respondents, fairly distributed across the four parties: the new-leftist Greens (GroenLinks, 14 percent), the new-rightist Populist Party (LPF, 27 percent), the old-leftist Labor Party (PvdA, 32 percent), and the old-rightist Conservative Party (VVD, 27 percent). These percentages match the shares won by the four parties in the actual elections fairly well: Greens (GroenLinks, 13 percent), Populist Party (LPF, 31 percent), Labor Party (PvdA, 28 percent), and Conservative Party (VVD, 28 percent), adding up to 100 percent and accounting for 55 percent of the number of actually cast votes during the elections. The Christian Democrats were the largest of the six parties that we exclude from our analysis (28 percent of the votes in the actual elections) and none of the five other parties was able to collect more than six percent of the votes.

Measurement

Class   We use the so-called EGP-class schema, designed by Erikson, Goldthorpe, and Portocarero, which assigns class positions to respondents on the basis of occupational title, self-employed status, and number of employees supervised (Erikson et al. 1979, Goldthorpe 1980: 39-42). We have relied on the coding procedure developed by Ganzeboom and Treiman (2005).[5]

Education   Following Kalmijn (1994), De Graaf and Kalmijn (2001) and Achterberg and Houtman (2006) we measure cultural capital as level of education, distinguishing six educational categories: 1) no more than elementary education; 2) lower vocational education (LBO, VMBO) or four-year secondary

---

5   We relied on either respondents' present occupation or last occupation (if retired or unemployed).

education (MULO, MAVO); 3) intermediary vocational education (MBO) or five-year secondary education (HAVO); 4) pre-university education (HBS, VWO, Gymnasium); 5) higher vocational education (HBO); 6) university education (MA).

Authoritarianism/libertarianism could be measured with eight items: 'Important to do what is told and follow rules', 'Important to behave properly', 'Important to follow traditions and customs' (all three with six response categories), 'Better for a country if almost everyone shares customs and traditions', 'Gays and lesbians free to live as they wish' (both with five response categories), 'Country's cultural life undermined or enriched by immigrants', 'Immigrants make country worse or better place to live', and 'Immigrants make countries' crime problems worse or better' (all three with five response categories). Principal component analysis produces a first factor with seven factor loadings between 0.45 and 0.67 and one (the one for the item on gays and lesbians) of 0.28. This first factor explains somewhat more than 30 percent of the variance: certainly not spectacular, but enough to construct a modestly reliable scale (Cronbach's $\alpha = 0.64$). Scores have been assigned as the means of the standardized items.

Economic conservatism/progressiveness could unfortunately be measured with no more than two Likert-type items: 'The government should take measures to reduce income differences' and 'Employees need strong trade unions to protect their working conditions and wages' (both with five response categories indicating the degree of (dis)agreement). The correlation between the answers to the two questions is 0.30 and a principal component analysis produces a first factor that explains no less than 65 percent of the variance. Although this is substantial, with only two items it is impossible to construct a reliable scale (Cronbach's α remains limited to 0.46). Scores have been assigned as the means of the two standardized items.

Hypotheses and Statistical Method

Our theory holds, firstly, that choosing between the old-leftist Labor Party (PvdA) and the old-rightist Conservative Party (VVD) constitutes class voting, while choosing between the new-rightist Populist Party (LPF) and the new-leftist Greens (GroenLinks) entails cultural voting. Because new politics is not so much assumed to *replace* old economic issues with new cultural ones, but rather to *add* the latter to the former, our theory furthermore predicts that choosing between the new-leftist Greens (GroenLinks) and the old-leftist Labor Party (PvdA), just like choosing between the new-rightist Populist Party (LPF) and the old-rightist Conservative Party (VVD), also entails cultural voting. The two remaining possible comparisons between pairs of parties—that is, these between the old-rightist Conservative Party (VVD) and the new-leftist Greens (GroenLinks) on the one hand and between the old-leftist Labor Party (PvdA) and the new-rightist Populist Party (LPF)—are meaningless for testing our theory. We therefore exclude these two comparisons from our analysis by not using multinomial-logit modeling (which would after all produce estimations for all six possible comparisons between the four parties), but by instead relying on four separate binary logistic regressions for the four theoretically meaningful pairs of parties only. In the subsequent analyses, we estimate log-odds ratios—showing the natural log of the odds of voting for a party as the ratio of the probability of voting for one party over the probability of voting for the other.[6] Higher log-odds ratios therefore mean that the probability to vote for one party outweighs the probability of voting for the other party. For negatively signed log-odds ratios the reverse is true.

Because our aim is to expose the weakness of the conventional measurement of class voting, we consider it wise to proceed carefully so as to prevent throwing out the baby with the bath water. We therefore test our ideas about cultural voting in the strictest and most conservative manner possible by biasing our analysis against it and hence biasing it in favor of finding strong class effects. We do so by entering education as a pseudo-interval variable with six categories rather than as a set of five dummies, hence allowing for linear effects of education only. Naturally, this reduces education's explanatory power in comparison to the alternative of dropping this assumption of linearity by modeling it as a series of dummy variables. We model EGP-class, on the other hand, as a series of six dummy variables. Another reason for doing so is of course that the seven EGP-classes, unlike the six educational categories, do not simply constitute a hierarchy. Although EGP-class and education are obviously quite strongly related—indeed, this is the very reason why it is necessary to control class effects for education effects and *vice versa*—the relationship between the two is not at all so strong so as to make it impossible to statistically disentangle the two (for details, see Houtman 2003: 24-46).

Results

Class Voting and Cultural Voting?

Does voting for the 'old' political parties constitute class voting, while that for the 'new' ones constitutes cultural voting? Table 7.1 demonstrates that voting for either the old-leftist Labor Party (PvdA) or the old-rightist Conservative Party (VVD) can indeed be conceived of as class voting. The odds of voting for the Labor Party (PvdA) are highest for those with the most precarious economic positions—skilled and unskilled manual workers as well as the poorly educated—, after all, while those with more favorable economic positions tend to vote for the Conservative Party (VVD). This difference in voting behavior is moreover caused

---

6   As a log-odds ratio is the natural logs of the odds ratio, these estimates can be conversed into odds ratios quite easily. Negatively-signed estimates are then transformed into odds ratios between zero and one, positively-signed log-odds ratios are transformed into odds ratios between one and infinity. We chose to present the log-odds ratios in our tables as these are easier to interpret.

Table 7.1 **Voting for the old-rightist Conservative Party (VVD) or the old-leftist Labor Party (PvdA) explained (1=Conservative Party, 2=Labor Party, log-odds ratios with standard errors in parentheses, N=580)**

Independent variables	Model 1	Model 2	Model 3	Model 4
Higher professionals (I)[1]	–	–	–	–
Lower professionals (II)	0.20 (0.23)	-0.05 (0.26)	0.19 (0.24)	-0.05 (0.26)
Non-manual workers (III)	0.04 (0.30)	-0.18 (0.33)	0.02 (0.30)	-0.18 (0.33)
Petty bourgeoisie (IV)	-0.68 (0.48)	-0.94 (0.52)	-0.78 (0.49)	-1.03 (0.53)
Higher working class (V)	0.25 (0.45)	0.35 (0.54)	0.20 (0.46)	0.27 (0.54)
Skilled manual workers (VI)	1.25** (0.49)	0.93 (0.54)	1.32** (0.49)	1.01 (0.54)
Semi- and unskilled manual workers (VII)	1.14** (0.36)	0.78 (0.40)	1.19** (0.37)	0.81* (0.40)
Education	-0.24* (0.11)	-0.04 (0.07)	-0.19** (0.06)	-0.19 (0.13)
Economic progressiveness		1.30*** (0.14)		1.31*** (0.15)
Libertarianism			0.46*** (0.13)	0.47** (0.15)
Constant	-0.03 (0.19)	0.40 (0.40)	-0.62 (0.48)	-1.17* (0.49)
Pseudo R^2 (Nagelkerke)	**0.10**	**0.32**	**0.13**	**0.34**

[1] Not included in analysis (reference category)
*p < 0.05; **p < 0.01; ***p < 0.001

by stronger desires for economic redistribution among the former as compared to the latter, precisely as the class theory of politics predicts. It is abundantly clear, in short, that voting for the old-leftist Labor Party (PvdA) and the old-rightist Conservative Party (VVD) can be characterized as class voting: class-based economic interests are decisive here.

The picture changes dramatically when we attempt to explain votes for the new-leftist Greens (GroenLinks) and the new-rightist Populist Party (LPF), however (Table 7.2). Although the poorly educated tend to vote for the Populist Party (LPF) and the well educated for the Greens (GroenLinks), distinctions

Table 7.2   **Voting for the new-rightist Populist Party (LPF) or the new-leftist Greens (GroenLinks) explained (1=Populist Party, 2=Greens, log-odds ratios with standard errors in parentheses, N=392)**

Independent variables	Model 1	Model 2	Model 3	Model 4
Higher professionals (I)[1]	–	–	–	–
Lower professionals (II)	-0.04 (0.31)	-0.06 (0.32)	0.03 (0.37)	-0.07 (0.39)
Non-manual workers (III)	0.58 (0.38)	0.45 (0.39)	0.61 (0.44)	0.46 (0.46)
Petty bourgeoisie (IV)	-0.30 (0.58)	-0.06 (0.60)	-0.25 (0.69)	0.06 (0.73)
Higher working class (V)	-0.30 (0.59)	-0.51 (0.60)	-0.44 (0.69)	-0.62 (0.70)
Skilled manual workers (VI)	-0.83 (0.75)	-1.25 (0.77)	-0.21 (0.80)	-0.54 (0.82)
Semi- and unskilled manual workers (VII)	0.51 (0.41)	0.45 (0.43)	0.32 (0.47)	0.25 (0.50)
Education	0.71*** (0.15)	0.46*** (0.08)	0.24** (0.09)	0.59*** (0.18)
Economic progressiveness		0.77*** (0.16)		0.87*** (0.21)
Libertarianism			1.73*** (0.21)	1.75*** (0.14)
Constant	-0.89** (0.26)	-2.70*** (0.51)	-6.96*** (0.83)	-6.05*** (0.73)
Pseudo R² (Nagelkerke)	**0.11**	**0.20**	**0.42**	**0.48**

[1]   Not included in analysis (reference category)
*p < 0.05; **p < 0.01; ***p < 0.001

between EGP classes have no explanatory value whatsoever in this case. And indeed, the votes for the Populist Party (LPF) by the poorly educated and for the Greens (GroenLinks) by the well educated are driven by high levels of authoritarianism and libertarianism, respectively, underscoring that education plays a cultural rather than an economic role here. Economic egalitarianism also leads to voting for the Greens (GroenLinks), to be sure, but its role is substantially weaker and the circumstance that it leads the well educated rather than the poorly educated to vote for a leftist party obviously flies in the face of the class theory of politics.

Table 7.3   Voting for the old-leftist Labor Party (PvdA) or the new-leftist Greens (GroenLinks) explained (1=Labor Party, 2=Greens, log-odds ratios with standard errors in parentheses, N=458)

Independent variables	Model 1	Model 2	Model 3	Model 4
Higher professionals (I)[1]	–	–	–	–
Lower professionals (II)	0.01 (0.29)	0.01 (0.29)	0.02 (0.30)	0.02 (0.30)
Non-manual workers (III)	0.53 (0.35)	0.53 (0.35)	0.51 (0.36)	0.51 (0.36)
Petty bourgeoisie (IV)	0.52 (0.62)	0.51 (0.62)	0.45 (0.63)	0.44 (0.63)
Higher working class (V)	-0.03 (0.59)	-0.04 (0.59)	-0.02 (0.60)	-0.03 (0.60)
Skilled manual workers (VI)	-1.22 (0.73)	-1.21 (0.73)	-1.09 (0.73)	-1.08 (0.74)
Semi- and unskilled manual workers (VII)	0.13 (0.39)	0.13 (0.39)	0.14 (0.40)	0.14 (0.40)
Education	0.40** (0.13)	0.22** (0.07)	0.12 (0.08)	0.22 (0.14)
Economic progressiveness		-0.04 (0.16)		-0.04 (0.17)
Libertarianism			0.64*** (0.16)	0.64*** (0.16)
Constant	-0.96*** (0.25)	-1.80*** (0.45)	-3.46*** (0.64)	-2.99*** (0.59)
Pseudo R² (Nagelkerke)	**0.07**	**0.07**	**0.12**	**0.12**

[1] Not included in analysis
*p < 0.05; **p < 0.01; ***p < 0.001

These findings confirm, in short, that voting for the new-leftist Greens (GroenLinks) and the new-rightist Populist Party (LPF) indeed cannot be understood as class voting, but rather constitutes cultural voting. While it is perfectly able to explain votes for old-leftist and old-rightist parties, then, the class theory of politics has nothing to offer when it comes to the explanation of votes for new-leftist and new-rightist parties. To satisfactorily account for the latter, the cultural significance of education needs to be acknowledged, so that in this case education needs to be treated as an indicator for cultural capital rather than class in an economic sense. Whereas the old politics of class is defined by a conflict between the rich and the

Table 7.4 **Voting for the old-rightist Conservative Party (VVD) or the new-rightist Populist Party (LPF) explained (1=Conservative Party, 2=Populist Party, log-odds ratios with standard errors in parentheses, N=514)**

Independent variables	Model 1	Model 2	Model 3	Model 4
Higher professionals (I)[1]	–	–	–	–
Lower professionals (II)	0.29 (0.25)	0.24 (0.25)	0.28 (0.26)	0.23 (0.26)
Non-manual workers (III)	0.07 (0.31)	-0.02 (0.32)	0.02 (0.33)	-0.07 (0.33)
Petty bourgeoisie (IV)	0.01 (0.43)	-0.02 (0.43)	0.03 (0.45)	-0.01 (0.45)
Higher working class (V)	0.49 (0.45)	0.35 (0.46)	0.58 (0.47)	0.45 (0.48)
Skilled manual workers (VI)	0.72 (0.52)	0.54 (0.53)	0.53 (0.53)	0.38 (0.54)
Semi- and unskilled manual workers (VII)	0.78* (0.38)	0.73 (0.38)	0.77* (0.39)	0.71 (0.39)
Education	-0.49*** (0.12)	-0.23** (0.07)	-0.23** (0.07)	-0.36** (0.13)
Economic progressiveness		0.30** (0.11)		0.28* (0.11)
Libertarianism			-0.80*** (0.14)	-0.79*** (0.14)
Constant	-0.13 (0.21)	0.92* (0.38)	2.95*** (0.53)	2.14*** (0.43)
Pseudo R² (Nagelkerke)	**0.10**	**0.12**	**0.19**	**0.24**

[1] Not included in analysis
*p < 0.05; **p < 0.01; ***p < 0.001

economically less well-off, in short, the new cultural politics pits a libertarian cultural elite against an authoritarian 'cultural proletariat.'

Two Lefts and Two Rights?

Does a cultural gap exist between those who vote for the new-leftist Greens (GroenLinks) and those who vote for the old-leftist Labor Party (PvdA), too? Table 7.3 points out that such is indeed the case. We do not so much find classes pitted against one another here, but rather the well educated cultural elite

**Table 7.5　　Voting for a rightist or a leftist party explained
(1=right, 2=left, log-odds ratios with standard errors in
parentheses, N=972)**

Independent variables	Model 1
Higher professionals (I)[1]	–
Lower professionals (II)	0.07 (0.18)
Non-manual workers	0.14 (0.23)
Petty bourgeoisie (IV)	-0.47 (0.36)
Higher working class (V)	-0.01 (0.34)
Skilled manual workers (VI)	0.70* (0.33)
Semi- and unskilled manual workers (VII)	0.71** (0.25)
Education	0.05 (0.04)
Constant	-0.53* (0.27)
Pseudo R² (Nagelkerke)	**0.02**

[1]　Not included in analysis (reference category)
*$p < 0.05$; **$p < 0.01$; ***$p < 0.001$

that tends to vote for the new-leftist Greens (GroenLinks) against the less well educated who tend to vote for the old-leftist Labor Party (PvdA). Consistent with this, the highly educated are not driven by class-based economic reasons, confirming the assumption of the theory of the new political culture that voting for the new-leftist Greens (GroenLinks) rather than the old-leftist Labor Party (PvdA) is culturally rather than economically driven.[7]

The gap between the new-rightist Populist Party (LPF) and the old-rightist Conservative Party (VVD) is basically identical as that between the new-leftist Greens (GroenLinks) and those who vote for the old-leftist Labor Party (PvdA).

7　In a previous publication we have already demonstrated that the same goes for voting for the new-leftist Greens (GroenLinks) rather than the old-leftist Socialist Party (SP) or *vice versa* (Achterberg and Houtman 2006).

Again, we find a predominantly cultural gap, with not so much economic classes, but rather educational categories pitted against one another, and the poorly educated voting for the new-rightist Populist Party (LPF) rather than the old-rightist Conservative Party (VVD) because they are more authoritarian (Table 7.4).

In striking contrast to what the virtual absence of literature about 'two rights' suggests, the gap that we find here is moreover even wider than that between the new-leftist Greens (GroenLinks) and the old-leftist Labor Party (PvdA). Variance explained is no less than twice as high as in the case of the old-leftist Labor Party (PvdA) and the new-leftist Greens (GroenLinks). By the time of the Dutch parliamentary elections of 2002, in short, the emergence of a new political culture had led not only to a bifurcation between 'new left' and 'old left' in Dutch politics, but to a similar gap between 'new right' and 'old right' as well.

The Alford Index and its Great Disappearance Act

Our findings point out that society's lower strata do not necessarily vote for leftist parties, just like the more privileged classes do not necessarily vote for rightist ones. If the working class votes for leftist parties, it is driven by class-based economic interests; if it votes for rightist ones, cultural capital and cultural voting motives are decisive. The reverse applies to the (upper) middle classes: if they vote for rightist parties, this is based on their class-based economic interests, while if they vote for leftist ones, cultural capital and cultural voting motives are decisive (see also Achterberg and Houtman 2006). Class voting and cultural voting hence work in opposite directions and tend to cancel one another out in a way that the Alford index misses and obscures. As a consequence, the Alford index cannot be relied on to ascertain levels of class voting, because a bivariate relationship between class and voting does not so much capture class voting, but rather the extent to which the latter is stronger than reversed cultural voting, that is, the net balance of class voting and cultural voting. In our case at hand here, the Alford index obscures that class voting and cultural voting are both strongly present in the Netherlands nowadays. This is demonstrated in Table 7.5, although manual workers are somewhat more likely than others to vote for leftist parties in the Netherlands nowadays, the differences are only very slight with EGP class explaining no more than a mere two percent of the differences in voting behavior. As we have seen, this does not mean that class voting is almost non-existent, as the traditional interpretation would be, but rather that class voting and cultural voting work in opposite directions.

In other words: although the traditional approach to class voting would lead to the conclusion that class voting is virtually non-existent in the Netherlands nowadays, it is in fact strongly present, but this presence is concealed by the Alford index.

Conclusion

Our findings point out that Inglehart's critics are correct in arguing that voting for new-rightist parties can be explained through basically the same mechanism as voting for new-leftist parties. In both instances we are dealing with cultural voting, that is, voting for a leftist party on the grounds of libertarian values generated by ample cultural capital, or, reversely, voting for a rightist party on the grounds of authoritarian values generated by limited cultural capital. Moreover, as we have seen, a cultural gap exists not only between those who vote for either of the two lefts (the new-leftist Greens [GroenLinks] and the old-leftist Labor Party [PvdA]), but also between those who vote for either of the two rights (the new-rightist Populist Party [LPF] and the old-rightist Conservative Party [VVD]). Voting for new left rather than old left emerges from a high level of libertarianism, rooted in a large amount of cultural capital, while voting for new right rather than old right on the contrary emerges from a high level of authoritarianism, rooted in a limited amount of cultural capital.

Distinguishing this cultural type of voting more systematically from class voting in future research requires replacing the Alford index with a more valid approach, because the former underestimates class voting by mixing it up with reversed cultural voting. Carefully distinguishing the two is even more important, because they can easily vary independently of one another. So, whereas Inglehart (1997: 254) is by and large correct in arguing that 'Postmaterialists come from middle-class backgrounds' and that 'middle-class Postmaterialists move left ... and working-class materialists move to the right', he may well be mistaken in suggesting that such a movement is necessarily 'conducive to a decline in class voting.' Declining Alford indices may after all not so much indicate declines in class voting, but rather increases in cultural voting, so that the decline of the familiar class-party alignments since World War II (Nieuwbeerta 1996) may not so much have been caused by a breakdown of class politics and a decline of class voting, but rather by a dramatic proliferation of cultural politics and an increase in cultural voting. For evidence that such is indeed the case, the reader is referred to Achterberg (2006a, 2006b), Houtman et al. (2008a) and Van der Waal et al. (2007).

Our findings clearly invoke the need for cross-national and historical analyses that disentangle class voting and cultural voting more carefully. A decline or increase of the Alford index may after all mean basically anything. When the Alford index declines, for instance, that may indeed mean that class voting has declined, as the conventional interpretation suggests. It may also mean that class voting has remained stable (while cultural voting has increased), however, or even that class voting has increased rather than decreased (while cultural voting has increased even more). It is hardly surprising, then, that Nieuwbeerta's (1995) attempt to explain the decline and cross-national variation of the Alford index since World War II has led him to reject, almost without exception, hypotheses derived from the class theory of politics about the role of socio-economic context variables such as the size of income differences, the living standard, the percentage of intergenerational class mobility, trade union density, the relative size of the working class, etcetera. Van der Waal et al. (2007) have meanwhile demonstrated that this explanatory impotence of the class approach of politics is indeed caused by the unacknowledged ambiguity of the Alford index, which measures cultural voting at least as much as it does class voting.

The drops in the Alford index during the heydays of the student protests of the 1960s and 1970s, for instance, are more likely to indicate increases in cultural voting than decreases in class voting, because of the sharply increased salience of cultural issues pertaining to individual liberty and democracy back then. The election victory of De Gaulle in France shortly after the vehement student unrest in Paris in May 1968, for instance, seems to have been caused by support by less-educated workers for De Gaulle's emphasis on restoring order one the one hand and well-educated young people expressing their support for the Left on the other (Inglehart 1977: 267-84). Although this produced a drop in the Alford index, it does hence not seem to signify a decline in class voting, but rather an increase in cultural voting. This suggests that a re-analysis of the actual causes underlying sharp drops or increases in the Alford index in the past may be quite illuminating from a theoretical point of view. Indeed, going even further back in history, it is likely that the election victory that brought the German national socialists to power in the 1930s was also based on cultural voting. In other words: there seem to be no good reasons to believe that cultural voting is something entirely new that has only emerged as late at the end of the 1960s (as Inglehart suggests), although it seems undeniable that it has become much stronger since then.

Although, reacting to his critics, Inglehart is now acknowledging the existence of new-rightist political currents, he argues that 'new rightist groups are a reaction against broader trends that are moving faster than these societies can assimilate them' and hence maintains confidently that they 'do not represent the wave of the future' (1997: 251). There is ample room for skepticism here. Inglehart's index for postmaterialism is after all hardly fit to detect 'the wave of the future', because it excludes the possibility of right-authoritarian postmaterialism by definition, thus enabling it to fly under its radar and remain undetected (Flanagan 1979, 1982, 1987). Moreover, and underscoring the severity of this shortcoming, the political salience of right-authoritarian issues has in fact increased even more strongly in Western industrial societies since World War II than that of left-libertarian ones (Achterberg 2006a, 2006b, Houtman et al. 2008a). Contrary to Inglehart's position, then, there are good reasons to assume that right-authoritarian politics is here to stay and grow, and his critics seem correct in arguing that the theory of the new political culture needs to be broadened, so as to incorporate its rightist-authoritarian branch alongside the left-libertarian one.

Our findings also point out that the bifurcation between studies into voting for new-leftist parties on the one hand and for new-rightist ones on the other is quite unfortunate. While the former are typically based on the theory of the new political culture, the latter tend to be based on the assumption that new-rightist parties are either 'protest parties', so that their voters are driven by political distrust and cynicism, or 'anti-immigrant parties', to the effect that their voters are driven by racist and ethnocentric appeals. Although it has been proposed that anti-immigrant parties can be distinguished from protest parties (for example, Fennema 1997), such a distinction proves hard to apply in practice. This is underscored by the circumstance that even during the very brief period 1994-1999 particular anti-immigrant parties seem to have changed into protest parties (Van der Brug and Fennema 2003). Attempts at constructing solid boundaries between these two types of parties thus seem artificial and hence produce unstable results.

Indeed, political cynicism and ethnocentrism are strongly related among themselves and to authoritarianism, while all of these are strongly and negatively related to postmaterialism, making it hardly surprising that they all drive new-rightist voting. Elchardus (1996) has demonstrated convincingly that a linear combination of these variables very well explains new-rightist Vlaams Blok voting in Flanders, Belgium. Like new-leftist parties, then, new-rightist ones are not single-issue parties either. Like the former, they deal with cultural issues in quite a general sense, although they are the former's mirror images, of course. Whereas the new-leftist parties emphasize the desirability of increasing individual liberty and tolerance for cultural diversity, the new-rightist ones emphasize the desirability of an orderly nation, conceiving of 'the people' as a homogeneous and undivided whole and conceiving of politicians who refuse to take 'the will of the people' seriously as traitors. New politics is a politics beyond class, in short—a cultural politics that focuses on issues of individual liberty, social order, and identity.

Chapter 8

One Nation without God?: Post-Christian Cultural Conflict in the Netherlands

With Peter Achterberg and Jeroen van der Waal

Introduction

The Netherlands has drawn attention from international observers because of the fierce tone of its debate on integration of immigrants since the year 2000. Throughout Europe there has been a 'moral panic' about ethnic minorities, but the Dutch case leaps to the eye because of its extremity (Vasta 2007). Along with the rise of the late populist politician Pim Fortuyn, a heated debate on ethnic minorities has developed. Fuelled by a public uproar over the alleged 'destruction of Dutch culture', Dutch policies have turned away from a focus on a multiculturalist 'group-based emancipation principle' and moved in the direction of assimilationism (Penninx 2006, see also Vasta 2007). But this has not gone without opposition. As the *European Commission against Racism and Intolerance* notes in their report on the Netherlands: 'integration and other issues relevant to ethnic minority groups … have been the subject of fundamental and deep questioning in political and public debate' (ECRI 2008: 34, see also Scholten and Holzhacker 2009: 96-8).

This sharp conflict on the question of how to deal with ethnic diversity has led many wondering, for the Netherlands is internationally renowned as a vanguard of secular tolerance (see Penninx 2006). Its image as a highly modernized and one of the least traditionally Christian countries in the world has been repeatedly corroborated in empirical research (Lechner 1996, 2008, Norris and Inglehart 2004). If traditional moral views on issues of abortion, euthanasia, gender roles and (homo-)sexuality are still held in the Netherlands, it is among the Christian share of its population. Therefore it does not come as a surprise that studies of the values of the Dutch population in highly secularized times indicate shared ideals of tolerance. As recently as 2004, Duyvendak noted that a discourse emphasizing cultural ideals of individual liberty and moral permissiveness is more deeply entrenched in the Netherlands than anywhere else, and cross-national research by Inglehart (1997) indeed shows that the Netherlands is one of the most morally permissive countries in the world (see also Inglehart and Welzel 2005).

The present-day Dutch combination of cultural and political conflict about how to deal with ethnic diversity on the one hand, and the country's longstanding tradition of secular moral permissiveness on the other, seems odd and begs for theoretical understanding. Classical theories about the cultural consequences of the decline of Christian religion provide a fertile starting point for the elaboration of this theoretical problem, particularly if these theories are next compared to actual changes in cultural and political conflict from the 1960s onwards. Our discussion results in a theory about the shape and origins of post-Christian cultural conflict, which will be tested by means of survey data collected in the Netherlands. Obviously, this country constitutes a theoretically instructive case for the study of the cultural consequences of secularization, because the Netherlands stands out as one of the most secularized countries in the world (Norris and Inglehart 2004)—'one nation without God', as Lechner has put it (2008: 135, see also Lechner 1996).

A Post-Christian Cultural Conflict?

Culture on the Ruins of Christian Morality

In the sociological rendition of the Enlightenment heritage, the process of modernization is understood as—at least potentially—liberating modern individuals from demands for conformity made in the name of Christian tradition and community (for example, Seidman 1994: 19-53) by establishing inalienable individual rights *vis-à-vis* the latter (Berting 1995). 'Modernity was held', as Featherstone (1995: 217-18) summarizes this position, 'to entail a relentless de-traditionalism in which collective orientations would give way to individualism, religious belief to secularization and the accumulated sediment of mores and everyday practices would surrender to progressive rationalization and the quest for "the new".'

These visions are echoed in contemporary accounts of the cultural consequences of the waning of Christian morality. According to this perspective, the erosion of traditional religious morality inspires all-embracing ideals of tolerance. As Emerson and Hartman set out:

> Modernization ... squeezes out religious influences from many of its spheres and greatly reduces religion's role in the others. ... Currently, postmodernization is a popular term used to describe the continued individualizing and relativizing of the world. ... Given this vast pluralism, societies and their governments are able to claim less and less as common to all. What rise to the top as shared values are tolerance and acceptance. These become the core values of highly modernized societies. (2006: 130)

Exploring 'how the shifting balance between modernization and tradition shapes human values', Inglehart and Welzel (2005: 4) signal a similar development in their book *Modernization, Cultural Change, and Democracy*: 'Collective emphasis shifts from collective discipline to individual liberty, from group conformity to human diversity ... giving rise to a syndrome we call self-expression values. These values bring increasing emphasis on the civil and political liberties that constitute democracy ... This reflects a humanistic transformation of modernity' (2005: 3). Again, the erosion of traditional Christian morality is portrayed as having unequivocal progressive consequences for cultural value orientations; although tendencies towards intolerance (authoritarianism and xenophobia) are not ignored, these are interpreted as 'retrogression' from the more general trend (2005: 4).

Strikingly, however, there have always been scholars who have taken a radically opposite stance and have hence envisioned the decline of traditional Christian morality as fuelling intolerance and ethnic hatred instead. This alternative perspective was already promoted in the thirties, when various theorists argued that decline of traditional morality would leave many uprooted and would produce an outcry for a more rather than a less coercive social order (Bain 1939). José Ortega y Gasset (1932), for instance, expected an eruption of illiberal sentiments in the wake of the erosion of traditional institutions and foresaw a quest for order by the uprooted masses and widespread violence against outgroups. A similar reasoning can be found in the work of Eric Hoffer (2002 [1951]) about the social bases of the radical and intolerant political movements that ravaged mid-twentieth century Europe: these movements, according to Hoffer, appealed especially to those who felt displaced after traditional institutions had lost their once unquestioned legitimacy.

Many a contemporary analysis echoes the latter point of view. Sztompka, for instance, worries about a 'dissolution of the moral space' (2002: 64), 'moral degradation', (idem: 66), and a 'moral vacuum' (idem: 70) underlying problems of order and trust in contemporary societies (see also Bellah et al. 1985, 1992, Elchardus and Smits 2002, Stivers 1994). A similar analysis leads Etzioni (2001, see also Etzioni 1995) to a pessimistic diagnosis of contemporary culture. In his view, the decline of Christian morality not only spawns problems such as anomie, distrust and crime, but also fuels antagonistic instead of tolerant attitudes: 'Without a shared moral culture, ordering life will have to rely on laws not undergirded by moral commitments, which ... has numerous ill consequences. ... social order most continually be constructed—or men (and women) be wolf to one another' (Etzioni 2001: 360).

According to one category of authors, in short, the decline of traditional Christian morality entails an increase of generalized tolerance, whereas others instead paint a grim picture of intolerance due to exactly the same process. In the next subsection we will compare the major cultural and political changes in the post-World War II era to these two radically diverging perspectives.

Culture Contested: New Left and New Right

The years following World War II resulted in a mass of formally free yet politically and professionally apathetic and subservient citizens (McGregor 1960, Mills 1951), numbed by newly acquired opportunities for consumption and anxious to keep up with the proverbial Joneses (Horkheimer and Adorno 2002 [1944], Riesman 1950,

Whyte 1956). As such, the fundamentally liberating promises of the decline of all-embracing Christian morality were not fulfilled, giving rise to cultural discontents that were expressed in the decades that followed.

From the 1960s onwards, this 'mass society' evoked major cultural discontents that sparked the counter culture of middle-class youngsters longing for liberty, personal authenticity and self-expression and rejecting conformist mainstream culture, commodification and mass production, and 'alienating' technological systems (Roszak 1969, Zijderveld 1970; see Chapter 1 of this book). A new political climate emerged in which conformist morals were fiercely criticized and in which individual freedom and the right for self-actualization were called for (Inglehart 1977). These 'new-leftist politics' of the time went hand in hand with the rise of various progressive 'new social movements', such as the peace movement, the feminist movement, and the homosexual rights movement (Kriesi 1989, Kriesi and Van Praag 1987, Zijderveld 1970), all calling for more individual freedom and recognition of and tolerance for non-traditional cultural identities (Kriesi 1998).

Various political scientists and sociologists have noted that the 'new-leftist' movements of the 1960s have nevertheless inspired a rightist counter reaction from the early 1980s onwards. New-rightist movements emerged (De Koster et al. 2008, Elchardus 1996) and authoritarian new-rightist parties surfaced and gained electoral power in many Western countries (see Chapter 7 of this book). Ignazi sets out how this authoritarian upsurge was fuelled by the rise of new-leftist libertarian movements in the 1960s and 1970s: new-rightist movements deem the erosion of social order brought about by the counter-cultural emphasis on individual freedom as problematic. The risen cultural heterogeneity leads to feelings of insecurity and disturbance and new-rightist political movements 'reflected the demands for identity (hence nationalism), for homogeneity (hence xenophobia), and for order, hierarchy and strong leadership (hence authoritarianism)' (Ignazi 2003: 202).

In short, new-leftist politics provoked a counter movement in which feelings of insecurity and uncertainty have been converted into a political agenda that was put forward by the new right. As such, issues of cultural homogeneity and social order versus cultural diversity and tolerance have become the focal point of present-day cultural conflict. It is important to note that the new-rightist counter movement in Europe did not address traditional Christian issues such as gender and sexuality. In a highly secularized country such as the Netherlands there is a virtual consensus on these issues, and the political left and (non-religious) right alike have come to accept gender equality and gay rights, even to the extent of being deployed to demonize traditional religious identities (Duyvendak 2004, see also Lechner 2008: 135, and Chapter 9 of this book for an elaboration).

The above suggests that the decline of Christian morality since the 1960s has spawned a post-Christian cultural conflict in Western countries. The rise of a post-Christian morality—which entails a rejection of traditional Christian stances on moral issues such as abortion, euthanasia, gender roles and (homo)sexuality—does not mean that political conflict revolving around cultural issues is a thing of the past. Accounts that imply either a decline or an increase in levels of cultural tolerance both simplify a complex cultural and political reality. The former neglect the progressive new-leftist cultural politics that emerged in the 1960s and 1970s, the latter overlook the new-rightist backlash from the 1980s onwards. Secularized Western countries seem instead to have witnessed the emergence of diametrically opposed political movements that clash over the question of how to deal with cultural diversity. What seems to characterize a radically secularized country like the contemporary Netherlands, then, is neither widespread ethnic intolerance, nor pervasive ethnic tolerance, but rather both of these.

Post-Christian Cultural Conflict?

The foregoing raises the question whether, how and why post-Christian morality is differently related to ethnic (in)tolerance for different social categories. In order to answer this question, it is important to take empirical research on tolerance into account. The tendency to include or exclude all sorts of ethnic outgroups proves closely related to various measures of authoritarianism (Meloen et al. 1996: 649), which is of course hardly surprising, because the latter were intended from the outset to tap not only into skepticism *vis-à-vis* democratic liberties and a rigid emphasis on maintenance of social order, but into ethnic intolerance as well (Adorno et al. 1950: 151). The authoritarianism / ethnic intolerance complex is furthermore frequently regarded as basically interchangeable with Christian morality, as measured by acceptance or rejection of traditional moral stances *vis-à-vis* issues like abortion, euthanasia, (homo-)sexuality and gender relations, without doubt due to their substantial interrelationship. Discussing indicators of 'overall tolerance', Inglehart et al. (2008: 269), for instance, lump together progressive post-Christian attitudes towards issues such as gender and homosexuality with tolerance of foreigners and 'other groups', and Inglehart and Welzel (2005: 56), too, consider tolerance of homosexuality 'a sensitive indicator of tolerance towards outgroups in general.' Other examples can be found in Vollebergh et al. (1999: 299), who combine items on tolerance towards homosexuals, male-female roles and freedom of abortion and euthanasia with items on patriotism and tolerance towards criminals into a single 'libertarian-authoritarian dimension', and in Flanagan and Lee (2003: 239-40), who combine items on freedom of speech, clarity of good and evil, and sexual permissiveness as 'libertarian' (see for yet other examples: Achterberg 2006a, 2006b, Achterberg and Houtman 2006, Fleishman 1988, Flere 2007, Middendorp 1989).

While the substantial correlation between Christian morality and authoritarianism/ethnic intolerance, of course, cannot be denied, our theoretical arguments above nonetheless suggest that there are good reasons to doubt that the two are mutually interchangeable and to question the habit of combining them into some sort of measure of 'overall tolerance.' Recent research does much to reinforce these doubts. It points out, firstly, that while orthodox Christians tend to embrace traditional values pertaining to issues like gender roles, euthanasia, abortion and the like, Christian orthodoxy is hardly or not at all related to authoritarianism

(De Koster and Van der Waal 2007: 453-4). Secondly, the well-established correlation between both dimensions proves solely caused by the circumstance that a rejection of Christian morality and aversion of authoritarianism go hand in hand, while the 'rightist' poles of Christian morality and authoritarianism scales are virtually unrelated (De Koster and Van der Waal 2007: 455-6).

These findings suggest that Christian morality and specific measures of ethnic intolerance can not only be distinguished analytically, but also disentangled empirically. Since the distinction between Christian morality and ethnic intolerance is crucial for an understanding of the theoretical problem addressed in this chapter, we will hence start our empirical assessment by testing the hypothesis that post-Christian morality and ethnic tolerance are interrelated more strongly than Christian morality and ethnic intolerance (hypothesis 1).

Corroboration of this hypothesis would validate the idea that Christian morality and ethnic intolerance are less closely related than they are typically assumed to be. Of course, this would call for an explanation, and differences in level of education might provide a first step towards solving our research puzzle. After all, the poles of the value dimensions that are expected to be correlated most strongly—that is, post-Christian morality and ethnic tolerance—are both embraced by the higher educated rather than the lower educated (for example, De Koster and Van der Waal 2007, Emler and Frazer 1999, Stubager 2008, 2009). The higher educated hence tend to embrace post-Christian morality and ethnic tolerance at the same time. This is in line with an abundance of research indicating that the higher educated tend to combine political values in a more 'coherent' fashion than the lower educated do (see for an overview Achterberg and Houtman 2009: 1650-1, Van der Waal et al. 2010). This suggests that the pattern predicted by the first hypothesis is caused by differences in educational level. Therefore we expect that the association between both value orientations is stronger among higher educational categories (hypothesis 2).

Obviously, these first two hypotheses are merely descriptive. Testing these makes clear whether and how post-Christian morality is differently related to ethnic (in)tolerance for different social categories, but it leaves the theoretically most important question to be answered: *why* would this be the case? In order to answer this question, it is important to note that research has shown time and again that authoritarianism and ethnic intolerance stem from an experienced absence of a meaningful social order, that is, from anomie or cultural insecurity (for example, Achterberg and Houtman 2009, Blank 2003, Lutterman and Middleton 1970, McDill 1961, Roberts and Rokeach 1956, Srole 1956), while Christian morality, on the other hand, plays a major role in endowing social life with metaphysical meaning and as such tends to counteract cultural insecurity (see Lukes 1967 and Zijderveld 2000 for theoretical treatments of how Christian religiosity ensures solidly grounded meaning). It is hence not only to be expected that Christian morality and ethnic intolerance are less closely related than they are frequently assumed to be, but also that ethnic intolerance is rooted in cultural insecurity, whereas Christian morality is not (hypothesis 3).

Key in understanding why both ethnic tolerance and ethnic intolerance thrive in the wake of the decline of Christian morality, is that the lower educated are more prone to cultural insecurity than the higher educated (Achterberg and Houtman 2009, McDill 1961), which can be understood with reference to what Gabennesch (1972) calls the smaller 'breadth of perspective' of the former, which makes them 'conceive of social reality as encompassing a superordinate normative dimension, an external locus where events are determined, where moral authority resides, and to which men must adapt themselves' (1972: 862-3). As such, they are more strongly affected by the absence of a meaningful social order. Because the lower educated are more inclined to conceive of the social order as natural and to take it for granted, they are more troubled if it is disturbed. This might provide the last part of the solution to our theoretical problem. As those with a post-Christian ideological profile face a world that is not provided with 'pre-given' meaning (Heelas 1996b), they are susceptible to cultural insecurity, and the above indicates this particularly holds for the lower educated. If cultural insecurity, in turn, indeed drives ethnic intolerance—as predicted by our third hypothesis—this could explain why the lower educated are less likely to combine post-Christian morality with ethnic tolerance. Thus, we expect that differences between educational categories in the association between post-Christian morality and ethnic tolerance can be explained by education-related differences in cultural insecurity (hypothesis 4). Technically speaking, we expect a positive interaction effect of post-Christian morality and education on ethnic tolerance that can be attributed to (and hence: explained away by) higher levels of cultural insecurity among the lower educated.

In short, our theoretical argument states that those with a post-Christian moral profile may either embrace or reject ethnic intolerance, dependent on education-related differences in cultural insecurity. This implies that in a highly secularized country as the Netherlands there is a post-Christian cultural *conflict* between the secular higher educated and the secular lower educated that is driven by differences in cultural insecurity. The agendas and social bases of new-leftist and new-rightist politics point exactly in the same direction of a post-Christian cultural conflict between the lower-educated and higher-educated secular. These parties do not pit against each other concerning Christian moral guidelines, but clash on questions pertaining to multiculturalism, ethnocentrism and authoritarianism, and that is why the tolerant higher educated form the social basis of the new left, while the intolerant lower educated disproportionately vote for the new right (Achterberg 2006a, 2006b, Houtman 2001, 2003, Houtman et al. 2008a, 2008b, Van der Waal et al. 2007).

Our theory suggests, in short, that secularization has not had the unambiguous cultural consequences suggested by those who have either hailed it as the dawning of a new era of cultural understanding and tolerance or deplored it as a major cause of ethnic conflict and hatred. Instead, it predicts that the emergence of a post-Christian society has spawned both of these simultaneously, that is, ethnic tolerance as much as ethnic intolerance, albeit among different segments of the population. We expect a post-Christian posture to lead to ethnic intolerance among the lower educated, due to their high levels of cultural insecurity, and to ethnic tolerance among their well-educated secular counterparts, due to their low levels of cultural insecurity.

Data and Methods

In order to test the hypotheses formulated above, we will analyze data on the theoretically salient case of the highly secularized Netherlands, collected in 2008 by *CentERdata*. This is an institute for data collection and research, specialized in online surveys. It maintains a panel representative for the Dutch population aged 16 years and older, the representativeness of which is carefully preserved.[1] A total of 2,423 individuals were selected to participate in the study, of which 2,121 respondents completed the questionnaire, yielding a response rate of 87.5 percent. A comparison with official statistics from *Statistics Netherlands* (Centraal Bureau voor de Statistiek) showed that our sample is representative for income level, educational level, age and gender.

To measure the extent to which respondents are characterized by *post-Christian morality* we have combined indicators of attitudes pertaining to gender roles with indicators of Christian religiosity. Conservative stances on traditional moral issues have in the Netherlands always been connected to Christian religiosity, and research demonstrates that traditional views on gender roles go hand in hand with other aspects of Christian morality (that is, traditional stances *vis-à-vis* issues like abortion, euthanasia, (homo-)sexuality and the like) and can as such be distinguished from authoritarianism (De Koster and Van der Waal 2007). Respondents were asked to indicate whether they agreed (1 totally disagree, 2 disagree, 3 neither agree nor disagree, 4 agree, 5 totally agree) with the following statements: 1) In a firm it is unnatural when women hold positions of authority over men; 2) After all boys can be educated more freely than girls; 3) A woman is more capable of bringing up small children than a man; 4) It is acceptable for a married couple to decide on principles not to have children although there are no medical objections; 5) It is not as important for a girl to get a good education as it is for a boy. We coded the 'don't know' answers as missing, and coded the items so that higher scores stand for a stronger rejection of traditional Christian views towards gender roles. The Christian religiosity of respondents is measured by means of questions on church membership (0, no denomination; 1, denomination) and church attendance (0, practically never; to 6, more than once a week),[2] which were coded so that higher scores stand for a less Christian profile. All seven items

---

1   Panel members who do not themselves own a computer with an Internet connection were provided the necessary equipment.

2   Apart from five Muslims, who were left out of the analysis, all respondents are either non-religious or belong to a Christian denomination.

were standardized, and a factor analysis indicates that there is a first factor with an eigenvalue of 2.31, explaining 33 percent of the variance. We have constructed a scale for *post-Christian morality* by calculating the mean score for respondents who have valid scores on at least five of the seven items. Higher scores on this scale (Cronbach's $\alpha = 0.63$) stand for a higher level of *post-Christian morality*.

In order to measure *ethnic tolerance*, we constructed scales for ethnocentrism, multiculturalism and authoritarianism, as well as a meta-scale based on these.

To measure *ethnocentrism* we used six Likert-type items, partly overlapping with those used by Eisinga and Scheepers (1989).[3] Respondents were asked whether they agreed (1 totally disagree, 2 disagree, 3 neither agree nor disagree, 4 agree, 5 totally agree) with the following statements: 1) Foreigners carry all kinds of dirty smells around; 2) With Moroccans you never know for certain whether or not they are going to be aggressive; 3) Most people from Surinam work quite slowly; 4) Most Turks are rather self-indulgent at work; 5) Foreigners living in the Netherlands should adapt to Dutch uses and customs; 6) The Netherlands should have never let foreign guest workers in our country. The 'don't know' answers were coded as missing. Factor analysis of the responses to these six items showed that there was a first factor with an eigenvalue of 3.39 explaining 56 percent of the variance. After standardizing and recoding the items, we have constructed a scale by calculating the mean score for respondents who have valid scores on at least four of the six items. Higher scores on this scale (Cronbach's $\alpha = 0.84$) stand for less ethnocentrism.

As the debate concerning whether ethnic minority groups should be accommodated in maintaining their cultural identities in the Netherlands primarily revolves around Muslim minorities, we included a measure for *multiculturalism*, consisting of six Likert-type items about Islam. Respondents were asked to indicate whether they agreed (1 totally disagree, 2 disagree, 3 neither agree nor disagree, 4 agree, 5 totally agree) with the following statements: 1) The Islamic tradition suits the Netherlands; 2) Muslims are good people; 3) I think that rightist parties are too extreme about Islam; 4) I think the Islam poses no problem to Dutch society; 5) In the Netherlands there is no room for Islam; 6) It is right that Islam is seen as a threat to our modern society. The 'don't know' answers were again coded as missing, and the last two items were recoded. Factor analysis of the responses to these six items showed that there was a first factor with an eigenvalue of 2.62 explaining 44 percent of the variance. After standardizing the items, we have constructed a scale for multiculturalism by calculating the mean score for respondents who have valid scores on at least four of the six items. Higher scores on this scale (Cronbach's $\alpha = 0.82$) stand for more multiculturalism (and hence indicate higher levels of ethnic tolerance).

We also used a common seven-item selection from the F-scale for *authoritarianism* by Adorno et al. (1950)—comparative research of Meloen et al.

---

3 Since some of the items of the original scale by Eisinga and Scheepers (1989) seem a bit outdated, they were replaced by others. The first four items are part of the original scale.

(1996) demonstrates that this is as good an indicator of aversion to ethnic tolerance as the scales developed by Altemeyer (1988) and Lederer (1983). Respondents were asked to indicate whether they agreed (1 totally disagree, 2 disagree, 3 neither agree nor disagree, 4 agree, 5 totally agree) with the following statements: 1) Young people often revolt against social situations that they find unjust: however, when they get older they ought to become resigned to reality; 2) What we need are fewer laws and institutions and more courageous, tireless and devoted leaders whom people can trust; 3) Most people fall short of your expectations when you get to know them better; 4) There are two sorts of people: the strong and the weak; 5) Most of our social problems would be solved if we could somehow get rid of the immoral, crooked and feebleminded people; 6) Ill-mannered people cannot expect decent people to want to mix with them; 7) Obedience and respect for authority are the most important virtues children should learn. Again, the 'don't know' answers were coded as missing. Factor analysis of the responses to these seven items showed that there was a first factor with an eigenvalue of 3.20 explaining 46 percent of the variance. After standardizing the items, we have constructed a scale by calculating the mean score for respondents who have valid scores on at least five of the seven items (Cronbach's $\alpha = 0.80$). This scale was reversed so that—in line with our measures of ethnic tolerance—higher scores on this scale stand for less authoritarianism.

Finally, we constructed a second-order scale for ethnic tolerance out of the scales for *ethnocentrism, multiculturalism* and *authoritarianism*. A secondary factor analysis on these three indicators indicated that there was a first factor with an eigenvalue of 1.89 explaining 63 percent of the variance. For each respondent a mean score was calculated so that higher scores on the *meta-scale ethnic tolerance* stand for more tolerance.

Cultural insecurity was measured by means of four items inspired by Srole's widely used anomie scale (Srole 1956, see also Achterberg and Houtman 2009). Respondents were asked whether they agreed (1 totally agree, 2 agree, 3 neither agree nor disagree, 4 disagree, 5 totally disagree, 6 don't know) with the following statements: 1) These days a person doesn't really know whom he can count on; 2) Succeeding in life mostly is a matter of luck; 3) It's hardly fair to bring children into the world, the way things look for the future; 4) Nowadays, what one feels or thinks does not count anymore. The 'don't know' answers were coded as missing. A factor analysis of the responses to these four items showed that there was a first factor with an eigenvalue of 2.23 explaining 56 percent of the variance. After standardizing the items, we have constructed a scale by calculating the mean score for respondents who have valid scores on at least three of the four items (Cronbach's $\alpha = 0.73$). Higher scores stand for more cultural insecurity.

Educational level was measured using the highest level attained. For the first part of our analysis, respondents have been recoded into three educational categories of roughly comparable size: low (only primary education and VMBO, 33 percent), medium (HAVO/VWO/MBO, 30 percent) and high (HBO/University, 37 percent). For our multiple linear regression analyses, it has subsequently been recoded into the number of years needed to attain a specific educational level, yielding a variable ranging from 8 to 18 years.

We include net monthly income in our analyses in order to control for explanations of ethnic intolerance focusing on weak economic positions (for example, Olzak 1992). To measure *income*, respondents were asked into which of four categories their monthly net household income fell: 1) 1,150 Euros or less (7 percent); 2) 1,151 to 1,800 (18 percent); 3) 1,801 to 2,600 (30 percent); and 4) 2,601 or more (45 percent).

Results

In order to assess whether post-Christian morality and ethnic tolerance can be disentangled empirically, we test our first hypothesis, which states that post-Christian morality and ethnic tolerance are interrelated more strongly than Christian morality and ethnic intolerance. To do so, we followed the approach used by De Koster and Van der Waal (2007): we divided our scale for post-Christian morality into two halves of roughly comparable sizes and correlated these with our measures of ethnic tolerance. The results are depicted in Table 8.1.

The first row of this table indicates that a substantial positive correlation exists between post-Christian morality and ethnic tolerance. The results depicted in the second and third row, however, indicate that this does not mean that both concepts are interchangeable: the association is much weaker at the 'Christian' side of the scale than at the 'post-Christian' side.[4] Hence, our first hypothesis is corroborated, which demonstrates that post-Christian morality and ethnic tolerance are less closely related than they are normally assumed to be. The two can be disentangled empirically and should not be simply lumped together in an overall indicator of tolerance. Instead, an explanation for their varying association is needed.

To shed light on this matter, we address our second hypothesis by focusing on the question of whether post-Christian morality is differently combined with ethnic tolerance by different educational groups. Firstly, we assess whether the association between post-Christian morality and various measures of ethnic tolerance is stronger among higher educational categories. Figure 8.1 indicates that this is the case indeed.

The pattern is the same for all four measures of ethnic tolerance employed. Post-Christian morality displays stronger positive associations with rejection of ethnocentrism, multiculturalism and rejection of authoritarianism as well as the meta-scale of these among the higher educated than among the lower educated. In fact, the correlations of post-Christian morality with multiculturalism and rejection of authoritarianism are not even significant for the lower educated (p = 0.15 and p = 0.26 respectively). The extent to which the lower educated are characterized by

---

4   These differences are statistically significant, except for those for the relationship between multiculturalism and post-Christian morality.

Table 8.1   **Associations of four measures of ethnic tolerance with scale for post-Christian morality (Pearson's *r*)**

	N	Ethnocentrism (reversed)	Multiculturalism	Authoritarianism (reversed)	Meta-scale ethnic tolerance
Post-Christian morality (total)	2,043	.21**	.15**	.16**	.22**
'Christian' part of scale	1,036	.08**	.14**	.01 ns	.09**
'Post-Christian' part of scale	1,007	.23**	.16**	.15**	.23**

ns not significant; ** p < 0.01

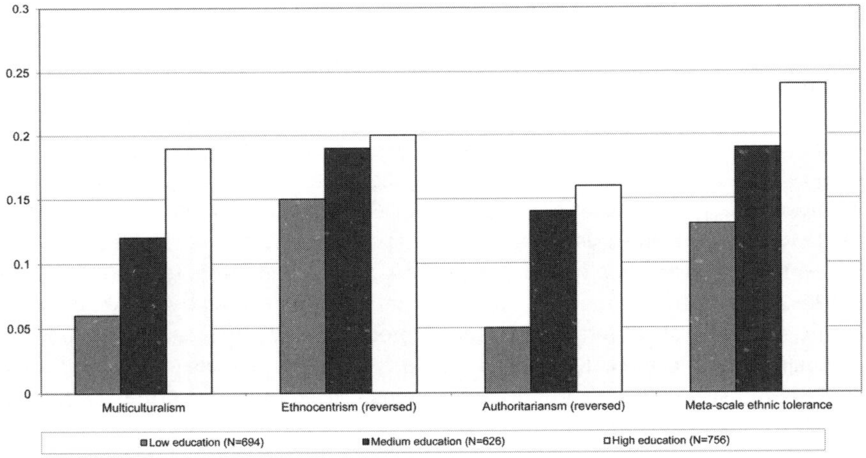

Figure 8.1   **Correlations between post-Christian morality and four scales of ethnic tolerance, by educational level**

post-Christian morality hence reveals no information at all about their support for multiculturalism or rejection of authoritarianism.

Although these simple, bivariate associations provide a first insight into the varying relationship between post-Christian morality and ethnic tolerance, additional analyses are of course needed to corroborate these findings. Therefore we applied four multivariate regression analyses—one for each measure of ethnic

Table 8.2   **Associations of four measures of ethnic tolerance with post-Christian morality and education (standardized coefficients, N=1,887)**

Independents	Ethnocentrism (reversed)	Multiculturalism	Authoritarianism (reversed)	Meta-scale ethnic tolerance
Education	.22**	.08**	.28**	.24**
Post-Christian morality	.15*	-.05 ns	.04 ns	.11*
Post-Christian morality *				
Education	.13*	.10*	.19**	.18**
Income	.05*	.02 ns	.01 ns	.04 ns
R²	.15	.04	.14	.17

ns not significant; * p < 0.05; ** p < 0.01

tolerance—in which education and the extent to which people adhere to post-Christian morality were both modeled as independent variables together with the control variable income. The results of these analyses are summarized in Table 8.2 above.

These analyses first indicate that post-Christian morality itself is not clearly related to either ethnic tolerance or intolerance. Rejection of ethnocentrism and the meta-scale of ethnic tolerance are directly positively affected by post-Christian morality, multiculturalism and rejection of authoritarianism are not. A stance on these latter issues appears not to be directly informed by post-Christian morality.

This already raises some doubt about frequently made claims of unequivocal cultural consequences of the decline of traditional Christian morality. In the light of this theoretical debate it is even more important to note that the analyses all display significant positive interaction effects of post-Christian morality and education. This indicates that post-Christian morality is differently combined with ethnic tolerance by the lower and the higher educated. It seems that whereas the former combine post-Christian morality with various forms of ethnic intolerance, post-Christian morality is associated with ethnic tolerance for the latter. The graphic display of the varying effect of post-Christian morality on the four measures of tolerance depicted in Figure 8.2 indicates that this is indeed the case.

Instead of a general inclination to either ethnic tolerance or intolerance, there are important differences between the lower and the higher educated when it comes to the consequences of a post-Christian morality. The fact that the line of the meta-scale crosses the axis demonstrates that post-Christian morality underlies ethnic intolerance among the lower educated, whereas it inspires ethnic tolerance among the higher educated. Zooming in on the subscales, the findings provide evidence

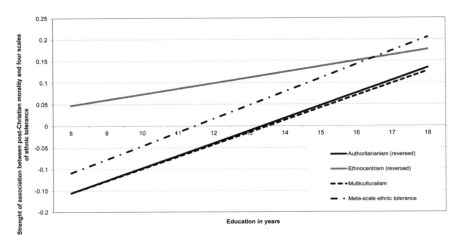

Figure 8.2   The association between post-Christian morality and four measures of ethnic tolerance, by education

that post-Christian morality leads the lower educated away from multiculturalism and towards authoritarianism, whereas for the higher educated post-Christian morality is associated with multiculturalism and rejection of authoritarianism. Only the scale for rejection of ethnocentrism does not cross the axis, but in line with the other analyses we see that post-Christian morality steers the higher educated more strongly away from ethnocentrism than the lower educated.

Overlooking these findings, we can conclude that post-Christian morality fuels ethnic intolerance for the lower educated and tolerance for the higher educated. The question that remains is how this pattern can be explained. To address this question we first test our third hypothesis, by looking at the relationship of both post-Christian morality and ethnic tolerance with cultural insecurity. In order to control for the substantial association between post-Christian morality and ethnic tolerance, we have calculated their partial correlations with cultural insecurity. These are depicted in Table 8.3.

In accordance with our expectations, these findings demonstrate that ethnic intolerance is rooted in cultural insecurity: people with higher levels of cultural insecurity are more inclined to ethnocentrism and authoritarianism, and less to multiculturalism. As predicted by our hypothesis, the association is reversed when it comes to post-Christian morality: a significant positive correlation exists between cultural insecurity and post-Christian morality, which indicates that the absence of a Christian morality indeed entails an experienced lack of a meaningful social order.

These findings pave the way for solving the final part of our theoretical puzzle. To do so, we need to assess whether education-related differences in cultural

Table 8.3   Partial correlations of post-Christian morality and four measures of ethnic tolerance with cultural insecurity (N=1,909)

	Cultural insecurity
Post-Christian morality (controlled for meta-scale ethnic tolerance)	.05*
Ethnocentrism (reversed) (controlled for post-Christian morality)	-.43**
Multiculturalism (controlled for post-Christian morality)	-.31**
Authoritarianism (reversed) (controlled for post-Christian morality)	-.46**
Meta-scale ethnic tolerance (controlled for post-Christian morality)	-.48**

* $p < 0.05$; ** $p < 0.01$

insecurity are responsible for the observation that post-Christian morality is associated with ethnic tolerance for the higher educated whereas it goes together with ethnic intolerance for the lower educated. Is it because the higher educated are less culturally insecure than the lower educated that they combine post-Christian morality with ethnic tolerance instead of with ethnic intolerance? To answer this question we test our fourth and last hypothesis, which technically states that the positive interaction effect between post-Christian morality and education can be attributed to lower levels of cultural insecurity among the higher educated.

Obviously, a necessary condition for this hypothesis to hold is that the higher educated are less culturally insecure. This turns out to be the case: the correlation between level of education and cultural insecurity is -0.31 ($p < 0.01$; N = 2,015). We perform the same multivariate regression analyses as shown in Table 8.2 above, but now we add our measure for cultural insecurity. The results of these analyses can be found in Table 8.4.

These analyses corroborate our hypothesis on the explanatory role of education-related differences in cultural insecurity. Due to the incorporation of cultural insecurity in the analyses, the positive interaction effect of post-Christian morality and education completely vanished for all four measures of ethnic tolerance. It is because the lower educated have higher levels of cultural insecurity than the higher educated that they combine post-Christian morality with ethnic intolerance instead of ethnic tolerance.

All in all, these findings demonstrate that the waning of Christian morality has not simply led to either ethnic tolerance or intolerance in the Netherlands, but rather to both of these. Because the lower educated are more culturally insecure, they combine post-Christian morality with ethnic intolerance, whereas post-Christian morality inspires ethnic tolerance among the less culturally insecure

Table 8.4   **Associations of four measures of ethnic tolerance with post-Christian morality, education and cultural insecurity (standardized coefficients, N=1,887)**

Independents	Ethnocentrism (reversed)	Multiculturalism	Authoritarianism (reversed)	Meta-scale ethnic tolerance
Education	.12**	.06*	.18**	.13**
Post-Christian morality	.15**	-.01 ns	.04 ns	.06 ns
Post-Christian morality*				
Education	.04 ns	.03 ns	.04 ns	.05 ns
Income	.01 ns	-.01 ns	-.04 ns	-.01 ns
Cultural insecurity	-.38***	-.28***	-.44***	-.45***
R^2	.27	.13	.33	.36

ns not significant; * $p < 0.05$; ** $p < 0.01$; ***$p < 0.001$

higher educated. While prior research has already repeatedly demonstrated that education positively affects ethnic tolerance (for example, Emler and Frazer 1999, Stubager 2008, 2009), our findings point out that this gap between the higher and the lower educated is wider among those with a post-Christian secular profile, which indicates that secularization has spawned a new and post-Christian cultural conflict between the higher and the lower educated.

Conclusion: Two Nations without God

Our findings do not merely provide insight into the logic of present cultural and political conflicts about multiculturalism and ethnic diversity in the Netherlands (for example, Penninx 2006), but have major theoretical implications for more general debates about the cultural consequences of secularization. The relevant literature is strikingly polarized between those who argue that the latter process entails the rise of all-encompassing tolerance (for example, Emerson and Hartman 2006: 130, Inglehart and Welzel 2005) and those who instead envision the emergence of a fertile breeding ground for ethnic hatred and intolerance towards outgroups (for example, Elchardus and Smits 2002, Etzioni 1995, 2001, Stivers 1994, Sztompka 2002).

Our findings demonstrate that, at least for the Netherlands, both of these accounts tell only half the story: both ethnic tolerance and ethnic intolerance thrive in the wake of the decline of Christian morality, and they do so among different social categories. The higher and the lower educated react differently to a society in which traditional Christian institutions no longer provide social life with unambiguous meaning. The lower educated who cannot draw upon traditional guidelines of thinking, feeling and acting are more culturally insecure than their higher educated counterparts, and because cultural insecurity provides a fertile breeding ground for ethnic intolerance, the post-Christian lower educated are ethnically intolerant, while the post-Christian higher educated are ethnically tolerant. In the Netherlands, the waning of Christian morality has thus spawned a new post-Christian cultural conflict about the question how to deal with ethnic diversity. As this conflict pitches the higher and lower educated against one another, the strongly secularized Netherlands is not just one nation without God, as Lechner (2008: 135, see also Lechner 1996) argues, but consists of two nations without God.

Apart from these insights into the cultural consequences of secularization, our results are relevant for scholars studying tolerance in a wider sense. Our study demonstrates that it is important to disentangle Christian morality from ethnic intolerance analytically as well as empirically. In the standard research practice, Christian morality is lumped together with authoritarianism and other measures of ethnic intolerance as indicators of some sort of overall intolerance or cultural conservatism (see Achterberg 2006a, 2006b, Achterberg and Houtman 2006, Flanagan and Lee 2003, Fleishman 1988, Flere 2007, Middendorp 1989, Vollebergh et al. 1999), but our study demonstrates that this is problematic since post-Christian morality and ethnic tolerance only go hand in hand among the higher educated. It therefore is problematic to, for example, consider tolerance of homosexuality 'a sensitive indicator of tolerance towards outgroups in general' (Inglehart and Welzel 2005: 56, see also Inglehart et al. 2008: 267).

Because we have only presented cross-sectional analyses for the Netherlands, strategically selected as one of the most secularized and morally permissive countries in the world, our findings clearly invite comparisons across time and between countries. A first important question for future research is whether due to the unfolding of processes of secularization, polarization over issues of Christian morality is perhaps giving way to the new type of cultural polarization that we find in the Netherlands today. If, indeed, a post-Christian polarization between the lower-educated and higher-educated secular segments of society about issues of ethnic diversity is increasingly replacing cultural polarization over issues of Christian morality, such would clearly contradict the familiar argument that cultural polarization in the West increasingly pits the religious and the secular against one another about Christian moral issues in particular (Inglehart and Baker 2000, Inglehart and Welzel 2005, see for a recent overview Fiorina and Abrams 2008). A second question for future research extends our analysis to a comparison between countries. Although the Netherlands is a vanguard of secularism (Norris and Inglehart 2004, see also Lechner 1996, 2008), and as such an atypical yet ideal case to study the issue at hand, other Western countries are, of course, also experiencing processes of secularization (Norris and Inglehart 2004). This informs the hypothesis that countries characterized by lower levels of Christian morality feature less polarization over Christian morality and more over multiculturalism and ethnic diversity.

Obviously, the case of the United States stands out for special attention, because it features higher levels of Christian religiosity than all other Western countries (Norris and Inglehart 2004), giving rise to the question whether our theoretical notions apply to the United States as well. On the one hand, American debates about the so-called 'culture wars' (Fiorina and Abrams 2008) and the 'new political culture' (Clark 1996, Clark and Hoffmann-Martinot 1998, Clark and Rempel 1997) seem to point in the direction of increased cultural polarization in the United States. On the other hand, these cultural conflicts seem to focus on moral issues such as abortion and homosexuality, which makes them radically different from the post-Christian type of cultural polarization found for the Netherlands. Recent studies have, however, cast doubt on the prevalence of conflict about these moral issues in the United States (see Fiorina et al. 2005, Fischer and Hout 2006, Hetherington 2009). Our theory suggests that a new cultural polarization may be on the rise in the United States, too, because the trend in Christian religiosity is unmistakably downward in this country as well (Hout and Fischer 2002, Norris and Inglehart 2004). Perhaps zooming in on the small but increasing proportion of the secular in the United States may hence produce surprising findings that may tell much about the new cultural conflicts that are looming as secularization proceeds in the United States.

Chapter 9
Secular Intolerance in a Post-Christian Society: The Case of Islam in the Netherlands

With Samira van Bohemen and Roy Kemmers

Introduction

The rise of populist anti-immigration parties in Western Europe has received wide attention in the scholarly literature (for example, Fennema 2005, Ignazi 1992, 2003, Kitschelt 1997, Minkenberg 1992, Van der Brug 2003). Time and again, researchers have concluded that support for such parties is mostly found among the lower educated (for example, Achterberg 2006a, 2006b, Houtman et al. 2008a, Kitschelt 1995, Minkenberg 1992). They are the ones who form 'an electoral potential ..., which feels attracted to an anti-immigrant message' (Van der Brug 2003: 103). Of course, this is hardly surprising given the consistent finding that the lower educated are more ethnically intolerant than the higher educated (Adorno et al. 1950, Dekker and Ester 1987, Grabb 1979, 1980, Lipset 1981, Lipsitz 1965).

In this light it is, however, highly remarkable that contemporary Dutch anti-immigrant politicians and opinion leaders have adopted a discourse that does not consist of plain ethnocentrism. Instead, their anti-immigrant arguments focus on a secular-liberal rejection of Islam, which in their view supports a system of beliefs that undermines democracy and threatens the rights of women and homosexuals (Uitermark 2010). The late populist politician Pim Fortuyn, for instance, labeled Islam as 'backward' and explained his discontent by saying, 'I don't feel like doing the emancipation of women and homosexuals all over again' (*de Volkskrant*, February 9, 2002).[1] A few years later, the Dutch feminist political activist Ayaan Hirsi Ali claimed that 'A large majority of Muslim women is beaten and enslaved. Given my liberal conviction, it is about time that I speak out against this practice.'[2] In a similar vein, the late Islam-critic Theo van Gogh argued that '[Muslims] hate our freedom' and that 'it is their conviction that the godless Netherlands should be destroyed' (2003: 103).

---

1   We have translated all quotes from opinion leaders and respondents from Dutch.

2   Available at: http://www.vpro.nl/programma/zomergasten/afleveringen/17869746/items/18934598/ [accessed: February 21, 2011].

Paradoxes of Individualization

Whereas anti-immigrant sentiments have traditionally been studied as expressions of ethnocentrism (for example, Billiet and De Witte 1995, Eisinga and Scheepers 1989, Pettigrew 1998, Poynting and Mason 2007), this secular liberal discourse suggests that there is more to contemporary Dutch Islam criticism than plain fear of the Other. As observed by Canovan, Dutch populists' 'reasons for opposing Muslim immigration and multicultural policies found some echoes on the Left' and '[cannot] simply be dismissed as right-wing xenophobia' (2005: 75-6). And Dutch sociologist Duyvendak states: 'this is the [present-day] paradox: the native Dutch population employs its widely shared values of tolerance to stigmatize and exclude Islamic immigrants' (2004: 13, our translation from Dutch). It is, however, still an open question whether the embracement of liberal values not only underlies rejectionist sentiments toward Islam among Dutch opinion leaders, but also among the public at large, and how this relates to the ethnocentric attitudes on which studies normally focus. Moreover, the observation that exclusionist parties, which typically receive support from the lower educated, employ a secular liberal discourse that is normally assumed to be distinctive of the higher educated (Houtman 2003) raises the question of whether and how educational groups differ when it comes to the relationship between a secular liberal discourse and anti-Islam sentiments. In order to empirically address these questions, we first discuss the relevant literature below.

Secular Intolerance of Islam in a Post-Christian Society

Standard Explanations: Ethnocentrism and Cultural Reification

In the social sciences a well-established research practice—which dates back to the 1950s, when Adorno et al. first published his seminal work *The Authoritarian Personality*—explains negative views on immigration, multiculturalism and ethnic diversity from ethnocentric prejudice (for example, Eisinga and Scheepers 1989, Lipset 1959, McDill 1961, Roberts and Rokeach 1956). Ethnocentrism refers to 'a tendency in the individual to be "ethnically centered," to be rigid in his acceptance of the culturally "alike" (the in-group) and in his rejection of the "unlike" (the out-group)' (Adorno et al. 1950: 102). Numerous studies have demonstrated that this 'cultural narrowness' is a major cause of negative sentiments toward minorities (for example, Billiet and De Witte 1995, Eisinga and Scheepers 1989, Pettigrew 1998, Poynting and Mason 2007). Moreover, it has frequently been shown that the lower educated are more ethnically intolerant than the higher educated (Adorno et al. 1950, Dekker and Ester 1987, Grabb 1979, 1980, Lipset 1981, Lipsitz 1965), resulting from their inability to handle cultural differences (Achterberg and Houtman 2009, McDill 1961, Van der Waal et al. 2010).

Drawing on Berger and Luckmann (1966), Gabennesch (1972) provides an interpretation of these findings by means of his conception of a 'reified' worldview. According to Gabennesch (1972: 858), 'the most crucial consequence of education

... is its tendency to broaden, multiply, and diversify the individual's sociocultural perspectives ... He may learn that his way of looking at things is just one of a surprisingly wide range of possible perspectives' some of which may 'diverge from frames of reference whose unrivaled supremacy the individual has accepted for years.' This 'breadth of perspective' is, however, greater among the higher educated. Their ability 'to recognize culture as socially produced and contingent' renders them tolerant of other cultures (Van der Waal 2010: 116). Gabennesch (1972: 863) argues that the lower educated, by contrast, maintain a 'view of social reality as if it were fixed instead of in process, absolute instead of relative, natural instead of general, as a product of forces which are more than human.' In other words, the lower educated reify their own ingroup culture and by consequence reject outgroup cultures.

Such differences between the lower and the higher educated may also be reflected in their attitudes toward Islam. Descriptive research indicates that no less than three-quarter of the lower educated in the Netherlands consider a Muslim way of life irreconcilable with Western values, against only one-third of the higher educated (Gijsberts and Lubbers 2009: 276). Cultural reification among the lower educated may provide an explanation for this difference. If this is actually the case, it is to be expected that the lower educated reject Islam because they are ethnocentric (hypothesis 1).

Although this explanation of negative sentiments toward Islam will most likely prove valid, it may only partly explain why so many lower educated in the Netherlands are attracted to an anti-Islam message. After all, what is remarkable about the case of Islam in contemporary Dutch public opinion is that rejection is justified from a distinctly secular liberal discourse (Korteweg 2006, Sniderman and Hagendoorn 2007, Sniderman et al. 2003). This discourse is constructed around core values of the Dutch present-day post-Christian society, such as individual liberty, gender equality and tolerance. Political protagonists of anti-Islam feelings like Fortuyn, Hirsi Ali, Van Gogh and Wilders argue that Islam threatens these values, framing it as a 'backward' culture (Korteweg 2006). Leftist politicians commonly respond by arguing that the real threat to the Dutch liberal morality is not Islam, but *intolerance* of Islam (Uitermark 2010). This suggests that a liberal morality holds different meanings for different social groups. This suggestion is elaborated upon below.

Secular Aversion to Religious Orthodoxy

The counter culture of the 1960s and 1970s played a decisive role in shaping the present-day liberal Dutch society. During this period, the Netherlands moved from being a highly 'pillarized' society in which the Christian churches played a crucial role, to becoming a secular society. The total amount of non-religious people rose from only 24 percent in 1958 to a majority of 63 percent in 2006. Both the Roman Catholic and the Protestant churches endured heavy blows to their congregation. Membership of the Roman Catholic Church dropped from 42 percent in 1958 to a mere 16 percent in 2006, and membership of the Protestant churches dropped from 32 percent in 1958 to only 14 percent in 2006 (Becker and De Wit 2000, Bernts et al. 2007).

In less than half a century, the Netherlands became a post-Christian society. A traditional morality made way for a cultural climate in which individual liberty and self-determination are leading principles (Inglehart 1997). Progressive ideas pertaining to the position of women and homosexuals are nowadays supported by the majority of the population, by both the higher and the lower educated (Duyvendak 2004, Keuzenkamp 2010). While the Christian churches lost their grounds, Islam became a more prominent player in the Dutch religious landscape, however. The minority groups that adhere to this religion seemingly support an orthodox morality and it is considered unlikely that they will give up on their religious beliefs in the same manner as the Dutch natives did (Becker et al. 1997). Now, how does the dominant Dutch liberal moral order relate to such a new presumedly orthodox religious minority?

Liberal values of individual liberty and tolerance are conventionally considered in non-reified terms. As such, they go hand in hand with relativism as a moral stance. Charles Taylor (1991), for instance, argued that ideas on proper conduct differ widely across post-Christian societies. As such, it has according to Taylor become a moral position not to judge the others' values and ways of life. The anthropologist Ahmed (1991: 213) contends that this 'turn towards a spirit of pluralism' also increases acceptance of Islam. He argues that when individual liberty and tolerance become unquestioned ideals, cultural differences lose their significance, so that a dialogue between the 'West' and Islam becomes possible. More concretely, what is argued here is that the relativism implied by a secular liberal morality goes together with acceptance of Islam. However, this most likely only goes for the higher educated, since they are inclined to have a non-reified outlook on culture. It thus seems that they are the ones who defend liberal relativism as a moral imperative.

This only represents one side of the coin, however. Sniderman et al. (2003) have shown that many Dutch natives openly condemn orthodox Muslim practices on the basis of a liberal value orientation (see also Sniderman and Hagendoorn 2007). In a similar vein, other studies have demonstrated that particularly liberal seculars reject orthodox Islamic practices such as the wearing of an Islamic veil (Saroglou et al. 2009, see also Sayyid 2009). These findings suggest that a liberal morality can also be reified, leading to a rejection of religiously orthodox belief systems. In this case, secular liberalism itself operates as a moral imperative: people essentialize values of individual liberty and tolerance and try to defend them *vis-à-vis* value systems that are considered to be at odds with this secular liberal morality (Duyvendak 2004, Lechner 2008). If this is actually the case, we should find that a liberal morality leads to rejection of Islam because of aversion to religious orthodoxy (hypothesis 2). Since the lower educated are generally disposed to cultural reification, they are most likely also the ones who are inclined to essentialize liberal values. If this is actually the case, a rejection of Islam out of aversion to religious orthodoxy is only to be found among the lower educated (hypothesis 3).

Should these hypotheses be confirmed, one question remains: how is the rejection of Islam on the basis of liberal essentialism related to the standard explanation that focuses on ethnocentrism? Although political protagonists of anti-Islam sentiments reject allegations of ethnocentrism and racism and claim that they are opposed to Islam purely on the basis of their liberal convictions, some argue that liberal intolerance of Islam is just another expression of ethnic intolerance (for example, Fekete 2004, Kundnani 2007). If this is the case indeed, we should find that aversion to religious orthodoxy only leads to a rejection of Islam among people who are ethnocentric (hypothesis 4).

Data and Methods

We have conducted our study by means of a triangular approach, combining analyses of survey data with qualitative analyses of focus group data. Because we are concerned with secular intolerance of Islam stemming from aversion to religious orthodoxy, we have selected the respondents not belonging to a religious denomination (N = 1,023) from our 2008 survey (see Chapter 8 of this book for details). This sample is representative for the secular Dutch population aged 16 years or older.

In addition, we have collected focus group data. A focus group can be described as 'a small group discussion focused on a particular topic and facilitated by a researcher' (Tonkiss 2004: 194). It can serve as a valuable addition to survey data, as 'people's knowledge and attitudes are not entirely encapsulated in reasoned responses to direct questions. Everyday forms of communication may tell as much, if not more, about what people know or experience' (Kitzinger 1995: 299). Focus groups are especially suited 'for exploring the attitudes, opinions, meanings and definitions *on the participants' own terms*' (Tonkiss 2004: 206, our emphasis, see also Cronin 2008: 234). In order to arrive at an understanding of both higher and lower educated natives' ways of discussing how to deal with an ethnically diverse landscape, we analyze the data of two focus groups, held with higher educated (university level—HE) and lower educated (not more than secondary education—LE) participants respectively.

A research team recruited the participants for the focus groups through their personal networks. They contacted people they were acquainted with personally or professionally, asking them if they knew any higher or lower educated natives who might be willing to join a discussion about living in an ethnically diverse society, after which the research team contacted the potential participants. The higher educated focus group consisted of 2 men and 3 women, the lower educated focus group of 2 men and 4 women. Such modestly sized groups are manageable without much interference of the moderator (Peek and Fothergill 2009: 37-8, see also Morgan 1997) and they tend to result in richer data than larger groups do

(Cronin 2008: 235). All respondents were between 30 and 65 years old and lived in or around the city of Rotterdam.

The group discussions were held in a conference room on the campus of Erasmus University Rotterdam during the summer of 2009. They lasted between 1.5 and 2 hours and were audio recorded and transcribed.[3] The discussions were moderated by a senior researcher, who introduced himself and the goal of the project before the discussion. He told the participants that we were interested to hear about the way they think and feel about living in an ethnically and culturally diverse society. The participants were encouraged to speak freely by explaining that 'right' or 'wrong' answers or opinions do not exist in this type of research. Moreover, they were given the guarantee that their opinions would be reported anonymously. The only rules stated were that the participants let each other finish, both for the clarity of the discussion and to facilitate transcription (and, by implication, analysis).

Measurement

Rejection of Islam was measured by means of six Likert-type items referring to issues concerning the place of Islam in Dutch society. Respondents were asked to indicate whether they agreed (1 totally disagree, 2 disagree, 3 neither agree nor disagree, 4 agree, 5 totally agree) with the following statements: 1) The Islamic tradition suits the Netherlands; 2) Muslims are good people; 3) I think that rightist parties are too extreme about Islam; 4) I think the Islam poses no problem to Dutch society; 5) In the Netherlands there is no room for Islam; 6) It is right that Islam is seen as a threat to our modern society. The 'don't know' answers were coded as missing, and the first four items were recoded. Factor analysis of the responses to these six items showed that there was a first factor with an eigenvalue of 3.44 explaining 57 percent of the variance. We have constructed a scale for rejection of Islam (Cronbach's $\alpha = 0.85$) by calculating the mean score for respondents who have valid scores on at least five of the six items.

Ethnocentrism was measured by means of six Likert-type items, four of which derived from the ethnocentrism scale created by Eisinga and Scheepers (1989), which measures negative prejudice toward outgroups. Respondents were asked whether they agreed (1 totally disagree, 2 disagree, 3 neither agree nor disagree, 4 agree, 5 totally agree) with the following statements: 1) Foreigners carry all kinds of dirty smells around; 2) With Moroccans you never know for certain whether or not they are going to be aggressive; 3) Most people from Surinam work quite slowly; 4) Most Turks are rather self-indulgent at work; 5) Foreigners living in the Netherlands should adapt to Dutch uses and customs; 6) The Netherlands should have never let foreign guest workers in our country. The 'don't know'

---

3   Devorah van den Berg's assistance in the transcription of the data is gratefully acknowledged.

answers were again coded as missing. Factor analysis revealed a first factor with an eigenvalue of 3.60, explaining 60 percent of the variance. We have constructed a scale for ethnocentrism (Cronbach's $\alpha = 0.86$) by calculating the mean score for respondents who have valid scores on at least four of the six items.

Aversion to religious orthodoxy was measured by means of seven Likert-type items. Respondents were asked whether they agreed (1 totally disagree, 2 disagree, 3 neither agree nor disagree, 4 agree, 5 totally agree) with the following statements: 1) Religious people are entitled to demand from the Dutch government that euthanasia is prohibited; 2) Religious people are entitled to demand from the Dutch government that abortion is prohibited; 3) Religious political parties are entitled to refuse homosexuals in their committee; 4) A religious leader is entitled to state out of his convictions that homosexuality is a disease that should be combated; 5) Religious men are entitled to demand from their wives that they cover their bodies when entering the public realm; 6) A religious leader is entitled to refuse to shake hands with a woman out of his convictions; 7) Religious primary schools are entitled to demand participation with prayer also of the non-religious children. The 'don't know' answers were again coded as missing. Factor analysis revealed one factor with an eigenvalue of 3.57, explaining 51 percent of the variance. After recoding all items, a scale (Cronbach's $\alpha = 0.83$) was constructed by calculating the mean scores for respondents with valid scores on at least six of these seven items.

Liberal morality was measured by means of seven Likert-type items indicating rejection of gender traditionalism and acceptance of progressive ideas on euthanasia and abortion. Respondents were asked whether they agreed (1 totally disagree, 2 disagree, 3 neither agree nor disagree, 4 agree, 5 totally agree) with the following statements: 1) In a firm it is unnatural when women hold positions of authority over men. 2) It is not as important for a girl to get a good education as it is for a boy; 3) After all boys can be educated more freely than girls; 4) A woman is more capable of bringing up small children than a man; 5) It should be possible that a doctor can relieve a person on his own request from his lively misery through euthanasia; 6) It is acceptable for a married couple to decide on principles not to have children although there are no medical objections; 7) It should be possible for a woman to have an abortion when she decides this. Again, the 'don't know' answers were coded as missing. Factor analysis revealed a first factor with an eigenvalue of 2.29, explaining 33 percent of the variance. After recoding the first four items, we have constructed a scale (Cronbach's $\alpha = 0.63$) by calculating the mean scores for respondents with valid scores on at least six of these seven items.

Educational level was measured by the highest level of education attained. We constructed a dichotomous variable, distinguishing between the higher educated (those who completed upper general intermediate school, higher vocational or university education; 48.2 percent) and the lower educated (those with lower levels of education; 51.4 percent). We also constructed a variable measuring the years needed to attain a specific level of education (ranging from 8 to 18 years), which is used in the regression analyses on the general secular population.

Two other control variables are included in the regression analyses. We controlled for the respondent's *age* (in years) and *gender*, which is coded 1 for males (53.5 percent) and 2 for females (46.5 percent).

Results

Cultural Conflict in a Liberal Moral Order?

In contemporary social sciences it is commonly asserted that secularization in the Netherlands gave way to a progressive liberal morality, in which values of individual liberty and tolerance are unequivocally supported by both the higher and the lower educated secular natives (Duyvendak 2004, Keuzenkamp 2010). At the same time, however, the higher and the lower educated differ when it comes to ethnic tolerance: in a highly secularized country such as the Netherlands a cultural conflict exists between the secular higher and lower educated (see Chapter 8 of this book). In order to assess what this means for the debate around Islam, we present the main parameters of this conflict in Table 9.1.

This table indicates that there are no major differences between higher and lower educated secular natives when it comes to the importance they attach to liberal values. Although the higher educated are somewhat more inclined to support a liberal morality (t (994) = -4.34; p < 0.001), the means of both groups are very high. This can also be exemplified with the total percentage of secular natives who disagree with traditional gender roles. For instance, 93 percent of the secular respondents rejects the idea that 'it is unnatural when a woman in an enterprise has leadership over a male co-worker.' These results substantiate the idea that liberal values are unequivocally supported by secular Dutch natives, no matter their educational background.

From the focus group discussions a similar picture emerges. Both the higher educated and the lower educated participants stress the importance they attach to the rights of women and homosexuals. Participant Jan Willem (HE), for instance, says that Dutch society is marked by its 'Western ideals: democracy, freedom of speech, equal rights for people: women, men, gays, etcetera. We should really stand for that.' Among the lower educated, similar attitudes are expressed. Participant Jannie (LE), for example, states that 'If you come to live here, you should be informed that there are gays here and that that's allowed and okay. And that a woman has just as many rights and is worth just as much as anyone.' This further illustrates that these liberal moral values pertaining to the rights of women and homosexuals are subscribed to by both the higher and the lower educated natives (Lechner 2008).

Another commonality between the secular higher and lower educated is that they combine this liberal value orientation with an aversion to religious orthodoxy. Table 9.1 shows that the higher and lower educated share an aversion to religious orthodoxy (t (974) = 1.06; p > 0.05). Again, scores are unanimously high. For

Table 9.1   Means and standard deviations of key variables, by level of education

	Mean (higher educated)	SD (higher educated)	Mean (lower educated)	SD (lower educated)	N
Liberal morality	4.26	0.49	4.12	0.53	996
Aversion to religious orthodoxy	4.33	0.73	4.37	0.67	955
Ethnocentrism	2.19	0.80	2.64	0.86	966
Rejection of Islam	2.66	0.87	2.96	0.86	976

instance, 80 percent of the secular natives rejects the idea that 'religious people are entitled to demand of the Dutch government that euthanasia is prohibited', and 82 percent rejects the idea that 'religious political parties are entitled to refuse homosexuals in their party committee.' Whereas the higher and lower educated do not differ in their aversion to religious orthodoxy, they do differ when it comes to tolerance to ethnic diversity. The lower educated are much more ethnocentric than the higher educated (t (953) = 8.32; p < 0.001) and they are also more inclined toward a rejection of Islam (t (964) = 5.39; p < 0.001).

How can this difference in rejection of Islam between the higher educated and the lower educated be explained? The finding that higher and lower educated secular natives all value a liberal morality, while they differ in their rejection of Islam, gives us reason to assume that liberal morality has different meanings for both social categories, sparking different stances toward religiously orthodox minority groups.

Rejection of Islam among the Lower Educated: A Matter of Cultural Reification?

Rejection of cultural diversity among the lower educated is conventionally understood as ethnocentric prejudice. This is the classical theoretical model of cultural reification, in which the lower educated are considered intolerant because of their 'cultural narrowness' (Adorno et al. 1950, see also Gabennesch 1972). Our first hypothesis predicts exactly this, that the lower educated reject Islam more so than the higher educated, because they are more ethnocentric. We tested this hypothesis by means of regression analysis (see Table 9.2).

Model 1 of Table 9.2 shows that the lower educated are indeed more inclined to reject Islam than the higher educated. Furthermore, model 2 shows that this is due to the fact that they are more ethnocentric: the negative relationship between level of education and rejection of Islam disappears completely as soon as ethnocentrism is taken into account, which has a strong positive effect on rejection of Islam. These findings corroborate our first hypothesis. The lower educated reject Islam more than the higher educated do, because of ethnocentric prejudice. This is,

Table 9.2   **Secular rejection of Islam explained by education, ethnocentrism, liberal morality, and aversion to religious orthodoxy (standardized coefficients, N=910)**

Independents	Model 1	Model 2	Model 3	Model 4
Educational level	-0.19***	-0.02 ns	-0.02 ns	-0.02 ns
Ethnocentrism		0.70***	0.69***	0.68***
Liberal morality			-0.03 ns	-0.06*
Aversion to religious orthodoxy				0.10***
Age	-0.08*	-0.10***	-0.11***	-0.11***
Female	-0.03 ns	0.00 ns	0.01 ns	0.00 ns
R^2	0.04	0.50	0.50	0.51

ns not significant; * $p < 0.05$; ** $p < 0.01$; ***$p < 0.001$

however, not a new insight—it rather confirms countless studies that have found that the lower educated are more inclined to reify their own ingroup culture, while simultaneously dismissing outgroup cultures (for example, Adorno et al. 1950, Dekker and Ester 1987, Grabb 1979, 1980, Lipset 1981, Lipsitz 1965).

With regard to negative sentiments toward Islam, we theorized that a liberal morality can itself also be reified so as to produce a form of liberal exclusionism. Adding liberal morality to our analysis in model 3 seemingly does not yield any effect. Model 4, however, demonstrates that this is because the negative relationship between liberal morality and rejection of Islam was suppressed. These findings indicate that those with a more liberal morality are, on the one hand, more positive toward Islam, whereas, on the other hand, they are more averse to religious orthodoxy, which in turn leads to a rejection of Islam. These findings corroborate our second hypothesis.

The important question that remains is if this tendency to essentialize liberalism is typical for the lower educated (as is the case with cultural reification in general), while the higher educated relativize it. If this is the case, we should find that for the lower educated aversion to religious orthodoxy leads to rejection of Islam, while this is not the case for the higher educated. In order to test this third hypothesis, we have constructed path models for the lower and higher educated respectively (see Figure 9.1 and 9.2).

Figure 9.1 shows that aversion toward religious orthodoxy indeed sparks rejection of Islam among the lower educated. This is, however, not the case for the higher educated (see Figure 9.2), for whom no such relationship exists. These findings are in line with our third hypothesis. Although the higher and the lower educated are equally intolerant of religious orthodoxy, only the latter essentialize it with the effect of rejecting Islam.

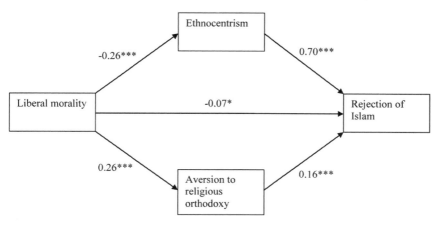

*p<0.05, **p<0.01, ***p<0.001; R^2 Rejection of Islam = 0.55,
R^2 Aversion to religious orthodoxy = 0.07, R^2 Ethnocentrism = 0.07
(Model controlled for age and gender)

**Figure 9.1   Secular rejection of Islam among the lower educated explained
by ethnocentrism, liberal morality, and aversion to religious
orthodoxy (standardized coefficients, one-sided tests, N=437)**

In the focus groups, these differences can be observed in more detail. Typical cases
are discussions on 'Islamic' practices of gender inequality, such as the practice
of men and women not shaking hands, marrying off, headscarves and burkas
(Sniderman and Hagendoorn 2007). When the lower educated natives discuss
the hand shaking practice, participant Richard (LE) argues that it is a manner of
politeness to shake hands and that refusing to do so is 'anti-social and insulting.'
Jannie (LE) says that refusing to shake hands is a sign of an 'utter lack of respect
for the person in front of you'—she calls the practice 'humiliating' and adds that
'[i]f you don't support such things, then you shouldn't come to live in a country
like [the Netherlands].' In the higher educated natives' focus group, on the other
hand, participant Caro (HE) states that '[t]he question of course is how much
assimilation you ask of people. I mean, the fact that relations between men and
women are different among Turks and Moroccans should not be an objection ...
unless it leads to excesses. That's when you have to intervene. But consider the
example of the hand shake. Do you mind that?' Maartje (HE) responds by saying
that 'I think those things are often made into such an issue.'

The higher educated natives often relativize the practices under discussion.
For instance, when discussing headscarves Maartje (HE) says she 'can remember
a picture that went all around the world of [former] Queen Juliana wearing a
headscarf. My mother also wore a headscarf whenever she left the house', to
which Henk (HE) adds 'moreover, in the whole of Gelderland [a Dutch province]
they walk around wearing those. ... ten years ago or so, you saw the same in

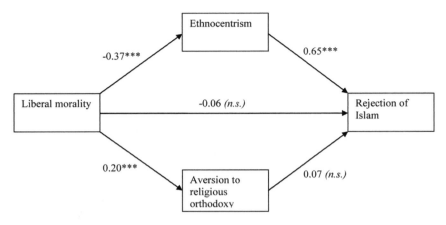

*p<0.05, **p<0.01, ***p <0.001; R^2 Rejection of Islam = 0.46,
R^2 Aversion to religious orthodoxy = 0.06, R^2 Ethnocentrism = 0.14
(Model controlled for age and gender)

**Figure 9.2   Secular rejection of Islam among the higher educated
explained by ethnocentrism, liberal morality, and aversion to
religious orthodoxy (standardized coefficients, one-sided tests,
N=473)**

other provinces. Girls wear skirts because they're not allowed to wear trousers.
I'm just saying.' And on the topic of marrying off, even though they agree that it
is undesirable, Maartje (HE) says that it happens less and less: 'of course, there's
always a certain group, but then I think in Staphorst [a Dutch Christian orthodox
town] you're also not allowed to decide for yourself who you marry', to which Henk
responds by saying that 'of course you can say marrying off isn't right. But what
you see nowadays in the Netherlands with people marrying too soon or having a
promiscuous lifestyle. That's not really splendid either.' Thus, the higher educated
natives relativize these practices by emphasizing that 'things like that' are not worse
than various Dutch cultural practices.

The lower educated see it the other way around. Participant Richard (LE)
argues that 'I think marrying off in itself does not have to be bad by definition, if
it's customary for certain people.' However, he continues by saying that 'when you
come to the Netherlands ... where other moral and social rules apply ... you should
ask yourself if you shouldn't adapt to those.' Angelique (LE) agrees and suggests
that 'there should be a questionnaire at the border with these things. You don't agree?
Then you're not allowed in. As a matter of speech.' The overall difference is that the
lower educated natives think that the liberal moral order needs to be defended by
taking measures, while the higher educated are reluctant to argue for interventions,
because they think that giving room for differences is an important part of those
liberal values.

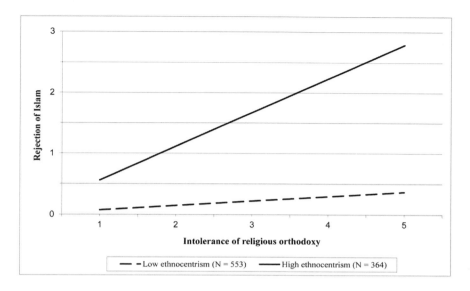

Figure 9.3   The relationship between aversion to religious orthodoxy and rejection of Islam, by level of ethnocentrism

Essentializing and Relativizing a Liberal Morality: The Basis of Cultural Conflict?

Now that we have established that the secular lower educated reject Islam because they essentialize liberal values, the question is how this relates to the standard explanation that focuses on ethnocentrism. Whereas critics of Islam commonly portray their fight as an aim to defend liberal values, others have suggested that liberal criticism of Islam is simply another expression of ethnic intolerance. In order to find out which is the case, we test our fourth hypothesis, which holds that aversion to religious orthodoxy only leads to a rejection of Islam among people who are ethnocentric. To do so, we have conducted regression analyses for those scoring high on ethnocentrism (> 2.5) and those scoring low (≤ 2.5) (see Figure 9.3).

Although no direct relationship exists between aversion to religious orthodoxy and ethnocentrism (Pearson's $r = -0.002$; $p > 0.05$), Figure 9.3 shows that aversion to religious orthodoxy only leads to rejection of Islam among people who are ethnocentric. Only the ethnocentric secular reject Islam because they are averse to religious orthodoxy: the relationship is insignificant ($p > 0.05$) for those who are not ethnocentric. This corroborates our fourth hypothesis. Secular people who are intolerant of ethnic diversity in general also reject Islam on the basis of aversion to religious orthodoxy inspired by liberal values. Because the lower educated are generally more ethnocentric than the higher educated, they are also the ones who are the most likely to essentialize their own liberal values in order to strengthen their exclusionist stance.

It is particularly clear from the focus group data that this difference between the liberal relativism of the secular higher educated and the liberal essentialism of the secular lower educated is a source of cultural conflict between both social groups: the higher and lower educated problematize *each other's* positions when it comes to discussions on ethnic tolerance. For instance, in the lower educated focus group Richard (LE) states that he thinks that 'our idea of a free country has gone out of hand. Anything goes nowadays', to which Jan cynically responds 'anything is possible, right?' 'Yes that's it, it's just out of control', Richard continues, 'I think the Netherlands have gone backwards in that sense very fast. Everything should be meddled with, just to be as tolerant as possible.' Angelique (LE) also thinks that 'there's just too little authority. It has gone so far that now we are in a real mess. ... They're letting things go too far.' So for this group, 'tolerance' is not a virtue, but an allegation toward people ('they') who are letting things go out of control.

The participants in the higher educated group, on the other hand, consider the problematization of ethnic diversity troublesome. Maartje (HE) says she thinks 'problems often have more to do with poverty than with people's cultural backgrounds', to which Jan Willem (HE) adds that problems with ethnic minorities are 'turned into a cultural difference by certain politicians.' José (HE) argues that 'in fact, every problem is viewed from a cultural background instead of from the actual problem', even 'to the point that everything is larded with cultural background.' So, while the lower educated participants problematize an abundance of tolerance (which is typically advocated by the higher educated), the higher educated criticize the problematization of cultural difference (which is typically advocated by the lower educated).

This indicates that the secular lower and the higher educated do not only diverge when it comes to the way they evaluate Islam in the light of their own liberal values: they also portray each other as part of the problem they perceive, which indicates that a conflict exists between both groups.

Conclusion

In this chapter we addressed the prevalence of anti-Islam sentiments in the post-Christian Dutch society. While previous studies have interpreted such sentiments as the result of ethnocentric prejudice (for example, Billiet and De Witte 1995, Pettigrew 1998)—which forms a standard explanation for negative stances *vis-à-vis* minorities—contemporary Dutch Islam criticism in the public debate has attained a distinctly liberal character, indicating that there seems to be more to it than 'classical' prejudice. Therefore, we have assessed whether and how anti-Islam sentiments among the general population are related to a liberal morality, how this differs between educational groups, and how this is related to the commonly used explanation pertaining to ethnocentric prejudice.

We have found that liberal values pertaining to gender roles are uncontested among both higher and lower educated Dutch natives (Duyvendak 2004). For the lower educated, this liberal morality proved to function as an additional source of rejection of Islam, based on aversion to religious orthodoxy. They are not only intolerant of Islam because of their ethnocentric prejudice, but also because they tend to essentialize their liberal moral values. The higher educated, in contrast, take a relativist position: for them, the importance they attach to a liberal morality does not inspire intolerance of Islam. Finally, following up on suggestions that liberal intolerance of Islam is simply another expression of ethnic intolerance (Fekete 2004, Kundnani 2007), we have demonstrated that liberal moral values are only employed to reject Islam by those who are ethnocentric.

This sheds light on the 'Dutch paradox of tolerance' that emerged with the rise of Dutch anti-Islam politics from 2002 onwards, most notably represented by the late Pim Fortuyn and Geert Wilders respectively: how can anti-Islam sentiments receive so much support in a country famous for its tolerance? Our findings indicate that ideals of individual liberty and tolerance do not unequivocally create a situation in which tolerance of cultural diversity prevails (Taylor 1991, see also Galston 1995): they can also function as a moral imperative according to which insufficient adherence to such values forms a basis for exclusion.

In addition, our results do not only show that higher and lower educated natives differ regarding the acceptance or rejection of Islam, they also indicate that these differences are a source of conflict between these two groups. Both the higher and the lower educated (implicitly) point out the other group as the source of a cultural conflict between the Dutch native majority and Islamic minorities. While the higher educated claim that conflicts between the Dutch native majority and Muslim minorities are aggravated by the rejectionist discourses of the lower educated, the latter accuse the former of providing too much room for anti-liberal Islamic practices. This opposition is found more prominently in the political debates between, for instance, Labor Party (PvdA) leader Job Cohen and the anti-Islamic Freedom Party (PVV) leader Geert Wilders. The former accuses the latter for excluding Muslims in the same way as Jews were excluded in the beginning of WWII (*Vrij Nederland*, December 15, 2010), while Wilders accuses Cohen of 'putting the doors wide open for Islam', which he characterizes as 'having a moral agenda' consisting of 'the oppression of women' (*De Telegraaf*, March 25, 2010). Thus, while leftist politicians argue that Wilders's representation of Muslims is stereotypical and stigmatizes an entire minority group, the Islam critics argue that the higher educated cultural elite in the Netherlands has deliberately closed its eyes for the problems caused by Muslim minorities. This opposition, which is found both among the public and among politicians, politicizes a tendency of social scientists to suggest 'interventions aimed at reducing anti-Muslim feelings' consisting of 'improving people's attitudes' by means of '[a]n emphasis on cultural diversity and multicultural recognition' (González et al. 2008: 681). Since the Islam critics in the public discourse as well as the lower educated participants in our focus group problematize exactly this discourse of the promotion of multiculturalism, policy suggestions such as these are unlikely to remain uncontested.

Bibliography

Achterberg, P. 2006a. *Considering Cultural Conflict: Class Politics and Cultural Politics in Western Societies.* Maastricht: Shaker.

Achterberg, P. 2006b. Class voting in the new political culture: Economic, cultural and environmental voting in 20 Western countries. *International Sociology,* 21(2), 237-61.

Achterberg, P. and Houtman, D. 2006. Why do so many people vote 'unnaturally'? A cultural explanation for voting behaviour. *European Journal for Political Research,* 45(1), 75-92.

Achterberg, P. and Houtman, D. 2009. Ideologically 'illogical'? Why do the lower-educated Dutch display so little value coherence? *Social Forces,* 87(3), 1649-70.

Adams, J. and Roscigno, V.J. 2005. White supremacists, oppositional culture and the world wide web. *Social Forces,* 84(2), 759-78.

Adler, P.A. and Adler, P. 2008. The cyber worlds of self-injurers: Deviant communities, relationships, and selves. *Symbolic Interaction,* 31(1), 33-56.

Adorno, T.W., Frenkel-Brunswik, E., Levinson, D.L. and Nevitt Sandford, R. 1950. *The Authoritarian Personality.* New York: Harper & Row.

Ahmed, A. 1991. Postmodernist perceptions of Islam: Observing the observer. *Asian Survey,* 31(3), 213-31.

Alexander, J.C. 2003. *The Meanings of Social Life: A Cultural Sociology.* Oxford: Oxford University Press.

Alford, R.R. 1967. Class voting in the Anglo-American political systems, in *Party Systems and Voter Alignments: Cross-National Perspectives,* edited by S.M. Lipset and S. Rokkan. New York: Free Press, 67-93.

Altemeyer, B. 1988. *Enemies of Freedom: Understanding Right-Wing Authoritarianism.* San Francisco: Jossey-Bass.

Althusser, L. 2006 [1971]. Ideology and ideological state apparatuses (notes towards an investigation), in *Media and Cultural Studies: Keyworks,* edited by M.G. Durham and D.M. Kellner. Oxford: Blackwell, 79-87.

Atkinson, W. 2007. Anthony Giddens as adversary of class analysis. *Sociology,* 41(3), 533-49.

Aupers, S. 2004. *In de ban van moderniteit: De sacralisering van het zelf en computertechnologie* [Under the Spell of Modernity: The Sacralization of Self and Computer Technology]. Amsterdam: Aksant.

Aupers, S. 2005. 'We are all gods': New age in the Netherlands 1960-2000, in *The Dutch and Their Gods,* edited by E. Sengers. Hilversum: Verloren, 181-201.

Aupers, S. 2007. 'Better than the real world': On the reality and meaning of online computer games. *Fabula*, 48(3/4), 250-69.

Aupers, S. forthcoming. Enchantment Inc.: Online gaming between spiritual experience and commodity fetishism, in *Things: Religion and the Question of Materiality*, edited by D. Houtman and B. Meyer. New York: Fordham University Press.

Aupers, S. and Houtman, D. 2003. Oriental religion in the secular west: Globalization and religious diffusion. *Journal of National Development*, 16(1/2), 67-86.

Aupers, S. and Houtman, D. 2005. 'Reality sucks': On alienation and cybergnosis. *Concilium: International Journal of Theology*, 1, 81-9.

Aupers, S., Houtman, D. and Van der Tak, I. 2003. 'Gewoon worden wie je bent': Over authenticiteit en anti-institutionalisme ['Simply becoming who you are': On authenticity and anti-institutionalism]. *Sociologische Gids*, 50(2), 203-23.

Baber, B.J. 1999. Can't see the forest for the trees? *Legal Assistant Today*, 17 (September/October), 84-5.

Baerveldt, C. 1996. New Age-religiositeit als individueel constructieproces [New age-religiosity as a process of individual construction], in *De kool en de geit in de nieuwe tijd: Wetenschappelijke reflecties op New Age* [The Fence, the Hare, and the Hounds in the New Age: Scientific Reflections on New Age], edited by M. Moerland. Utrecht: Jan van Arkel, 19-31.

Bain, R. 1939. Cultural integration and social conflict. *American Journal of Sociology*, 44(4), 499-509.

Bakardjieva, M. 2005. *Internet Society: The Internet in Everyday Life*. London: Sage.

Barker, E. 1994. Whatever next?, in *Religions sans frontières: Present and Future Trends of Migration, Culture and Communication*, edited by R. Cipriani. Rome: Presidenza del Consiglio dei Ministri, 367-76.

Barlow, J.P. 1993. *A Declaration of the Independence of Cyberspace*. Available at: http://homes.eff.org/~barlow/Declaration-Final.html [accessed: September 20, 2008].

Barthes, R. 1986. *Mythologies*. London: Paladin.

Bartle, R.A. 2004. *Designing Virtual Worlds*. Berkeley, CA: New Riders Publishers.

Barzilai-Nahon, K. and Barzilai, G. 2005. Cultured technology: The Internet and religious fundamentalism, *The Information Society*, 21(1), 25-40.

Baudrillard, J. 1993 [1976]. *Symbolic Exchange and Death*. London: Sage.

Bauman, Z. 1987. *Legislators and Interpreters: On Modernity, Post-Modernity, and Intellectuals*. Cambridge: Polity Press.

Bauman, Z. 1995. *Life in Fragments: Essays in Postmodern Morality*. Oxford: Blackwell.

Bauman, Z. 1997. *Postmodernity and Its Discontents*. Cambridge: Polity Press.

Bauman, Z. 1998. *Globalization: The Human Consequences*. Cambridge: Polity Press.

Bauman, Z. 2000. *Liquid Modernity*. Cambridge: Polity Press.

Bauman, Z. 2001a. *The Individualized Society*. Cambridge: Polity Press.
Bauman, Z. 2001b. *Community: Seeking Safety in an Insecure World*. Cambridge: Polity Press.
Bauman, Z. 2004. *Identity*. Cambridge: Polity Press.
Beck, U. 1992. *Risk Society: Towards a New Modernity*. London: Sage.
Beck, U. and Beck-Gernsheim, E. 1996. Individualization and 'precarious freedoms': Perspectives and controversies of a subject-orientated sociology, in *Detraditionalization: Critical Reflections on Authority and Identity*, edited by P. Heelas, S. Lash and P. Morris. Oxford: Blackwell, 24-48.
Beck, U. and Beck-Gernsheim, E. 2002. *Individualization: Institutionalized Individualism and its Social and Political Consequences*. London: Sage.
Becker, H.S. 1966. *Outsiders: Studies in the Sociology of Deviance*. New York: Free Press.
Becker, J.W., De Hart, J. and Mens, J. 1997. *Secularisatie en alternatieve zingeving in Nederland* [Secularization and Alternative Religion in the Netherlands]. The Hague: SCP.
Becker, J.W. and De Wit, J.S.J. 2000. *Secularisatie in de jaren negentig: Kerklidmaatschap, veranderingen in opvattingen en een prognose* [Secularization in the Nineties: Church Membership, Changes in Attitudes and a Prognosis]. The Hague: SCP.
Bell, D. 1976. *The Cultural Contradictions of Capitalism*. New York: Basic Books.
Bellah, R.N., Madsen, R., Sullivan, W.M., Swidler, A. and Tipton, S.M. 1985. *Habits of the Heart: Individualism and Commitment in American Life*. New York: Harper & Row.
Bellah, R.N., Madsen, R., Sullivan, W.M., Swidler, A. and Tipton, S.M. 1992. *The Good Society*. New York: Vintage Books.
Benedikt, M. 1991. Introduction, in *Cyberspace: First Steps*, edited by M. Benedikt. Cambridge, MA: MIT Press, 1-25.
Berger, P.L., Berger, B. and Kellner, H. 1973. *The Homeless Mind: Modernization and Consciousness*. New York: Vintage Books.
Berger, P.L. and T. Luckmann. 1966. *The Social Construction of Reality: A Treatise in the Sociology of Knowledge*. New York: Doubleday.
Berlin, I. 1969. Two concepts of liberty, in I. Berlin, *Four Essays on Liberty*. London: Oxford University Press, 118-72.
Berman, M.A. 1999. New ideas, big ideas, fake ideas. *Across the Board*, 36(1), 28-32.
Bernts, T., Dekker, G. and De Hart, J. 2007. *God in Nederland 1996-2006* [God in the Netherlands 1996-2006]. Kampen: Ten Have.
Berting, J. 1995. Modernisation, human rights and the search for fundamentals, in *The Search for Fundamentals: The Process of Modernisation and the Quest for Meaning*, edited by L. van Vucht Tijssen, J. Berting and F.J. Lechner. Dordrecht: Kluwer, 201-16.
Besecke, K. 2005. Seeing invisible religion: Religion as a societal conversation about transcendent meaning. *Sociological Theory*, 23(2), 179-96.

Billiet, J. and De Witte, H. 1995. Attitudinal dispositions to vote for a 'new' extreme right-wing party: The case of 'Vlaams Blok'. *European Journal of Political Research*, 27(2), 181-202.

Bittarello, M.B. 2008. Another time, another space: Virtual worlds, myths and imagination. *Online - Heidelberg Journal of Religions on the Internet*, 3(1).

Blanchard, A. and Horan, T. 2000. Virtual communities and social capital, in *Social Dimensions of Information Technology*, edited by G. David Garson. Hershey: Idea Group Publishing, 5-20.

Blanchard, A.L. and Markus, M.L. 2004. The experienced 'sense' of a virtual community: Characteristics and processes. *The DATA BASE for Advances in Information Systems*, 35(1), 65-79.

Blank, T. 2003. Determinants of national identity in East and West Germany: An empirical comparison of theories on the significance of authoritarianism, anomie, and general self-esteem. *Political Psychology*, 24(2), 259-88.

Blevins, K.R. and Holt, T.J. 2009. Examining the virtual subculture of Johns. *Journal of Contemporary Ethnography*, 38(5), 619-48.

Boltanski, L. and Chiapello, E. 2005. *The New Spirit of Capitalism*. London: Verso.

Borsook, P. 2000. *Cyberselfish: A Critical Romp through the Terribly Libertarian Culture of High Tech*. New York: PublicAffairs.

Bourdieu, P. 1984. *Distinction: A Social Critique of the Judgement of Taste*. Cambridge, MA: Harvard University Press.

Bovbjerg, K.M. 2001. *Følsomhedens etik: Tilpasning af personligheden i New Age og moderne management* [Ethics of Sensitivity: Adaptation of the Personality in New Age and Modern Management]. Højbjerg: Hovedland.

Braham, J. 1999. The spiritual side. *Industry Week*, 248(3), 48-56.

Brannen, J. and Nilsen, A. 2005. Individualisation, choice and structure: A discussion of current trends in sociological analysis. *Sociological Review*, 53(3), 412-28.

Brasher, B.E. 2001. *Give me that Online Religion*. San Francisco: Jossey-Bass.

Braverman, H. 1974. *Labor and Monopoly Capital: The Degradation of Work in the Twentieth Century*. New York: Monthly Review Press.

Brown, C.G. 2001. *The Death of Christian Britain: Understanding Secularisation, 1800-2000*. London: Routledge.

Bruce, S. 1998. Good intentions and bad sociology: New age authenticity and social roles. *Journal of Contemporary Religion*, 13(1), 23-36.

Bruce, S. 2002. *God is Dead: Secularisation in the West*. Oxford: Blackwell.

Burris, V., Smith, E. and Strahm, A. 2000. White supremacist networks on the Internet. *Sociological Focus*, 33(2), 215-35.

Caiani, M. and Wagemann, C. 2009. Online networks of the Italian and German extreme right: An explorative study with social network analysis. *Information, Communication & Society*, 12(1), 66-109.

Campbell, C. 2002 [1972]. The cult, the cultic milieu and secularization, in *The Cultic Milieu: Oppositional Subcultures in an Age of Globalization*, edited by J. Kaplan and H. Lööw. Walnut Creek: AltaMira Press, 12-25.

Campbell, C. 2007. *The Easternization of the West: A Thematic Account of Cultural Change in the Modern Era*. Boulder, CO: Paradigm.

Campbell, H. 2005. Spiritualising the Internet: Uncovering discourses and narratives of religious Internet usage. *Online - Heidelberg Journal of Religions on the Internet*, 1(1).

Campbell, H. 2010. *When Religion Meets New Media*. London: Routledge.

Campbell, J.E. 2004. *Getting It On Online: Cyberspace, Gay Male Sexuality, and Embodied Identity*. New York: Harrington Park Press.

Canovan, M. 2005. *The People*. Cambridge: Polity Press.

Carnevale, F.A. 2007. Revisiting Goffman's *Stigma*: The social experience of families with children requiring mechanical ventilation at home. *Journal of Child Health Care*, 11(1), 7-18.

Castells, E. 2000. *The Rise of the Network Society (Volume 1: The Information Age): Economy, Society and Culture (Second Revised Edition)*. Oxford: Blackwell.

Castronova, E. 2005. *Synthetic Worlds: The Business and Culture of Online Worlds*. Chicago: University of Chicago Press.

Chandler, C.R. 1984. Durkheim and individualism: A comment on Messner. *Social Forces*, 63(2), 571-3.

Chau, M. and Xu, J. 2007. Mining communities and their relationships in blogs: A study of online hate groups. *International Journal of Human-Computer Studies*, 65(1), 57-70.

Chaves, M. 1994. Secularization as declining religious authority. *Social Forces*, 72(3), 749-74.

Clark, T.N. 1996. Structural realignment in American city politics: Less class, more race, and a new political culture. *Urban Affairs Review*, 31(3), 367-403.

Clark, T.N. 1998. Assessing the new political culture by comparing cities around the world, in *The New Political Culture*, edited by T.N. Clark and V. Hoffman-Martinot. Boulder, CO: Westview, 93-194.

Clark, T.N. 2001. The debate over 'Are social classes dying?', in *The Breakdown of Class Politics: A Debate on Post-Industrial Stratification*, edited by T.N. Clark and S.M. Lipset. Baltimore: Johns Hopkins University Press, 273-319.

Clark, T.N. and Hoffmann-Martinot, V. (eds). 1998. *The New Political Culture*. Boulder, CO: Westview.

Clark, T.N. and Lipset, S.M. (eds). 2001. *The Breakdown of Class Politics: A Debate on Post-Industrial Stratification*. Baltimore: Johns Hopkins University Press.

Clark, T.N. and Rempel, M. (eds). 1997. *Citizen Politics in Post-Industrial Societies*. Boulder, CO: Westview.

Coser, L.A. 1977. *Masters of Sociological Thought: Ideas in Historical and Social Context (Second Edition)*. New York: Macmillan.

Costea, B., Crump, N. and Amiridis, K. 2007. Managerialism and 'infinite human resourcefulness': A commentary on the 'therapeutic habitus', 'derecognition of finitude' and the modern sense of self. *Journal for Cultural Research*, 11(3), 245-64.

Covey, S.R. 1989. *The Seven Habits of Highly Effective People: Restoring the Character Ethic.* New York: Simon & Schuster.

Cronin, A. 2008. Focus groups, in *Researching Social Life (Third Edition)*, edited by N. Gilbert. London: Sage, 226-44.

Curott, P. 2001. 'Foreword', in *Witchcraft and the Web: Weaving Pagan Traditions Online*, by M.M. Nightmare. Toronto: ECW Press, 15-19.

Curry, P. 2004. *Defending Middle-Earth: Tolkien, Myth and Modernity (Revised Edition).* New York: Houghton Mifflin.

Dalton, R.J., Flanagan, S.C. and Beck, P.A. 1984. *Electoral Change in Advanced Industrial Democracies: Realignment or Dealignment?* Princeton: Princeton University Press.

Davie, G. 1994. *Religion in Britain since 1945: Believing without Belonging.* Oxford: Blackwell.

Davis, E. 1998. *TechGnosis: Myth, Magic and Mysticism in the Age of Information.* New York: Three Rivers Press.

Dawson, L.L. and Cowan, D.E. 2004. Introduction, in *Religion Online: Finding Faith on the Internet*, edited by L.L. Dawson and D.E. Cowan. New York: Routledge, 1-16.

De Beer, P. 2007. How individualized are the Dutch? *Current Sociology*, 55(3), 389-413.

De Graaf, P.M. and Kalmijn, M. 2001. Trends in the intergenerational transmission of cultural and economic status. *Acta Sociologica*, 44(1), 51-66.

Dekker, P. and Ester, P. 1987. Working-class authoritarianism: A re-examination of the Lipset thesis. *European Journal of Political Research*, 15(4), 395-415.

Dekker, P. and Ester, P. 1996. Depillarization, deconfessionalization, and de-ideologization: Empirical trends in Dutch society (1958-1992). *Review of Religious Research*, 37(4), 325-41.

Dekker, P., Ester, P. and Van den Broek, A. 1999. Fixing left and right: Value orientations according to Middendorp and Inglehart, in *Ideology in the Low Countries: Trends, Models and Lacunae*, edited by H. de Witte and P. Scheepers. Assen: Van Gorcum, 151-76.

De Koster, W. 2010. *'Nowhere I Could Talk Like That': Togetherness and Identity on Online Forums.* Unpublished PhD dissertation. Rotterdam: Erasmus University.

De Koster, W. and Van der Waal, J. 2007. Cultural value orientations and Christian religiosity: On moral traditionalism, authoritarianism, and their implications for voting behavior. *International Political Science Review*, 28(4), 451-67.

De Koster, W., Van der Waal, J. Achterberg, P. and Houtman, D. 2008. The rise of the penal state: Neo-liberalisation or new political culture? *British Journal of Criminology*, 48(6), 720-37.

De Mul, J. 2002. *Cyberspace Odyssee* [Cyberspace Odyssey]. Kampen: Klement.

Dery, M. 1996. *Escape Velocity: Cyberculture at the End of the Century.* New York: Grove Press.

Deshotels, T.H. and Forsyth, C.J. 2007. Postmodern masculinities and the eunuch. *Deviant Behavior*, 28(3), 201-18.

De Witte, H. 1990. *Conformisme, radicalisme en machteloosheid: Een onderzoek naar de sociaal-culturele en sociaal-economische opvattingen van arbeiders in Vlaanderen* [Conformity, Radicalism and Powerlessness: A Study of the Socio-Cultural and Socio-Economic Attitudes of Workers in Flanders]. Leuven: HIVA.

Dibbell, J. 2001. A rape in cyberspace: Or how an evil clown, a Haitian trickster spirit, two wizards, and a cast of dozens turned a database into a society, in *Reading Digital Culture*, edited by D. Trend. Oxford: Blackwell, 199-213.

DiMaggio, P., Hargittai, E., Neuman, W.R. and Robinson, J.P. 2001. Social implications of the Internet. *Annual Review of Sociology*, 27, 307-36.

Driskell, R.B. and Lyon, L. 2002. Are virtual communities true communities?: Examining the environments and elements of community. *City & Community*, 1(4), 373-90.

Duffy, M.E. 2003. Web of hate: A fantasy theme analysis of the rhetorical vision of hate groups online. *Journal of Communication Inquiry*, 27(3), 291-312.

Durkheim, E. 1964 [1893]. *The Division of Labor in Society.* New York: Free Press.

Durkheim, E. 1964 [1895]. *The Rules of Sociological Method.* New York: Free Press.

Durkheim, E. 1965 [1912]. *The Elementary Forms of Religious Life.* New York: Free Press.

Durkheim, E. 1973 [1898]. Individualism and the intellectuals, in *Emile Durkheim on Morality and Society*, edited by R.N. Bellah. Chicago: University of Chicago Press, 43-57.

Duyvendak, J.W. 2004. *Een eensgezinde, vooruitstrevende natie: Over de mythe van 'de' individualisering en de toekomst van de sociologie* [A United, Progressive Nation: On the Myth of 'the' Individualization and the Future of Sociology]. Amsterdam: Vossiuspers.

Eisinga, R. and P. Scheepers. 1989. *Etnocentrisme in Nederland: Theoretische en empirische verkenningen* [Ethnocentrism in the Netherlands: Theoretical and Empirical Explorations]. Nijmegen: ITS.

Elchardus, M. 1996. Class, cultural re-alignment and the rise of the populist right, in *Changing Europe: Some Aspects of Identity, Conflict and Social Justice*, edited by A. Erskine. Aldershot: Avebury, 41-63.

Elchardus, M. 2009. Self-control as social control: The emergence of symbolic society. *Poetics*, 37(2), 146-61.

Elchardus, M. and Smits, W. 2002. *Anatomie en oorzaken van het wantrouwen* [Anatomy and Causes of Distrust]. Brussels: VUB Press.

Ellwood, R.S. 1994. *The Sixties Spiritual Awakening: American Religion Moving from Modern to Postmodern.* New Brunswick: Rutgers University Press.

Emerson, M.O. and D. Hartman. 2006. The rise of religious fundamentalism. *Annual Review of Sociology*, 32, 127-44.

Emler, N. and Frazer, E. 1999. Politics: The education effect. *Oxford Review of Education*, 25(1/2), 251-73.

Erikson, R., Goldthorpe, J.H. and Portocarero, L. 1979. Intergenerational class mobility in three Western European societies: England, France and Sweden. *British Journal of Sociology*, 30(4), 415-41.

Ess, C., Kawabata, A. and Kurosaki, H. 2007. Cross-cultural perspectives on religion and computer-mediated communication. *Journal of Computer-Mediated Communication*, 12(3), 939-55.

Etzioni, A. 1995. Old chestnuts and new spurs, in *New Communitarian Thinking: Persons, Virtues, Institutions and Communities*, edited by A. Etzioni. Charlottesville: University Press of Virginia, 16-34.

Etzioni, A. 2001. On social and moral revival. *Journal of Political Philosophy*, 9(3), 356-71.

Etzioni, A. 2004. On virtual, democratic communities, in *Community in the Digital Age: Philosophy and Practice*, edited by A. Feenberg and D. Barney. Lanham: Rowman & Littlefield, 225-38.

Etzioni, A. and Etzioni, O. 1999. Face-to-face and computer-mediated communities: A comparative analysis. *The Information Society*, 15(4), 241-48.

European Commission against Racism and Intolerance (ECRI). 2008. *Third Report on the Netherlands*. Strasbourg: Council of Europe.

Evans, G. (ed.) 1999. *The End of Class Politics?: Class Voting in Comparative Context*. Oxford: Oxford University Press.

Evans, G., Heath, A. and Lalljee, M. 1996. Measuring left-right and libertarian-authoritarian values in the British electorate. *British Journal of Sociology*, 47(1), 93-112.

Eysenbach, G. and Till, J.E. 2001. Ethical issues in qualitative research on Internet communities. *British Medical Journal*, 323(7321), 1103-5.

Featherstone, M. 1995. Postmodernism and the quest for meaning, in *The Search for Fundamentals: Modernisation and the Quest for Meaning*, edited by L. van Vucht Tijssen, J. Berting and F. J. Lechner. Dordrecht: Kluwer, 217-35.

Feenberg, A. and Bakardjieva, M. 2004. Virtual community: No 'killer implication'. *New Media & Society*, 6(1), 37-43.

Fekete, L.L. 2004. Anti-Muslim racism and the European security state. *Race & Class*, 46(1), 3-29.

Felling, A. and Peters, J. 1986. Conservatism: A multidimensional concept. *Netherlands' Journal of Sociology*, 22(1), 36-60.

Fennema, M. 1997. Some conceptual issues and problems in the comparison of anti-immigrant parties in Western Europe. *Party Politics*, 3(4), 473-92.

Fennema, M. 2005. Populist parties of the right, in *Movements of Exclusion: Radical Right-Wing Populism*, edited by J. Rydgren. Halifax: Nova Science Publishers, 1-24.

Fenton, S. 1984. *Durkheim and Modern Sociology*. Cambridge: Cambridge University Press.

Fernback, J. 1999. There is a there there: Notes toward a definition of cybercommunity, in *Doing Internet Research: Critical Issues and Methods for Examining the Net*, edited by S. Jones. Thousand Oaks: Sage, 203-20.

Fernback, J. 2007. Beyond the diluted community concept: A symbolic interactionist perspective on online social relations. *New Media & Society*, 9(1), 49-69.

Fernback, J. and Thompson, B. 1995. *Virtual Communities: Abort, Retry, Failure?* Available at: http://www.well.com/~hlr/texts/VCcivil.html [accessed: July 12, 2006].

Fiorina, M.P. and Abrams, S.J. 2008. Political polarization in the American public. *Annual Review of Political Science*, 11, 563-88.

Fiorina, M.P., Abrams, S.J. and Pope, J.C. 2005. *Culture War? The Myth of a Polarized America*. New York: Pearson Longman.

Fischer, C.S. and Hout, M. 2006. *Century of Difference: How America Changed in the Last One Hundred Years*. New York: Russell Sage Foundation.

Fiske, J. 1998. *Understanding Popular Culture*. London: Routledge.

Flanagan, S.C. 1979. Value change and partisan change in Japan: The silent revolution revisited. *Comparative Politics*, 11(April), 253-78.

Flanagan, S.C. 1982. Changing values in advanced industrial societies: Inglehart's silent revolution from the perspective of Japanese findings. *Comparative Political Studies*, 14(4), 403-44.

Flanagan, S.C. 1987. Value change in industrial societies: Reply to Inglehart. *American Political Science Review*, 81(4), 1303-19.

Flanagan, S.C. and Lee, A-R. 2003. The new politics, culture wars, and the authoritarian-libertarian value change in advanced industrial democracies. *Comparative Political Studies*, 36(3), 235-70.

Fleishman, J.A. 1988. Attitude organization in the general public: Evidence for a bidimensional structure. *Social Forces*, 67(1), 159-84.

Flere, S. 2007. Gender and religious orientation. *Social Compass*, 54(2), 239-53.

Foster, D. 1997. Community and identity in the electronic village, in *Internet Culture*, edited by D. Porter. London: Routledge, 23-37.

Frank, T.C. 1998. *The Conquest of Cool: Business Culture, Counter Culture, and the Rise of Hip Consumerism*. Chicago: University of Chicago Press.

Freeman, D. 2004. *Creating Emotions in Games: The Craft and Art of Emotioneering*. Boston, Indianapolis: New Riders.

Fukuyama, F. 2002. *Our Posthuman Future: Consequences of the Biotechnology Revolution*. New York: Farrar, Straus and Giroux.

Furedi, F. 2003. *Therapy Culture: Cultivating Vulnerability in an Uncertain Age*. London: Routledge.

Gabennesch, H. 1972. Authoritarianism as world view. *American Journal of Sociology* 77(5): 857-75.

Galston, W.A. 1995. Two concepts of liberalism. *Ethics*, 105(3), 516-34.

Gans, H. 1999 [1972]. *Popular Culture and High Culture: An Analysis and Evaluation of Taste*. New York: Basic Books.

Ganzeboom, H.B.G. and Treiman, D.J. 2005. *International Stratification and Mobility File: Conversion Tools*. Available at: http://www.fsw.vu.nl/~h. ganzeboom/ismf [accessed: July 1, 2007].

Gergen, K.J. 1991. *The Saturated Self: Dilemmas of Identity in Contemporary Life*. New York: Basic Books.

Gerstenfeld, P.B., Grant, D.R. and Chiang, C-P. 2003. Hate online: A content analysis of extremist Internet sites. *Analyses of Social Issues and Public Policy*, 3(1), 29-44.

Giddens, A. 1991. *Modernity and Self-identity: Self and Society in the Late Modern Age*. Cambridge: Polity Press.

Giddens, A. 1994. Living in a post-traditional society, in *Reflexive Modernization: Politics, Tradition and Aesthetics in the Modern Social Order*, edited by U. Beck, A. Giddens and S. Lash. Cambridge: Polity Press, 56-109.

Gijsberts, M. and Lubbers, M. 2009. Wederzijdse beeldvorming [Mutual representation], in *Jaarrapport integratie* [Annual Report Integration], edited by M. Gijsberts and J. Dagevos. The Hague: SCP.

Glaser, J., Dixit, J. and Green, D.P. 2002. Studying hate crime with the Internet: What makes racists advocate racial violence? *Journal of Social Issues*, 58(1), 177-93.

Goffman, E. 1986 [1963]. *Stigma: Notes on the Management of Spoiled Identity*. New York: Simon & Schuster.

Goldschmidt Salamon, K.L. 2001. 'Going global from the inside out': Spiritual globalism in the workplace, in *New Age Religion and Globalization*, edited by Mikael Rothstein. Aarhus: Aarhus University Press, 150-72.

Goldthorpe, J.H. 1980. *Social Mobility and Class Structure in Modern Britain*, Oxford: Clarendon Press.

González, K.V., Verkuyten, M., Weesie, J. and Poppe, E. 2008. Prejudice towards Muslims in the Netherlands: Testing integrated threat theory. *British Journal of Social Psychology*, 47(4), 667-85.

Goudsblom, J. 1985. Levensbeschouwing en sociologie [Ideology and sociology]. *Amsterdams Sociologisch Tijdschrift*, 12(1), 3-21.

Gouldner, A.W. 1958. Introduction, in *Emile Durkheim: Socialism and Saint Simon*, edited by A.W. Gouldner. Yellow Springs: Antioch Press, i-xxix.

Grabb, E.G. 1979. Working-class authoritarianism and tolerance of outgroups: A reassessment. *Public Opinion Quarterly*, 43(1), 36-47.

Grabb, E.G. 1980. Marxist categories and theories of class: The case of working-class authoritarianism. *Pacific Sociological Review*, 23(4), 359-76.

Grant, D., O'Neil, K. and Stephens, L. 2004. Spirituality in the workplace: New empirical directions in the study of the sacred. *Sociology of Religion*, 65(3), 265-83.

Green, S., Davis, C., Karshmer, E., Marsh, P. and Straight, B. 2005. Living stigma: The impact of labeling, stereotyping, separation, status loss, and discrimination in the lives of individuals with disabilities and their families. *Sociological Inquiry*, 75(2), 197-215.

Hall, S. 1980. Encoding/decoding, in *Culture, Media, Language*, edited by S. Hall, D. Hobson, A. Lowe and P. Willis. London: Hutchinson, 128-39.

Halman, L. and R. de Moor. 1994. Religion, churches and moral values, in *The Individualizing Society: Value Change in Europe and North America*, edited by P. Ester, L. Halman and R. de Moor. Tilburg: Tilburg University Press, 37-65.

Hamilton, M. 2000. An analysis of the festival for mind-body-spirit, London, in *Beyond New Age: Exploring Alternative Spirituality*, edited by S. Sutcliffe and M. Bowman. Edinburgh: Edinburgh University Press, 188-200.

Hammer, O. 2001. *Claiming Knowledge: Strategies of Epistemology from Theosophy to the New Age*. Leiden: Brill.

Hammer, O. 2004. Contradictions of the new age, in *The Encyclopedic Sourcebook of New Age Religions*, edited by J. Lewis. Buffalo: Prometheus, 415-19.

Hanegraaff, W.J. 1996. *New Age Religion and Western Culture: Esotericism in the Mirror of Secular Thought*. Leiden: Brill.

Hanegraaff, W.J. 2001. Prospects for the globalization of new age: Spiritual imperialism versus cultural diversity, in *New Age Religion and Globalization*, edited by M. Rothstein. Aarhus: Aarhus University Press, 15-30.

Hanegraaff, W.J. 2002. New age religion, in *Religion in the Modern World: Traditions and Transformations*, edited by L. Woodhead, P. Fletcher and H. Kawanami. London: Routledge, 249-63.

Hara, N. and Estrada, Z. 2005. Analyzing the mobilization of grassroots activities via the Internet: A case study. *Journal of Information Science*, 31(6), 503-14.

Hardey, M. 2002. Life beyond the screen: Embodiment and identity through the Internet. *Sociological Review*, 50(4), 570-85.

Hayes, J. 1999. Business gurus divine spiritual answers to labor issues. *Nation's Restaurant News*, 33(2), 66.

Heath, A.F., Evans, G. and Martin, J. 1994. The measurement of core beliefs and values: The development of balanced socialist/laissez faire and libertarian/authoritarian scales. *British Journal of Political Science*, 24(1), 115-32.

Heath, J. and Potter, A. 2004. *Nation of Rebels: Why Counterculture Became Consumer Culture*. New York: HarperCollins.

Hechter, M. 2004. From class to culture. *American Journal of Sociology*, 110(2), 400-45.

Heelas, P. 1996a. *The New Age Movement: The Celebration of the Self and the Sacralisation of Modernity*. Oxford: Blackwell.

Heelas, P. 1996b. Introduction: Detraditionalization and its rivals, in *Detraditionalization: Critical Reflections on Authority and Identity*, edited by P. Heelas, S. Lash and P. Morris. Oxford: Blackwell, 1-20.

Heelas, P., Woodhead, L., Seel, B., Szerszynski, B. and Tusting, K. 2005. *The Spiritual Revolution: Why Religion is Giving Way to Spirituality*. Oxford: Blackwell.

Heim, M. 1993. *The Metaphysics of Virtual Reality*. Oxford: Oxford University Press.

Helland, C. 2004. Popular religion and the world wide web: A match made in (cyber)heaven, in *Religion Online: Finding Faith on the Internet*, edited by L.L. Dawson and D.E. Cowan. New York: Routledge, 23-36.

Hetherington, M.J. 2009. Putting polarization in perspective. *British Journal of Political Science*, 39(2), 413-48.

Hijmans, E. 1996. The logic of qualitative media content analysis: A typology. *Communications*, 21(1), 93-108.

Hoffer, E. 2002 [1951]. *The True Believer: Thoughts on the Nature of Mass Movements*. New York: Harper & Row.

Hoffman-Martinot, V. 1991. Grüne and Verts: Two faces of European ecologism, in *West European Politics*, 14(4), 70-95.

Højsgaard, M.T. and Warburg, M. 2005. Introduction: Waves of research, in *Religion and Cyberspace*, edited by M.T. Højsgaard and M. Warburg. London: Routledge, 1-11.

Hopson, J. 2001. *Behavioral Game Design*. Available at: http://www.gamasutra.com/view/feature/3085/behavioral_game_design.php [accessed: March 21, 2011].

Horkheimer, M. and Adorno, T.W. 2002 [1944]. *Dialectic of Enlightenment: Philosophical Fragments*. Stanford: Stanford University Press.

Hout, M., Brooks, C. and Manza, J. 1993. The persistence of classes in post-industrial societies. *International Sociology*, 8(3), 259-78.

Hout, M. and C.S. Fischer. 2002. Why more Americans have no religious preference: Politics and generations. *American Sociological Review*, 67(2), 165-190.

Houtman, D. 1996. Cultureel kapitaal, sociale stratificatie en onderwijsoriëntatie [Cultural capital, social stratification and orientation towards education]. *Sociologische Gids*, 43(6), 413-34.

Houtman, D. 2001. Class, culture, and conservatism: Reassessing education as a variable in political sociology, in *The Breakdown of Class Politics: A Debate on Post-Industrial Stratification*, edited by T.N. Clark and S.M. Lipset. Baltimore: Johns Hopkins University Press, 161-95.

Houtman, D. 2003. *Class and Politics in Contemporary Social Science: 'Marxism Lite' and Its Blind Spot for Culture*. New York: Aldine de Gruyter.

Houtman, D. 2008. *Op jacht naar de echte werkelijkheid: Dromen over authenticiteit in een wereld zonder fundamenten* [The Hunt for Real Reality: Dreams of Authenticity in a World without Foundations]. Amsterdam: Pallas Publications.

Houtman, D., Achterberg P. and Derks, A. 2008a. *Farewell to the Leftist Working Class*. New Brunswick: Transaction Press.

Houtman, D., Achterberg, P. and Duyvendak, J.W. 2008b. De verhitte politieke cultuur van een ontzuilde samenleving [The heated political culture of a de-pillarized society], in *De grote kloof: Verhitte politiek in tijden van verwarring*

[The Big Gap: Heated Politics in an Era of Confusement], edited by B. Snels and N. Thijssen. Amsterdam: Boom, 61-80.

Houtman, D. and Aupers, S. 2007. The spiritual turn and the decline of tradition: The spread of post-Christian spirituality in 14 Western countries, 1981-2000. *Journal for the Scientific Study of Religion*, 46(3), 305-20.

Houtman, D. and Duyvendak, J.W. 2009. Boerka's, boerkini's en belastingcenten: Culturele en politieke polarisatie in een post-Christelijke samenleving [Burkas, burkinis and tax money: Cultural and political polarization in a post-Christian society], in *Polarisatie: Bedreigend en verrijkend* [Polarization: Threatening and Enriching], edited by *Raad voor Maatschappelijke Ontwikkeling*. Amsterdam: SWP Publishers, 102-19.

Houtman, D. and Mascini, P. 2002. Why do churches become empty, while new age grows? Secularization and religious change in the Netherlands. *Journal for the Scientific Study of Religion*, 41(3), 455-73.

Humphreys, S. 2008. Ruling the virtual world: Governance in massively multiplayer online games. *European Journal of Cultural Studies*, 11(2), 149-71.

Hurenkamp, M. and Kremer, M. 2005. De spanning tussen keuzevrijheid en tevredenheid [The tension between freedom of choice and satisfaction], in V*rijheid verplicht: Over tevredenheid en de grenzen van keuzevrijheid* [Freedom obliges: On Satisfaction and the Limits of Freedom of Choice], edited by M. Hurenkamp and M. Kremer. Amsterdam: Van Gennep, 7-19.

Ignazi, P. 1992. The silent counter-revolution: Hypotheses on the emergence of extreme right-wing parties in Europe. *European Journal of Political Research*, 22(1), 3-34.

Ignazi, P. 2003. *Extreme Right Parties in Western Europe*. Oxford: Oxford University Press.

Inglehart, R. 1977. *The Silent Revolution: Changing Values and Political Styles among Western Publics*. Princeton: Princeton University Press.

Inglehart, R. 1987. Value change in industrial societies. *American Political Science Review*, 81(4), 1289-303.

Inglehart, R. 1990. *Culture Shift in Advanced Industrial Society.* Princeton: Princeton University Press.

Inglehart, R. 1997. *Modernization and Postmodernization: Cultural, Economic, and Political Change in 43 Countries*. Princeton: Princeton University Press.

Inglehart, R. and W.E. Baker. 2000. Modernization, cultural change, and the persistence of traditional values. *American Sociological Review*, 65(1), 19-51.

Inglehart, R., Foa, R., Peterson, C. and Welzel, C. 2008. Development, freedom, and rising happiness: A global perspective (1981-2007). *Perspectives on Psychological Science*, 3(4), 264-85.

Inglehart, R. and C. Welzel. 2005. *Modernization, Cultural Change and Democracy: The Human Development Sequence*. Cambridge: Cambridge University Press.

Jameson, F. 1991. *Postmodernism, or, the Cultural Logic of Late Capitalism.* Durham, NC: Duke University Press.

Jansz, J. 2005. The emotional appeal of violent video games for adolescent males. *Communication Theory*, 15(3), 219-41.

Jenkins, H. 2006. *Fans, Bloggers, and Gamers: Exploring Participatory Culture.* New York: New York University Press.

Joinson, A.N. 2005. Internet behaviour and the design of virtual methods, in *Virtual Method: Issues in Social Research on the Internet*, edited by C. Hine. Oxford: Berg, 21-34.

Kalmijn, M. 1994. Assortative mating by cultural and economic occupational status. *American Journal of Sociology*, 100(2), 422-52.

Karaflogka, A. 2003. Religion on – religion in cyberspace', in *Predicting Religion: Christian, Secular and Alternative Futures*, edited by G. Davie, P. Heelas and L. Woodhead. Aldershot: Ashgate, 191-202.

Kelemen, M. and Smith, W. 2001. Community and its 'virtual' promises: A critique of cyberlibertarian rhetoric. *Information, Communication & Society*, 4(3), 370-87.

Kellner, D. 1992. Popular culture and the construction of postmodern identities, in *Modernity and Identity*, edited by S. Lash and J. Friedman. Oxford: Blackwell, 141-77.

Kelly, R.V. 2004. *Massively Multiplayer Online Role-Playing Games: The People, the Addiction and the Playing Experience.* London: McFarland & Company.

Kelly, K.D. and Chambliss, W.L. 1966. Status consistency and political attitudes. *American Sociological Review*, 31(3), 375-82.

Kendall, L. 1999. Recontextualizing 'cyberspace': Methodological considerations for on-line research, in *Doing Internet Research: Critical Issues and Methods for Examining the Net*, edited by S. Jones. Thousand Oaks: Sage, 57-74.

Keuzenkamp, S. 2010. De houding van Nederlanders tegenover homosexualiteit [Dutch attitudes towards homosexuality], in *Steeds gewoner, nooit gewoon: Acceptatie van homosexualiteit in Nederland* [Increasingly Common, Never Normal: Acceptance of Homosexuality in the Netherlands], edited by S. Keuzenkamp. The Hague: SCP, 1-24.

King, B. and J. Borland. 2003. *Dungeons and Dreamers: The Rise of Computer Game Culture, From Geek to Chic.* New York: McGraw-Hill.

King, S.A. 1996. Researching Internet communities: Proposed ethical guidelines for the reporting of the results. *The Information Society*, 12(2), 119-27.

Kitschelt, H.P. 1997. *The Radical Right in Western Europe: A Comparative Analysis.* Ann Arbor: University of Michigan Press.

Kitzinger, J. 1995. Introducing focus groups. *British Medical Journal*, 311(2), 299-302.

Kivits, J. 2005. Online interviewing and the research relationship, in *Virtual Methods: Issues in Social Research on the Internet*, edited by C. Hine. Oxford: Berg, 35-49

Klatch, R.E. 1999. *A Generation Divided: The New Left, the New Right, and the 1960s*. Berkeley: University of California Press.

Kline, S., Dyer-Witheford, N. and De Peuter, G. 2003. *Digital Play: The Interaction of Technology, Culture, and Marketing*. Montreal: McGill-Queen's University Press.

Kohn, M.L. 1977 [1969]. *Class and Conformity: A Study in Values (Second Edition)*. Chicago: University of Chicago Press.

Kohn, M.L. and Schooler, C. 1983. *Work and Personality: An Inquiry into the Impact of Social Stratification*. New York: Ablex.

Kohn, M.L. and Slomczynski, K.M. 1990. *Social Structure and Self Direction: A Comparative Analysis of the United States and Poland*. Oxford: Blackwell.

Komito, L. 1998. The net as foraging society: Flexible communities. *The Information Society*, 14(1), 97-106.

Korteweg, A.C. 2006. The murder of Theo van Gogh: Gender, religion and the struggle over immigrant integration in the Netherlands, in *Migration, Citizenship, Ethnos*, edited by Y.M. Bodemann and G. Yurdakul. New York: Palgrave-MacMillan, 147-66.

Kriesi, H-P. 1989. New social movements and the new class in the Netherlands. *American Journal of Sociology*, 94(5), 1078-116.

Kriesi, H-P. 1998. The transformation of cleavage politics: The 1997 Stein Rokkan lecture. *European Journal of Political Research*, 33(2), 165-85.

Kriesi, H-P. and Van Praag, P. 1987. Old and new politics: The Dutch peace movement and the traditional political organizations. *European Journal of Political Research*, 15(3), 319-46.

Krippendorff, K. 2004. *Content Analysis: An Introduction to Its Methodology (Second Edition)*. London: Sage.

Kundnani, A. 2007. Integrationism: The politics of anti-Muslim racism. *Race & Class*, 48(4), 24-44.

Lau, K.J. 2008. *New Age Capitalism: Making Money East of Eden*. Pennsylvania: University of Pennsylvania Press.

Lechner, F.J. 1996. Secularization in the Netherlands? *Journal for the Scientific Study of Religion*, 35(3), 252-64.

Lechner, F.J. 2008. *The Netherlands: Globalization and National Identity*. New York and London: Routledge.

Lederer, G. 1983. *Jugend und Autorität: Über den Einstellungswandel zum Autoritarismus in der Bundesrepublik Deutschland und den USA*. Opladen: Westdeutscher Verlag.

Levin, B. 2002. Cyberhate: A legal and historical analysis of extremists' use of computer networks in America. *American Behavioral Scientist*, 45(6), 958-88.

Lijphart, A. 1968. *The Politics of Accommodation: Pluralism and Democracy in the Netherlands*, Berkeley, CA: University of California Press.

Link, B.G. and Phelan, J.C. 2001. Conceptualizing stigma. *Annual Review of Sociology*, 27(1), 363-85.

Lipset, S.M. 1959. Democracy and working-class authoritarianism. *American Sociological Review*, 24, 482-502.

Lipset, S.M. 1981. *Political Man: The Social Bases of Politics (Expanded Edition).* Baltimore: Johns Hopkins University Press.

Lipsitz, L. 1965. Working-class authoritarianism: A re-evaluation. *American Sociological Review*, 30(1), 103-9.

Luckmann, T. 1967. *The Invisible Religion: The Problem of Religion in Modern Society.* New York: Palgrave Macmillan.

Luckmann, T. 1996. The privatisation of religion and morality, in *Detraditionalisation: Critical Reflections on Authority and Identity*, edited by P. Heelas, S. Lash and P. Morris. Oxford: Blackwell, 72-86.

Luhrmann, T.M. 1989. *Persuasions of the Witch's Craft: Ritual Magic in Contemporary England.* Cambridge, MA: Harvard University Press.

Lukes, S. 1967. Alienation and anomie, in *Philosophy, Politics, and Society: Third Series*, edited by P. Lasslet and W.G. Runciman. Oxford: Blackwell, 134-56.

Lutterman, K.G. and R. Middleton. 1970. Authoritarianism, anomia, and prejudice. *Social Forces*, 48(4), 485-92.

Lyon, D. 2000. *Jesus in Disneyland: Religion in Postmodern Times.* Oxford: Polity Press.

Lyons, P. 1996. *New Left, New Right and the Legacy of the Sixties.* Philadelphia: Temple University Press.

Mann, C. and Stewart, F. 2000. *Internet Communication and Qualitative Research: A Handbook for Researching Online.* London: Sage.

Manzo, J.F. 2004. On the sociology and social organization of stigma: Some ethnomethodological insights. *Human Studies*, 27(4), 401-16.

Marcuse, H. 1964. *One-Dimensional Man: Studies in the Ideology of Advanced Industrial Society.* Boston, MA: Beacon Press.

Markham, A.N. 1998. *Life Online: Researching Real Experience in Virtual Space.* Walnut Creek: AltaMira Press.

Marks, R.B. 2003. *Everquest Companion: The Inside Lore of a Game World.* New York: McGraw-Hill.

Marwick, A. 1998. *The Sixties: Cultural Revolution in Britain, France, Italy, and the United States, c. 1958-c. 1974.* New York: Oxford University Press.

Mascini, P. and Houtman, D. 2011. Resisting the toleration of illegal activities: A rightist backlash? *British Journal of Criminology*, 51(4), 690-706.

Mayo, E. 1949. *Hawthorne and the Western Electric Company: The Social Problems of an Industrial Civilisation.* London: Routledge.

McDill, E.L. 1961. Anomie, authoritarianism, prejudice, and socioeconomic status: An attempt at clarification. *Social Forces*, 39(3), 239-45.

McGonigal, J. 2011. *Reality is Broken: Why Games Make us Better and How They Can Change the World.* New York: Penguin.

McGregor, D. 1960. *The Human Side of Enterprise.* New York: McGraw-Hill.

McMillan, D.W. and Chavis, D.M. 1986. Sense of community: A definition and theory. *Journal of Community Psychology*, 14(1), 6-23.

Mehra, B., Merkel, C. and Bishop, A.P. 2004. The Internet for empowerment of minority and marginalized users. *New Media & Society*, 6(6), 781-802.

Meloen, J.D., Van der Linden, G. and De Witte, H. 1996. A test of the approaches of Adorno et al., Lederer and Altemeyer of authoritarianism in Belgian Flanders: A research note. *Political Psychology*, 17(4), 643-56.

Middendorp, C.P. 1989. Models for predicting the Dutch vote along the left-right and the libertarianism-authoritarianism dimensions. *International Political Science Review*, 10(4), 279-308.

Middendorp, C.P. 1991. *Ideology in Dutch Politics: The Democratic System Reconsidered (1970-1985)*, Assen: Van Gorcum.

Mills, C.W. 1951. *White Collar: The American Middle Classes*. New York: Oxford University Press.

Minkenberg, M. 1992. The new right in Germany: The transformation of conservatism and the extreme right. *European Journal of Political Research*, 22(1), 55-81.

Mitchell, R.E. 1966. Class-linked conflict between two dimensions of liberalism-conservatism. *Social Problems*, 13(Spring), 418-27.

Mitroff, I.I. and E.A. Denton. 1999a. *A Spiritual Audit of Corporate America: A Hard Look at Spirituality, Religion, and Values in the Workplace*. San Francisco: Jossey-Bass.

Mitroff, I.I. and E.A. Denton. 1999b. A study of spirituality in the workplace. *Sloan Management Review*, 40(4), 83-92.

Morgan, D.L. 1997. *Focus Groups as Qualitative Research*. London: Sage.

Mughan, A. 2000. *Media and the Presidentialization of Parliamentary Elections*. London: Palgrave Macmillan.

Nadesan, M.H. 1999. The discourses of corporate spiritualism and evangelical capitalism. *Management Communication Quarterly*, 13(1), 3-42.

Naisbitt, J. and P. Aburdene. 1990. *Mega-Trends 2000*. London: Pan Books.

Neal, C. 1999. A conscious change in the workplace. *Journal for Quality and Participation*, 22(2), 27-30.

Newman, J. 2004. *Videogames*. London: Routledge.

Nieckarz Jr., P.P. 2005. Community in cyber space? The role of the Internet in facilitating and maintaining a community of live music collecting and trading. *City & Community*, 4(4), 403-23.

Nieuwbeerta, P. 1995. *The Democratic Class Struggle in Twenty Countries, 1945-1990*. Amsterdam: Thesis.

Nieuwbeerta, P. 1996. The democratic class struggle in postwar societies: Class voting in twenty countries, 1945-1990. *Acta Sociologica*, 39(4), 345-84.

Nieuwbeerta, P. 2001. The democratic class struggle in postwar societies: Traditional class voting in twenty countries, 1945-1990, in *The Breakdown of Class Politics: A Debate on Post-Industrial Stratification*, edited by T.N. Clark and S.M. Lipset. Baltimore: Johns Hopkins University Press, 121-35.

Nieuwbeerta, P. and De Graaf, N.D. 1999. Traditional class voting in twenty postwar societies, in *The End of Class Politics? Class Voting in Comparative Perspective*, edited by G. Evans. Oxford: Oxford University Press, 23-58.

Nightmare, M.M. 2001. *Witchcraft and the Web: Weaving Pagan Traditions Online*. Toronto: ECW Press.

Nip, J.Y.M. 2004. The relationship between online and offline communities: The case of the queer sisters. *Media, Culture & Society*, 26(3), 409-28.

Noble, D. 1997. *The Religion of Technology: The Divinity of Man and the Spirit of Invention*. New York: Penguin.

Norris, P. and Inglehart, R. 2004. *Sacred and Secular: Religion and Politics Worldwide*. New York: Cambridge University Press.

Noveck, B. and Balkin, J. (eds). 2006. *The State of Play: Law, Games, and Virtual Worlds*. New York: New York University Press.

Nunn, C.Z., Crockett, Jr., H.J. and Williams, Jr., J.A. 1978. *Tolerance for Nonconformity: A National Survey of Americans' Changing Commitment to Civil Liberties*. San Francisco: Jossey-Bass.

O'Kane, J.M. 1970. Economic and noneconomic liberalism, upward mobility potential, and Catholic working class youth. *Social Forces*, 40(4), 499-506.

O'Leary, S.D. 2004. Cyberspace as sacred space: Communicating religion on computer networks, in *Religion Online: Finding Faith on the Internet*, edited by L.L. Dawson and D.E. Cowan. New York: Routledge, 37-58.

Olson, D.V.A. and Carroll, J.W. 1992. Religiously based politics: Religious elites and the public. *Social Forces*, 70(3), 765-86.

Olzak, S. 1992. *The Dynamics of Ethnic Competition and Conflict*. Stanford: Stanford University Press.

Ortega y Gasset, J. 1932. *The Revolt of the Masses*. New York: W.W. Norton & Company.

Paccagnella, L. 1997. Getting the seats of your pants dirty: Strategies for ethnographic research on virtual communities. *Journal of Computer-Mediated Communication*, 3(1). Available at: http://jcmc.indiana.edu/vol3/issue1/paccagnella.html.

Page, R.M. 1984. *Stigma*. London: Routledge.

Pakulski, J. and Waters, M. 1996. *The Death of Class*. London: Sage.

Papadakis, M.C. 2003. *Computer-Mediated Communities: The Implications of Information, Communication, and Computational Technologies for Creating Community Online*. Arlington: SRI International.

Peek, L. and Fothergill, A. 2009. Using focus groups: Lessons from studying daycare centers, 9/11, and hurricane Katrina. *Qualitative Research*, 9(1), 31-59.

Penczak, C. 2001. *City Magick: Urban Rituals, Spells, and Shamanism*. York Beach: Weiser Books.

Penninx, R. 2006. Dutch immigrant integration policies before and after the Van Gogh murder. *Journal of International Migration and Integration*, 7(2), 241-54.

Peters, T.J. and Waterman, Jr., R.H. 1982. *In Search of Excellence: Lessons from America's Best-Run Companies*. New York: Harper & Row.

Pettigrew, T.F. 1998. Reactions toward the new minorities of Western Europe. *Annual Review of Sociology*, 24(1), 77-103.

Pontifical Council for Social Communications. 2002. *Ethics in Internet*. Available at: http://www.vatican.va/roman_curia/pontifical_councils/pccs/documents/rc_pc_pccs_doc_20020228_ethics-Internet_en.html [accessed: March 16, 2006].

Possamai, A. 2003. Alternative spiritualities and the cultural logic of late capitalism. *Culture and Religion*, 4(1), 31-45.

Poynting, S. and Mason, V. 2007. The resistible rise of Islamophobia: Anti-Muslim racism in the UK and Australia before 11 September 2001. *Journal of Sociology*, 43(1), 61-86.

Protestantse Kerk in Nederland (PKN). 2005. *Leren leven van de verwondering: Visie op het leven en werken van de kerk in haar geheel* [Learning to Live of Amazement: Outlook on the Life and Works of the Church in Its Unity]. Utrecht: Protestantse Kerk in Nederland. Available at: http://www.pkn.nl/3/site/uploaded Docs/www 51818_PLD_verwondering(1)(1)(1).pdf [accessed: March 16, 2006].

Radkau, J. 2009. *Max Weber: A Biography*. Cambridge: Polity Press.

Ransford, H.E. 1972. Blue collar anger: Reactions to student and black protest. *American Sociological Review*, 37(3), 333-46.

Reid, E. and Chen, H. 2007. Internet-savvy U.S. and Middle Eastern extremist groups. *Mobilization*, 12(2), 177-92.

Rempel, M. and Clark, T.N. 1997. Post-industrial politics: A framework for interpreting citizen politics since the 1960s, in *Citizen Politics in Post-Industrial Societies*, edited by M. Rempel and T.N. Clark. Boulder, CO: Westview, 9-56.

Riesman, D. 1950. *The Lonely Crowd: A Study of the Changing American Character*. New Haven: Yale University Press.

Rigby, S. and Ryan, R. 2007. *Rethinking Carrots: A New Method For Measuring What Players Find Most Rewarding and Motivating About Your Game*. Available at: http://www.gamasutra.com/features/20070116/rigby_01.shtml [accessed: April 28, 2008].

Ritzer, G. and Jurgenson, N. 2010. Production, consumption, prosumption: The nature of capitalism in the age of the digital "prosumer". *Journal of Consumer Culture*, 10(1), 13-36.

Roberts, A.H. and Rokeach, M. 1956. Anomie, authoritarianism, and prejudice: A replication. *American Journal of Sociology*, 61(4), 355-58.

Roberts, L.D., Smith, L.M. and Pollock, C. 2002. Mooing till the cows come home: The search for sense of community in virtual environments, in *Psychological Sense of Community: Research, Applications, and Implications*, edited by A.T. Fisher, C.C. Sonn and B.J. Bishop. New York: Kluwer, 223-45.

Roberts, R. 1994. Power and empowerment: New age managers and the dialectics of modernity/postmodernity? *Religion Today*, 9(3), 3-13.

Robins, K. 2000. Cyberspace and the world we live in, in *The Cybercultures Reader*, edited by D. Bell and B.M. Kennedy. London: Routledge, 77-95.

Roeland, J. 2009. *Selfation: Dutch Evangelical Youth Between Subjectivization and Subjection*. Unpublished PhD dissertation. Amsterdam: Free University.

Rorty, R. 1980. *Philosophy and the Mirror of Nature*. Oxford: Blackwell.

Roszak, T. 1969. *The Making of a Counter Culture: Reflections on the Technocratic Society and its Youthful Opposition*. Garden City: Doubleday.

Rotenstreich, N. 1989. *Alienation: The Concept and its Reception*, Leiden: Brill.

Rushkoff, D. 1999. *Playing the Future: What We Can Learn from Digital Kids*. New York: Riverhead Books.

Sanders, T. 2005. Researching the online sex work community, in *Virtual Methods: Issues in Social Research on the Internet*, edited by C. Hine. Oxford: Berg, 67-79.

Saroglou, V., Lamkaddem, B., Van Pachterbeke, M. and Buxant, C. 2009. Host society's dislike of the Islamic veil: The role of subtle prejudice, values, and religion. *International Journal of Intercultural Relations*, 333(3), 419-28.

Sayyid, S. 2009. Contemporary politics of secularism, in *Secularism, Religion and Multicultural Citizenship*, edited by G.B. Levey and T. Modood. Cambridge: Cambridge University Press, 164-85.

Schafer, J.A. 2002. Spinning the web of hate: Web-based hate propagation by extremist organizations. *Journal of Criminal Justice and Popular Culture*, 9(2), 69-88.

Schäfer, M.T. 2009. Participation inside? User activities between design and appropriation, in *Digital Material: Tracing New Media in Everyday Life and Technology*, edited by M. van den Boomen, S. Lammes, A. Lehmann and J. Raessens. Amsterdam: Amsterdam University Press, 147-58.

Scheepers, P., Eisinga, R. and Van Snippenburg, L. 1992. Working-class authoritarianism: Evaluation of a research tradition and an empirical test. *Netherlands' Journal of Social Sciences*, 28(2), 103-26.

Scholten, P. and R. Holzhacker. 2009. Bonding, bridging and ethnic minorities in the Netherlands: Changing discourses in a changing nation. *Nations and Nationalism*, 15(1), 81-100.

Schwartz, B. 2004. *The Paradox of Choice: Why More Is Less*. New York: Harper & Collins.

Second Vatican Council. 1971. *Communio et progressio*. Available at: http://www.vatican.va/roman_curia/pontifical_councils/pccs/documents/rc_pc_pccs_doc_23051971_communio_en.html [accessed: March 16, 2006].

Seidman, S. 1994. *Contested Knowledge: Social Theory in the Postmodern Era*. Cambridge: Blackwell.

Seigel, J. 1987. Autonomy and personality in Durkheim: An essay on content and method. *Journal of the History of Ideas*, 48(3), 483-507.

Sheldon, L. 2004. *Character Development and Storytelling for Games*. Boston: Thomson Course Technology.

Simi, P. and Futrell, R. 2006. Cyberculture and the endurance of white power activism. *Journal of Political and Military Sociology*, 34(1), 115-42.

Simi, P. and Futrell, R. 2009. Negotiating white power activist stigma. *Social Problems*, 56(1), 89-110.

Slater, D. 1997. *Consumer Culture and Modernity.* Cambridge: Polity Press.

Slater, D. 2002. Social relationships and identity online and offline, in *Handbook of New Media: Social Shaping and Consequences of ICTs*, edited by L. Lievrouw and S. Livingstone. London: Sage, 533-46.

Smith, C., Emerson, M., Gallagher, S., Kennedy, P. and Sikkink, D. 1998. *American Evangelism: Embattled and Thriving.* Chicago: University of Chicago Press.

Sniderman, P. and Hagendoorn, L. 2007. *When Ways of Life Collide: Multiculturalism and its Discontents in the Netherlands.* Princeton: Princeton University Press.

Sniderman, P., Hagendoorn, L. and Prior, M. 2003. De moeizame acceptatie van moslims in Nederland [The arduous acceptance of Muslims in the Netherlands]. *Mens & Maatschappij*, 78(3), 199-217.

Srole, L. 1956. Social integration and certain corollaries: An exploratory study. *American Sociological Review* 21(6): 709-16.

Stark, R. 1999. Secularization RIP. *Sociology of Religion*, 60: 249-73.

Stark, R. and Bainbridge, W.S. 1985. *The Future of Religion: Secularization, Revival and Cult Formation.* Berkeley, CA: University of California Press.

Stenger, N. 1991. Mind is a leaking rainbow, in *Cyberspace: First Steps*, edited by M. Benedikt. Cambridge, MA: MIT Press, 49-58.

Stivers, R. 1994. *The Culture of Cynicism: American Morality in Decline.* Oxford: Blackwell.

Stouffer, S.A. 1955. *Communism, Conformity, and Civil Liberties: A Cross-Section of the Nation Speaks Its Mind.* New York: Wiley.

Stubager, R. 2008. Education effects on authoritarian-libertarian values: A question of socialization. *British Journal of Sociology*, 59(2), 327-50.

Stubager, R. 2009. Education-based group identity and consciousness in the authoritarian-libertarian value conflict. *European Journal of Political Research*, 48(2), 204-33.

Sutcliffe, S.J. and Bowman, M. (eds). 2000. *Beyond New Age: Exploring Alternative Spirituality.* Edinburgh: Edinburgh University Press.

Swets, J.A. and R.A. Bjork. 1990. Enhancing human performance: An evaluation of 'new age' techniques considered by the U.S. Army. *Psychological Science*, 1(2), 85-96.

Sztompka, P. 2002. On the decaying moral space: Is there a way out? *European Review*, 10(1), 63-72.

Tanis, C. 2007. Online social support groups, in *The Oxford Handbook of Internet Psychology*, edited by A.N. Joinson, K.Y.A. McKenna, T. Postmes and U-D. Reips. Oxford: Oxford University Press, 139-53.

Tateo, L. 2005. The Italian extreme right on-line network: An exploratory study using an integrated social network analysis and content analysis approach, *Journal of Computer-Mediated Communication*, 10(2). Available at: http://onlinelibrary.wiley.com/doi/10.1111/j.1083-6101.2005.tb00247.x/full

Taylor, C. 1991. *The Ethics of Authenticity.* Cambridge, MA: Harvard University Press.

Taylor, T.L. 2006. *Play Between Worlds: Exploring Online Game Culture*. Cambridge: MIT Press.

Thiesmeyer, L. 1999. Racism on the web: Its rhetoric and marketing. *Ethics and Information Technology*, 1(2), 117-25.

Thompson, K.C. 2001. Watching the stormfront: White nationalists and the building of community in cyberspace. *Social Analysis*, 45(1), 32-52.

Tonkiss, F. 2004. Using focus groups, in *Researching Society and Culture (Second Edition)*, edited by C. Seale. London: Sage, 193-206.

Traynor, J.B. 1999. Total life planning: A new frontier in work-life benefits. *Employee Benefit Journal*, 24(4), 29-32.

Turkle, S. 1995. *Life on the Screen: Identity in the Age of the Internet*. New York: Simon & Schuster.

Turner, J. 1999. Spirituality in the workplace. *CA Magazine*, 132(10), 41-2.

Uitermark, J. 2010. *Dynamics of Power in Dutch Integration Politics*. Unpublished PhD dissertation. Amsterdam: University of Amsterdam.

Van der Brug, W. 2003. How the LPF fuelled discontent: Empirical tests of explanations of LPF-support. *Acta Politica*, 38(1), 89-106.

Van der Brug, W. and Fennema, M. 2003. Protest or mainstream: How the European anti-immigrant parties have developed into two separate groups by 1999. *European Journal of Political Research*, 42(1), 55-76.

Van der Waal, J. 2010. *Unraveling the Global City Debate: Economic Inequality and Ethnocentrism in Contemporary Dutch Cities*. Unpublished PhD dissertation. Rotterdam: Erasmus University.

Van der Waal, J., Achterberg, P. and Houtman, D. 2007. Class is not dead – it has been buried alive: Class voting and cultural voting in postwar Western societies (1956-1990). *Politics & Society*, 35(3), 403-26.

Van der Waal, J., Achterberg, P., Houtman, D., De Koster, W. and Manevska, K. 2010. 'Some are more equal than others': Economic egalitarianism and welfare chauvinism in the Netherlands. *Journal of European Social Policy*, 20(4), 350-63.

Van Gogh, T. 2003. *Allah weet het beter* [Allah Knows Better]. Amsterdam: XTRA Producties.

Van Hoog, S. (ed.) 2001. *Klikgids 2002: Wegwijzer voor de natuurgerichte gezondheidszorg en bewustwording* [Click Directory 2002: Guide for Nature-Oriented Medicine and Consciousness-Raising]. Deventer: Buro Klik.

Vasta, E. 2007. From ethnic minorities to ethnic majority policy: multiculturalism and the shift to assimilationism in the Netherlands. *Ethnic and Racial Studies*, 30(5), 713-40.

Veugelers, J.W.P. 2000. Right-wing extremism in contemporary France: A 'silent counterrevolution'? *Sociological Quarterly*, 41(1), 19-40.

Visscher, Q. 2010. Elke Christen z'n eigen zender [Every Christian his own channel]. *Trouw*, May 6, 2010.

Vollebergh, W.A.M., Iedema, J. and Meeus, W. 1999. The emerging gender gap: Cultural and economic conservatism in the Netherlands 1970-1992. *Political Psychology*, 20(2), 291-321.

Ward, K.J. 1999. Cyber-ethnography and the emergence of the virtually new community. *Journal of Information Technology*, 14(1), 95-105.

Watson, N. 1997. Why we argue about virtual community: A case study of the phish.net fan community, in *Virtual Culture: Identity & Communication in Cybersociety*, edited by S.G. Jones. London: Sage, 102-32.

Wattenberg, M. 1991. *The Rise of Candidate-Centered Politics: Presidential Elections of the 1980s*. Cambridge, MA: Harvard University Press.

Watts Miller, W. 1996. *Durkheim, Morals and Modernity*. Montreal: McGill-Queen's University Press.

Weakliem, D. 1991. The two lefts? Occupation and party choice in France, Italy, and the Netherlands. *American Journal of Sociology*, 96(6), 1327-61.

Weber, M. 1948 [1919]. Science as a vocation, in *From Max Weber: Essays in Sociology*, edited by H.H. Gerth and C.W. Mills. London: Routledge, 129-56.

Weber, M. 1949 [1922]. *The Methodology of the Social Sciences*. New York: Free Press.

Weber, M. 1978 [1921]. *Economy and Society (Two Volumes)*. Berkeley/Los Angeles: University of California Press.

Weber, M. 1963 [1922]. *The Sociology of Religion*. Boston, MA: Beacon Press.

Welch, J. 1998. The new seekers: Greed is good. *People Management*, 4(25), 28-33.

Wellman, B. 1997. The road to utopia and dystopia on the information highway. *Contemporary Sociology*, 26(4), 445-9.

Wellman, B. and Hampton, K. 1999. Living networked on and offline. *Contemporary Sociology*, 28(6), 648-54.

Wenjing, X. 2005. Virtual space, real identity: Exploring cultural identity of chinese diaspora in virtual community. *Telematics and Informatics*, 22(4), 395-404.

Wertheim, M. 1999. *The Pearly Gates of Cyberspace: A History of Space from Dante to the Internet*. New York: W.W. Norton & Company.

Whine, M. 2000. Far right extremists on the Internet, in *Cybercrime: Law Enforcement, Security and Surveillance in the Information Age*, edited by D. Thomas and B.D. Loader. London: Routledge, 234-50.

Whyte, Jr., W.H. 1956. *The Organization Man*. New York: Simon & Schuster.

Wilbur, S.P. 1997. An archaeology of cyberspaces: Virtuality, community, identity, in *Internet Culture*, edited by D. Porter. London: Routledge, 5-22.

Wilson, B. 1976. *Contemporary Transformations of Religion*. Oxford: Oxford University Press.

Wilson, B. 1982. *Religion in Sociological Perspective*. Oxford: Oxford University Press.

Wojcieszak, M. 2010. 'Don't talk to me': Effects of ideologically homogeneous online groups and politically dissimilar offline ties on extremism. *New Media & Society*, 12(4), 637-55.

Woodcock, B.S. 2008. *An Analysis of MMOG Subscription Growth: Version 21.0.* Available at: http://www.mmogchart.com [accessed: March 21, 2011].

Woodhead, L. 2010. Real religion and fuzzy spirituality? Taking sides in the sociology of religion, in *Religions of Modernity: Relocating the Sacred to the Self and the Digital*, edited by Stef Aupers and Dick Houtman. Leiden: Brill, 31-48.

Yang, C-C. 2000. The use of Internet among academic gay communities in Taiwan: An exploratory study. *Information, Communication & Society*, 3(2), 153-72.

Yee, N. 2001. *The Virtual Skinner Box*. Available at: http://www.nickyee.com/eqt/skinner.html [accessed: March 21, 2011].

Yee, N. 2007. Motivations of play in online games. *Journal of CyberPsychology and Behavior*, 9(6), 772-5.

Zhou, Y., Reid, E., Qin, J., Chen, H. and Lai, G. 2005. US domestic extremist groups on the web: Link and content analysis. *IEEE Intelligent Systems*, 20(5), 44-51.

Zijderveld, A.C. 1970. *The Abstract Society: A Cultural Analysis of Our Time.* New York: Doubleday.

Zijderveld, A.C. 2000. *The Institutional Imperative: The Interface of Institutions and Networks*. Amsterdam: Amsterdam University Press.

Index